THE ANCHOR BOOK OF LATIN QUOTATIONS

Norbert Guterman held several degrees from the Sorbonne, contributed to many French and American literary magazines, and earned a considerable reputation for himself as a translator. He is author (with Henri Lefebvre) of *La Conscience Mystifiée* and co-editor-translator, with Francis Steegmuller, of *Sainte-Beuve: Selected Essays*. He died in 1984.

THE ANCHOR BOOK OF

Latin Quotations

WITH ENGLISH TRANSLATIONS

Compiled by Norbert Guterman

ANCHOR BOOKS
DOUBLEDAY
NEW YORK   LONDON   TORONTO   SYDNEY   AUCKLAND

An Anchor Book

PUBLISHED BY DOUBLEDAY

a division of Bantam Doubleday Dell Publishing Group, Inc.
666 Fifth Avenue, New York, New York 10103

ANCHOR BOOKS, DOUBLEDAY, and the portrayal of an anchor
are trademarks of Doubleday, a division of Bantam Doubleday
Dell Publishing Group, Inc.

The Anchor Book of Latin Quotations was originally published
by Anchor Books in 1966
as *A Book of Latin Quotations*.

Grateful acknowledgment is made to the following for permission to quote:

JONATHAN CAPE, LIMITED. From *The Eclogues* and *Georgics*, of Vergil, translated by C. D. Lewis. Reprinted by permission of the publisher.

THE CATHOLIC UNIVERSITY OF AMERICA PRESS. From *The City of God*, by St. Augustine. Reprinted by permission of the Fathers of the Church of the Catholic University of America.

DOUBLEDAY, ANCHOR BOOKS. From *The Confessions of St. Augustine*, translated by J. K. Ryan. Copyright © 1960 by Doubleday & Company, Inc. Reprinted by permission of the publisher.

HARVARD UNIVERSITY PRESS. From material from The Loeb Classical Library. Reprinted by permission of the publisher.

MACMILLAN COMPANY, LTD. From *Physical Enquiries*, by Seneca, translated by John Clarke. Reprinted by permission of the publisher.

OXFORD UNIVERSITY, THE CLARENDON PRESS. From *Poems*, by Horace, translated by E. C. Wickham. Reprinted by permission of The Clarendon Press, Ltd.

Library of Congress Cataloging-in-Publication Data
Guterman, Norbert, 1900–1984
    [Book of Latin quotations]
    The Anchor book of Latin quotations :
    with English translations / compiled by Norbert Guterman.
        p.   cm.
    Originally published under title:
    A book of Latin quotations, 1966.
    1. Quotations, Latin.   2. Quotations,
Latin—Translations into English.
I. Title.   II. Title: Book of Latin quotations.
PN6080.G8   1990   90–237
089′.71—dc20   CIP
ISBN 0-385-41391-2

INTRODUCTION

For more than two centuries Latin has been steadily losing ground as an international language. Even in our own lifetime we have witnessed its disappearance from many colleges and university curricula: the charge has long been that it uselessly clutters up young minds, and that room had to be made for the growing body of scientific knowledge. Recently we have seen the beginning of the dislodgment of Latin from what is probably its last stronghold, the Roman Catholic Mass. True, it was employed at the last ecumenical council as the international language of the clergy, but one wonders whether this will ever be the case again. Is the recent vogue of the charming Latin translations of *Winnie the Pooh* and *Alice in Wonderland* (by Alexander Lenard and Clide Harcourt Carruthers respectively) a sign of the tenacity of the old language and its appeal to the literary mind? Or is it rather a confirmation of its loss of any serious functional role, and its degradation to a level of luxury? Has Latin become just "a fun thing"?

The practical arguments put forward by its defenders —*e.g.*, that its study helps to develop logical thinking, serves as an invaluable aid in learning other languages, etc. —are not really convincing: not that they are false, but they do not prove that Latin is indispensable. Along these lines, other disciplines—mathematics, logic, modern languages— may well be as beneficial. For my part, I simply happen to enjoy the Latin language—the sound of its vowels and the forms of its inflections, its ruggedness, its majesty, and its conciseness. Even the comparatively diffuse Cicero, of whom Quintilian says that not a word can be added to his copious flow, seems a model of economy when one reads many a modern novel, speech, critical review, or even a presidential sentence. For those with a sense of history Latin is almost as important as Greek; and it must not be forgotten that during many centuries Greek thought and literature influenced European literatures through the medium of Latin. As has often been pointed out, it was not Aristophanes, Menander, and Euripides who shaped the European drama, but their Latin adapters and imitators, Plautus, Terence, and Seneca.

The passages collected in this book have been "quotations" for well over a thousand years. Many of them exist only because they were "quoted," the works from which they are taken having been lost. In the case of the most celebrated poets whose works survive in toto or nearly so, a collection of passages which have never been quoted during the last two millennia would make a very slim book indeed. In preparing the present selection I tried not to omit historically famous texts, but in general the standard has been double—both timelessness and timeliness of interest. Another kind of double standard governed the choice of translations: they are meant to serve both as a convenience for readers with some knowledge of Latin and as an acceptable approximation of the original for non-Latinists. I have taken the liberty of slightly modifying a few of the older translations; in passages torn from their context this was sometimes sheer necessity. For the errors, near-errors, and non-errors in those given without a translator's name I alone am responsible.

NORBERT GUTERMAN

THE ANCHOR BOOK OF LATIN QUOTATIONS

APPIUS CLAUDIUS CAECUS

c. 355 – c. 275 B.C.

Est unusquisque faber ipsae suae fortunae.

Tui animi compote es, ne quid fraudis stuprique ferocia pariat.

Negotium populo romano melius quam otium committi.

LIVIUS ANDRONICUS

c. 280 – 204 B.C.

Mirum videtur quod sit factum iam diu?
Aiax Mastigophorus

Praestatur laus virtuti, sed multo ocius
verno gelu tabescit. *Id.*

2

APPIUS CLAUDIUS

According to Cicero, Appius Claudius was the author of a collection of apothegms inspired by the philosophy of Pythagoras. Only a few lines attributed to him have come down to us. He is best known as the builder of the first aqueduct and the Via Appia. As censor (312 B.C.) and consul (307 and 296 B.C.) he favored the plebeians. In 280 B.C., old and infirm, he was carried in a litter to the senate and persuaded it to reject Pyrrhus's peace proposals, enunciating the principle that Rome must never negotiate with an invader.

Every man is the artisan of his own fortune.

Be master of your soul, lest your untamed nature bring forth deceit or disgrace.

The Roman people understand work better than leisure.

LIVIUS ANDRONICUS

Livius Andronicus, probably a Greek, was brought to Rome from Tarentum as a child; he was part of "the spoils of war." He was merely a translator—the first to be known by name in European literature—but it was he who introduced epic poetry, lyrical poetry, and drama into the Latin language. For about two centuries his roughhewn version of the *Odyssey* figured in the school curriculum: Horace and Vergil memorized it as schoolboys. Only bits of his work have survived.

Does it seem marvelous because it was done long ago?

Praise is bestowed on virtue but vanishes more quickly than frost in spring.

Lepus tute es; et pulpamentum quaeris!

Ex incertis fabulis

Virum mihi, Camena, insece versutum . . .

Odissia I, 1

Namque nullum
peius macerat humanum quamde mare saevum;
vires cui sunt magnae topper confringent
inportunae undae. *Id., VIII, 138–39*

Cum socios nostros Ciclops impius mandisset . . .

Id., XX, 19

GNAEUS NAEVIUS

C. 270 – C. 200 B.C.

Semper pluris feci ego
potioremque habui libertatem quam pecuniam.

Agitatoria

Quasi pila
in choro ludens datatim dat se et communem facit.
alii adnutat, alii adnictat, alium amat alium tenet.
alibi manus est occupata, alii pervelit pedem;
anulum dat alii spectandum, a labris alium invocat,
cum alio cantat, at tamen alii suo dat digito litteras.

Tarentilla

4

You're a rabbit yourself, and yet you're out for game!

Tell me, O Muse, of the cunning hero . . .

For there is no worse torment for a man than the cruel sea; even if he has great strength, it will soon be broken by the wild waves.

When the wicked Cyclops had crunched my comrades in his jaws . . .

NAEVIUS

Naevius, a plebeian, fought in the First Punic War (264–241 B.C.). He wrote satires, the first national epic (*Bellum Poenicum*), which influenced Vergil, and the first Roman historical plays. He incurred the wrath of the powerful Metelli with his ambiguous remark, *Fato Metelli Romae fiunt consules* (this translates either as "It is fate that . . ." or "It is fatal that—the Metelli occupy consulships at Rome"). Metellus (consul in 206 B.C.) replied with the threat, *Dabunt malum Metelli Naevio poetae:* "The Metelli will give the poet Naevius the apple"—here the word *malum* can mean either "prize" or "punishment." Under an ancient law forbidding public criticism of officials, he was imprisoned and later exiled to Utica in North Africa, where he died. His proud epitaph was preserved by Aulus Gellius.

I have always valued freedom more highly than money, and preferred it.

Like a ball in a circle game, she lets herself be handled by one man after another, making herself common property. She nods to one, winks at another; she favors one, yet hugs another. While her hand is busy at one place, her foot is rubbing against another man's. She lets one man admire her ring, while inviting another with her lips. She sings with one man, the while writing a love note to another with her finger in the air.

Cedo qui vestram rem publicam tantam amisistis tam cito?
Proveniebant oratores novi, stulti adulescentuli.

Ex incertis fabulis

Desubito famam tollunt si quam solam videre in via.

Danae

Laetus sum laudari me abs te, pater, a laudato viro.

Hector proficiscens

Ingenio arbusta ubi nata sunt non obsitu . . .

Lycurgus

Oderunt di homines iniuros.   *Id.*

Odi summussos; proinde aperte dice quid sit quod times.

Ex incertis fabulis

Pati necesse est multa mortales mala.   *Id.*

Seseque i perire mavolunt ibidem
quam cum stupro redire ad suos popularis.

Bellum Poenicum

Immortales mortales si foret fas flere
flerent divae Camenae Naevium poetam.
itaque postquamst Orchi traditus thesauro,
obliti sunt Romae loquier lingua latina.

Epigramma

Q: Tell me, how come your great commonwealth was lost so speedily?
A: We were overrun by a new lot of orators, a bunch of silly youngsters.

The moment they see a woman alone in the street, they cry scandal.

I am glad it is you, Father, a man highly praised, who praises me.

Where trees have grown by nature's art, not planted by human hands . . .

The gods hate unjust men.

I loathe whisperers: say out loud what it is you fear.

Mortals must bear many ills.

They would rather perish on the spot than go back in disgrace to their countrymen.

Were it proper for the immortals to mourn for men, the divine Muses would lament the poet Naevius. And once death had taken him to her underground vaults, at Rome they forgot how to speak Latin. [*Epitaph on himself*]

TITUS MACCIUS PLAUTUS

c. 255 – 184 b.c.

Ita cuique comparatum est in aetate hominum;
ita divis est placitum, voluptatem ut maeror comes
consequatur.   *Amphitruo, 634*

Plus aegri ex abitu viri, quam ex adventu voluptatis cepi.
                                          Id., 641

Non ego illam mihi dotem duco esse, quae dos dicitur,
sed pudicitiam et pudorem et sedatum cupidinem,
deum metum, parentum amorem et cognatum concordiam,
tibi morigera atque ut munifica sim bonis, prosim probis.
                                          Id., 839

Argentum accepi, dote imperium vendidi.
                                          Asinaria, 87

Diem aquam solem lunam noctem, haec argento non emo:
caeterum quae volumus uti Graeca mercamur fide.
                                          Id., 198

Lupus est homo homini, non homo, quom qualis sit non
novit.   *Id., 495*

Nam multum loquaces merito omnes habemur,
nec mutam profecto repertam ullam esse
aut hodie dicunt aut ullo in saeclo.   *Aulularia, 124*

8

PLAUTUS

Plautus was born at Sarsina, a small town in Umbria. In his youth he earned some money as a stage carpenter, lost it in trade, and worked in a flour mill. His plays are free adaptations of Greek comedies. According to Aulus Gellius, at one time he was believed to have written 130 comedies, but Varro recognized only 21 as authentic, 19 as doubtful, and the rest as spurious. All the authentic plays have survived, though one is not complete.

(Tr. Paul Nixon)

It is our human lot, it is heaven's will, for sorrow to come after joy.

I have felt more unhappy at his going than happy at his coming.

Personally I do not feel that my dowry is what people call a dowry, but purity and honor and self-control, fear of God, love of parents and affection for my family, and being a dutiful wife to you, sir, lavish of loving kindness and helpful through honest service.

Sold myself! Gave my authority for a dowry!

Daylight, water, sunlight, moonlight, darkness—for those things I have to pay no money; everything else we wish to use we purchase on Greek credit.

Man is no man, but a wolf, to a stranger.

Awful chatterboxes—that's the name we all have, and it fits. And then the common saying: "Never now, nor through the ages, never any woman dumb."

Quae indotata est, ea in potestate est viri;
dotatae mactant et malo et damno viros.   *Id., 535*

Quem di diligunt
adulescens moritur, dum valet sentit sapit.
Bacchides, 816

Enim vero di nos quasi pilas homines habent.
Captivi, Prologus, 22

Tum denique homines nostra intellegimus bona,
quom quae in potestate habuimus, ea amisimus.
Id., 142

Ut saepe summa ingenia in occulto latent.
Id., 165

Fere maxima pars morem hunc homines habent: quod sibi
volunt,
dum impetrant, boni sunt;
sed id ubi iam penes sese habent,
ex bonis pessimi et fraudulentissimi
fiunt.   *Id., 232*

Mos est oblivisci hominibus
neque novisse cuius nihili sit faciunda gratia.
Id., 985

Qui utuntur vino vetere sapientis puto
et qui libenter veteres spectant fabulas.
Casina, Prologus, 5

A wife that doesn't bring you a penny—a husband has some control over her; it's the dowered ones that pester the life out of their husbands with the way they act up and squander.

He whom the gods love dies young, while he has strength and senses and wits.

Ah yes, the gods use us mortals as footballs!

We mortals realize the value of blessings only when we have lost them.

How often does it happen that the greatest talents are shrouded in obscurity!

Generally speaking, men have a habit of being fine fellows so long as they are seeking some favor, but when they have obtained it, there's a change, and your fine fellows turn into villainous cheats of the worst description.

It's a regular thing to forget a fellow and cut him if his good will can't help you at all.

Those be wise men, in my opinion, who take old wine and those who love to see old plays.

Ubi amor condimentum inerit, cuivis placituram escam
  credo;
neque salsum neque suave esse potest quicquam, ubi amor
  non admiscetur:
fel quod amarumst, it mel faciet, hominem ex tristi
  lepidum et lenem.   *Id.*, *221*

Credo ego Amorem primum apud homines carnificinam
  commentum.   *Cistelaria*, *203*

> Qui e nuce nuculeum esse volt, frangit nucem;
> qui volt cubare, pandit saltum saviis.   *Curculio*, *55*

> Antiquom poetam audivi scripsisse in tragoedia,
> mulieres duas peiores esse quam unam. res itast.
>   *Id.*, *591*

Argentariis male credi qui aiunt, nugas praedicant.
nam et bene et male credi dico; id adeo hodie expertus
  sum.
non male creditur qui numquam reddunt, sed prorsum
  perit.   *Id.*, *679*

> Pulchra edepol dos pecuniast.
> Quae quidem pol non maritast.
>   *Epidicus*, *179*

Humanum amarest; humanum autem ignoscerest.
                                          Mercator, *320*

> Utinam lex esset eadem quae uxori est viro;
> nam uxor contenta est, quae bona est, uno viro;
> qui minus vir una uxore contentus siet?   *Id.*, *823*

When you spice a dish with love, it'll tickle every palate, I do believe. Not a thing can be either salt or sweet without a dash of love: it will turn gall, bitter though it may be, to honey—an old curmudgeon to a pleasing and polished gentleman.

I do believe it was Love that first devised the torturer's profession here on earth.

The man that wants to eat the kernel, cracks the nut; the man that wants to get the girl clears the way with kisses.

An old dramatist, so I've heard, once wrote in a tragedy that two women are worse than one. They are.

People that say bankers are ill trusted talk rubbish. Why, they are well trusted and ill trusted both, I tell you—and what is more, I have proved it myself this very day. Money is not ill trusted to men that never repay you; it is gone for good.

Lord, man, a fat dowry and good money. —Gad, yes, if it comes without the wife.

To love is human; to be indulgent is human too.

I wish there were the same rule for the husband and the wife. Now a wife, a good wife, is content with just her husband; why should a husband be less content with just his wife?

Novo modo tu homo amas, siquidem te quicquam quod
   faxis pudet;
nihil amas, umbra es amantis magis quam amator.

Miles gloriosus, 624

Hospes nullus tam in amici hospitium devorti potest,
quin, ubi triduom continuom fuerit, iam odiosus siet;
verum ubi dies decem continuos sit, east odiorum Ilias:
tam etsi dominus non invitus patitur, servi murmurant.

Id., 741

Mulier profecto natast ex ipsa Mora;
nam quaevis alia quae morast aeque, mora
minor ea videtur quam quae propter mulieremest.
hoc adeo fieri credo consuetudine.   *Id., 1292*

Purpura aetati occultandaest, aurum turpi mulieri;
pulchra mulier nuda erit quam purpurata pulchrior.

Mostellaria, 288

Qui amans egens ingressus est princeps in Amoris vias,
superavit aerumnis suis aerumnas Herculi.   *Persa, 1*

Pater, avos, proavos, abavos, atavos, tritavos
quasi mures semper edere alienum cibum,
neque edacitate eos quisquam poterat vincere.

Id., 57

Tacitast melior mulier semper quam loquens.

Rudens, 1114

Miserum istuc verbum et pessimum est, habuisse, et nihil
   habere.   *Id., 1321*

Ut cuique homini res paratast, perinde amicis utitur:
si res firma, item firmi amici sunt; sin res laxe labat,
itidem amici conlabuscunt.   *Stichus, 520*

A new kind of lover you are, if you're actually ashamed of anything you do! You are not in love, you're no lover, you're only the shadow of a lover!

No guest can accept the hospitality of a friend like this without becoming an affliction after three days' stay; but after a ten days' stay he becomes a whole Iliad of affliction. Even though the master is no unwilling sufferer, the servants grumble.

Woman is certainly the daughter of Delay personified! Why, any other delay, even one of equal length, seems shorter than what a woman lets you in for. I really do believe they do it just out of habit.

Purple belongs to shady years, jewels to ugly women; a pretty girl is prettier undressed than dressed in purple.

The lover that first set out on the highways of love with an empty purse went in for harder labors than Hercules.

My father, grandfather, great-grandfather, great-great-grandfather, great-great-great-grandfather, and his father too always ate other folks' food, just like mice, and not a soul could beat them at edacity.

A woman's always worth more seen than heard.

That's a dismal word, the very worst of worst, "had," when what you have is nothing.

On anyone's financial standing hangs his status with friends: if he is in a sound financial state, his friends are sound; once that state begins wavering wildly, his friends waver likewise.

Numquam edepol temere tinnit tintinnabulum:
nisi qui illud tractat aut movet, mutumst, tacet.

Trinummus, 1004

Pluris est oculatus testis unus quam auriti decem;
qui audiunt audita dicunt, qui vident plane sciunt.

Truculentus, 485

Strenui nimio plus prosunt populo quam arguti et cati;
facile sibi facunditatem virtus argutam invenit,
sine virtute argutum civem mihi habeam pro praefica,
quae alios conlaudat, eapse sese vero non potest.

Id., 493

Non enim possunt militares pueri dauco exducier.

Id., 907

Ut illum di perdant, primus qui horas repperit
quique adeo primus statuit hic solarium;
qui mihi comminuit misero articulatim diem.
nam unum me puero venter erat solarium,
multo omnium istorum optimum et verissimum.
ubi is te monebat, esses, nisi cum nil erat;
nunc etiam quom est non estur, nisi Soli libet.
itaque adeo iam oppletum oppidum est solariis:
maior pars populi aridi reptant fame.

Boeotia, fragment

Postquam est mortem aptus Plautus, comoedia luget,
scaena est deserta, dein risus ludus iocusque
et numeri innumeri omnes conlacrumarunt.

ENNIUS

Born at Rudiae (the present-day Rutigliano) in Calabria, Ennius served in the Roman army as a centurion during the Second Punic War. Cato brought him to Rome, and he became a Roman citizen in 184 B.C. His copious production included tragedies and comedies adapted from the Greek, satires, epigrams, a didactic poem on nature, a poem on mythology, a poem on Scipio's victory over Hannibal, and the *Annals*, a history of Rome in eighteen books. This last introduced the Greek hexameter into Latin. Later writers revered him as "the father of Roman poets." Vergil often drew upon him; Lucretius, Cicero, Ovid, Propertius admired him; as late as the second century A.D. passages from the *Annals* were recited in public. His style is vigorous, marked by bold imagery and by frequent use of alliteration and onomatopeia. Occasionally ponderous, it is charming in its very awkwardness. Judging from the surviving fragments (a total of about a thousand lines, chiefly from the *Annals*), Ovid's verdict, *ingenio maximus, arte rudis* ("lofty in genius, crude in workmanship"), seems just. Ennius used to say that he had three "brains," in as much as he could speak three languages (Greek, Oscan, and Latin). According to Gellius, the passage about the good companion and reliable friend (fifth quotation below) is a self-portrait.

Muses, whose feet are treading great Olympus.

In the woods, a vulture was devouring the wretched man. Alas! into what an atrocious grave were his limbs sinking!

And the trumpet's taratantara spluttered its terrible din.

She looked up at the sky studded with glittering stars.

Vocat quocum bene saepe libenter
mensam sermonesque suos rerumque suarum
comiter inpertit, magnam cum lassus diei
partem trivisset de summis rebus regendis. . . .
quoi res audacter magnas parvasque iocumque
eloqueretur sed cura, malaque et bona dictu
evomeret si qui vellet tutoque locaret;
quorum multa volup ac gaudia clamque palamque,
ingenium quoi nulla malum sententia suadet
ut faceret facinus levis aut malus.   *Id., VII*

Pellitur e medio sapientia, vi geritur res,
spernitur orator bonus, horridus miles amatur;
haud doctis dictis certantes, sed maledictis . . .
                                   Id., VIII

Unus homo nobis cunctando restituit rem.
Noenum rumores ponebat ante salutem;
ergo postque magisque viri nunc gloria claret.
                                   Id., XII

Labitur uncta carina, volat super impetus undas.
                                   Id., XIV

Moribus antiquis res stat Romana virisque.
                       Id. Ex incertis libris

Quomque caput caderet, carmen tuba sola peregit
et pereunte viro raucus sonus aere cucurrit.   *Ibid.*

Oscitat in campis caput a cervice revulsum
semianimesque micant oculi lucemque requirunt.
                                   Ibid.

Amicus certus in re incerta cernitur.
        Ibid. (Quoted by Cicero, De Amicit., 64)

He sent for a man with whom he was often happy to share his table, and to talk about private affairs after a tiring day spent dealing with the most serious business of government. . . . To him he would speak frankly of matters great and small, tell jokes, and, if he so wished, speak well or ill of anything, confident of the other's discretion. With this companion he spent many an agreeable, happy hour, both with others and alone. He had such a disposition that he never deliberately perpetrated a misdeed nor lightly gave offense.

Wisdom is driven out from our midst, brute force rules the state, the honest orator is scorned, the rude soldier is worshiped. Instead of learned arguments, litigants resort to abuse.

By his delaying tactics one man [Fabius Maximus Cunctator] restored our fortunes. He never put rumors before our safety; and so today his glory shines the brighter.

The well-greased keel, rushing on, flies over the white waves.

On ancient ways and heroes stands the Roman state.

When his head was severed, the trumpet blared on, and as the warrior lay dying, a hoarse sound issued from the brass.

His head, severed at the neck, rolled down the field, the half-alive eyes twitching and longing for light.

A friend in need is a friend indeed.

Qui vicit non est victor nisi victus fatetur.   *Ibid.*

Capitibus nutantes pinos rectosque cupressos.
                                              Ibid.

Otio qui nescit uti . . .
plus negoti habet quam quom est negotium in negotio;
nam cui quod agat institutumst non ullo negotio
id agit, id studet, ibi mentum atque animum delectat
suum:
otioso in otio [aeger] animus nescit quid velit.
                                              Iphigenia

Qui ipse si sapiens prodesse non quit, nequiquam sapit.
                                              Medea

Ea libertas est qui pectus purum et firmum gestitat;
aliae res obnoxiosae nocte in obscura latent.   *Phoenix*

Ego deum genus esse semper dixi et dicam caelitum,
sed eos non curare opinor quid agat humanum genus;
nam si curent, bene bonis sit, male malis; quod nunc abest.
                                              Telamo

Superstitiosi vates inpudentesque harioli,
aut inertes aut insani aut quibus egestas imperat,
qui sibi semitam non sapiunt, alteri monstrant viam;
quibus divitias pollicentur, ab iis drachumam ipsi petunt.
De his divitiis sibi deducant drachuman, reddant cetera.
                                              Ibid.

Flagiti principium est nudare inter cives corpora.
                                              Ex fabulis incertis

Quem metuunt oderunt, quem quisque odit periise expetit.
                                              Ibid.

Numquam poetor nisi si podager.   *Saturae*

The victor is not truly victor unless the vanquished admits it.

The pines, heads nodding, and the cypresses standing straight.

A man who does not know how to enjoy leisure works harder than a man who works hard when he works. For a man who does what he has to do, does it effortlessly, devotedly, with delight of heart and mind. In leisure ill-employed, the mind is sick, not knowing what it wants.

A wise man whose wisdom serves him not is wise in vain.

Freedom is having a pure and dauntless heart; all else is slavery and lies hidden in darkness.

I have always said and will go on saying, there is a race of gods in heaven, but I do not believe that they concern themselves with what the human race is doing; for if they did, good men would fare well, and bad men ill, which is not the case now.

Superstitious prophets, shameless haruspices, lazy, mad, driven by poverty, who cannot find their own way yet show it to others, who promise riches to the very men they ask for a drachma—why don't they just take a drachma for themselves from those riches, and hand over the rest?

The beginning of shame is baring the body in public.

Whom men fear, they hate; whom a man hates he wishes dead.

I never poetize save when I rheumatize.

Simia quam similis turpissima bestia nobis! *Ibid.*

Enni poeta salve qui mortalibus
versus propinas flammeos medullitus! *Saturae*

Hic est ille situs cui nemo civis neque hostis
quibit pro factis reddere opis pretium. *Id.*

Aspicite o cives senis Enni imaginis formam.
Hic vestrum pinxit maxima facta patrum.
Nemo me lacrimis decoret nec funera fletu
faxit. Cur? Volito vivus per ora virum.
Epigrammata

MARCUS PORCIUS CATO
234 – 149 B.C.

Est interdum praestare mercatoris rem quaerere, nisi tam
periculosum sit, et item fenerari, si tam honestum sit.
De Agri Cultura, I, 1

The monkey, that most repulsive animal, how like ourselves!

Hail, poet Ennius, you who pour out to mortals flaming verses from your inmost being!

Here lies a man [Scipio Africanus] whom neither fellow citizen nor foe can ever properly repay for his exploits.

Look, O citizens, upon the features of Ennius in his old age. It was he depicted your fathers' noblest deeds. Let no one adorn me with tears or weep at my funeral. Why? I yet do live, quick on the lips of men.

[Lines written for his own tomb]

CATO

Cato, called "the Censor" or "the Elder," to distinguish him from later Catos, was consul in 195 B.C., and censor in 184; in the latter office he tried to reform Roman morals, sparing no one and banning foreign habits and customs. (However, he studied Greek in his old age.) On his return to Rome from an official visit to Carthage, he ended all his speeches in the senate with the famous phrase *Ceterum censeo Carthaginem esse delendam* —"Also, I think Carthage should be destroyed." His treatise on farming, *De agri cultura,* is the oldest surviving Latin prose work. Of his speeches and other works, which included a history of Rome, only fragments remain. "Without question he had a stern temper," Livy says of him, "but he had a soul unconquerable by appetites, an unwavering integrity, and a contempt for influence and wealth. . . . Not even old age, which weakens everything, could break down his mind."

Trade may sometimes be better for making money, but it involves grave risk; the same is true of usury, but it is far less honorable [than farming].

Vendat oleum, si pretium habeat, vinum, frumentum quod supersit vendat; boves vetulos, armenta delicula, oves deliculas, lanam, pelles, plostrum vetus, ferramenta vetera, servum senem, servum morbosum, et siquid aliut supersit, vendat. Patrem familias vendacem, non emacem esse oportet. *Id., II, 7*

Vilicus ne sit ambulator, sobrius siet semper, ad cenam nequo eat. Familiam exerceat, consideret, quae dominus imperaverit fiant. Ne plus censeat sapere se quam dominum. . . . Parasitum nequem habeat. . . . Haruspicem, augurem, hariolum, Chaldaeum nequem consuluisse velit. . . . Primus cubit surgat, postremus cubitum eat. *Id., V, 2, 4, 5*

Res rustica sic est: si unam rem sero feceris, omnia opera sero facies. *Id., V, 7*

Per imbrem in villa quaerito quid fieri possit. Ne cessetur, munditias facito. Cogitato, si nihil fiet, nihilo minus sumptum futurum. *Id., XXXIX, 2*

Quid est agrum bene colere? bene arare. Quid est secundum? arare. Quid tertium? stercorare. *Id., LXI*

Emas, non quod opus est, sed quod necesse est: quod non opus est, asse carum est.
(*Quoted by Seneca, Epistulae, XCIV, 28*)

Vita humana prope uti ferrum est. Si exerceas, conteritur; si non exerceas, tamen rubigo interficit. Itidem homines exercendo videmus conteri. Inertia atque torpedo plus detrimenti facit, quam exercitio.
Carmen de moribus (*Quoted by Aulus Gellius, XI, 3*)

Fures privatorum in nervo atque in compedibus aetatem agunt; fures publici in auro atque in purpura.
Praeda militibus dividenda (*Id., XI, 18*)

Sell the oil, if it fetches a good price, sell whatever excess there be of wine and grain; sell off the worn-out oxen, defective cattle, defective sheep, wool, hides, the old wagon, old tools, the aged slave, the sickly slave, and all else that is of no use. The proprietor of an estate should be eager to sell, not to buy.

Your manager should never leave his duties; he should stay sober and never dine out. He should keep the slaves busy and see that what the master ordered is done. He must not suppose he knows more than the master. . . . He must not tolerate parasites. . . . He is not to consult haruspices, augurs, diviners, or astrologers. . . . He should be the first up in the morning, the last to bed.

This is how it is with farming: if you put off doing one thing, you will be late with everything.

On a rainy day see what can be done around the house. Rather than stand idle, tidy things up. Remember, though no work is done, the expenses do not stop.

What is good farming? Good plowing. What is the second thing? Plowing. What third? Manuring.

Buy not what you can use, but what you cannot do without. What you do not need is dear at any price.

Human life nearly resembles iron. When you use it, it wears out; when you don't use it, rust consumes it. We see that men are worn out by work, but laziness and sluggishness do more damage.

Those who steal from private individuals spend their lives in stocks and chains; those who steal from the public treasure go dressed in gold and purple.

Scio solere plerisque hominibus rebus secundis atque pro-
lixis atque prosperis animum excellere atque superbiam
atque ferociam augescere atque crescere. . . . Advorsae
res edomant et docent quid opus siet facto, secundae res
laetitia transvorsum trudere solent a recte consulendo atque
intellegendo.   *Pro Rhodiensibus* (*Id., XIII, 25*)

Orator est vir bonus dicendi peritus.
          (*Quoted by Quintilian, Institutio Oratoria, XII, i, 1*)

MARCUS PACUVIUS

C. 220 – C. 130 B.C.

Men servasse ut essent qui me perderent?
          Armorum iudicium

Flucti flacciscunt, silescunt venti, mollitur mare.
          Chryses

O flexanima atque omnium regina rerum oratio!
          Hermiona

Conqueri fortunam advorsam, non lamentari decet;
id viri est officium, fletus muliebri ingenio additust.
          Niptra

          Patria est, ubicumque est bene.   *Teucer*

I know that most men's spirits are lifted when the times are prosperous, rich, and happy, so that their pride and arrogance grow. . . . Adversity chastens them and teaches them what should be done; good fortune, which leads them to rejoice, usually makes them stray from right counsels and clear thinking.

An orator is a good man skilled in speaking.

PACUVIUS

Highly praised by Cicero as a tragic poet, Pacuvius, a nephew of Ennius, was born at Brundisium (Brindisi). He lived in Rome where he gained fame as a painter; later he devoted himself to writing. His works include fourteen plays and a satire. Only fragments of the plays survive. According to Suetonius, the line from *Armorum iudicium* quoted below was put to music and sung at the funeral of Julius Caesar.

Did I save them that they might destroy me?

The waves grow gentler, the winds abate, the sea's appeased.

O Eloquence who moves men's minds, queen of the universe!

For a man it is proper to complain of adverse fortune, but not to wail at it; weeping belongs to a woman's nature.

Wherever we are content, that is our country.

Adulescens, tam etsi properas te hoc saxum rogat
Ut sese aspicias, deinde quod scriptum est legas.
Hic sunt poetae Pacuvi Marci sita
Ossa. Hoc volebam nescius ne esses. Vale.

Epigramma

Fortunam insanam esse et caecam et brutam perhibent
  philosophi . . .
Insanam autem esse aiunt quia atrox incerta instabilisque
  sit;
caecam ob eam rem esse iterant quia nil cernat quo sese
  adplicet;
brutam quia dignum atque indignum nequeat internoscere.
Sunt autem alii philosophi qui contra Fortunam negant
esse ullam sed temeritate res regi omnes autumant.
Id magis verisimile esse usus reapse experiundo edocet.

Ex incertis fabulis

CAECILIUS STATIUS

c. 219 – 166 B.C.

In senectute hoc deputo miserrimum,
  sentire ea aetate eumpse esse odiosum alteri.

Ephesio

Facile aerumnam ferre possunt si inde abest iniuria;
etiam iniuriam, nisi contra constant contumeliam.

Fallacia

Hi sunt inimici pessumi fronte hilaro corde tristi.

Hypobolimaeus

Young man, though you hurry past, this stone would have you look at it and read what is written here. Here lie the bones of the poet Marcus Pacuvius. I would not have you wholly ignorant of him. Farewell.   [*Epitaph on himself*]

Philosophers say that Fortune is foolish, blind, stupid . . . Foolish, they say, because she is cruel, uncertain, fickle; blind, because she does not see whither she goes; stupid because she cannot distinguish between the deserving and the undeserving. However, there are other philosophers who deny that Fortune exists, who maintain that all things are governed by Chance. This is actually the more likely opinion, in the light of ordinary experience.

CAECILIUS

Caecilius Statius was born at Milan, brought to Rome as a prisoner of war, and then manumitted. He followed Plautus as a writer of comedies. Forty titles are known, but only a few fragments have survived. Horace praised his plays—ironically?—for their *gravitas* (dignity), ranking him among the authors "whom mighty Rome learns by heart" and "lists on her muster-roll of poets from the days of Livius Andronicus to our own."

In my opinion, the most wretched thing in old age is the feeling of being hateful to others.

People can bear hardship easily so long as there is no injury, and even injury so long as they do not have to cope with insult.

Your worst enemies are those whose faces are cheerful while their hearts are bitter.

Placere occepit graviter, postquam emortuast.

Plocium

Edepol, senectus, si nihil quicquam aliud viti
adportes tecum, cum advenis, unum id sat est
quod diu vivendo multa quae non volt videt.   *Ibid.*

Vivas ut possis quando nec quis ut velis.   *Ibid.*

Serit arbores quae saeclo prosint alteri.

Synephebi

In civitate fiunt facinora capitalia,
nam ab amico amante argentum accipere meretrix noenu
vult.   *Ibid.*

Deum qui non summum putet
aut stultum aut rerum esse inperitum existumem.
cui in manu sit, quem esse dementem velit.
quem sapere, quem insanire, quem in morbum inici.

Ex incertis fabulis

Homo homini deus est si suum officium sciat.   *Ibid.*

I began to like her tremendously once she died.

Egad, old age, if you bring no other evil, you bring this one: the more things a man does not want to see, he is obliged to see the longer he lives.

Live as you can since you cannot live as you would.

He plants trees to be useful to another generation.

Outrageous things are going on in our city: there is a prostitute who refused money from her lover!

A man who does not believe that [Love] is the greatest of the gods is either foolish or inexperienced, in my opinion. This god drives mad whom he pleases, he has the power to make wise, demented, or sick.

Man is to man a god when he recognizes his duty.

PUBLIUS TERENTIUS AFER

c. 185 – 159 b.c.

Hoc tempore
obsequium amicos, veritas odium parit.

Andria, 67

Davos sum, non Oedipus.   *Id., 194*

Facile omnes quom valemus recta consilia aegrotis damus.

Id., 309

Amantium irae amoris integratiost.   *Id., 555*

Homo sum: humani nil a me alienum puto.

Heauton Timorumenos, 77

Ius summum saepe summast malitia.   *Id., 796*

Nullumst iam dictum quod non sit dictum prius.

Eunuchus, 41

TERENCE

Terence, son of a Libyan slave, was born at Carthage. He was taken to Rome, where his owner, the senator Terentius Lucanus, gave him a liberal education and eventually freed him. Talented and handsome, he became a favorite of prominent personages. He staged six plays, all of which have come down to us. Cicero and Horace admired him for the urbanity and polish of his plays; Caesar praised his love of "pure speech." Terence has been regarded as the creator of the comedy of manners, influencing writers like Congreve, Sheridan, and Diderot. He was never a popular success; he tells us how the audience walked out on a play of his, once to attend a boxing match, once a gladiatorial show in the neighborhood. In 160 B.C. he went to Greece to study and improve his art, and while there wrote a number of plays. They were all lost at sea when he sent his manuscripts to Rome in advance of his own return. He lived just long enough to learn of this misfortune; he died at Stymphalis in Arcadia.

Nowadays flattery wins friends, truth begets hatred.

I'm Davus, not Oedipus. [i.e., *I can't solve riddles.*]

When in health, we all have good advice for the sick.

Lovers' quarrels renew their love.

I am a man: I hold that nothing human is alien to me.

The law at its most rigorous is often injustice at its worst.

Nothing is ever said that has not been said before.

In amore haec omnia insunt vitia: iniuriae,
suspiciones, inimicitiae, indutiae,
bellum, pax rursum: incerta haec si tu postules
ratione certa facere, nihilo plus agas
quam si des operam ut cum ratione insanias.

Id., 59

Di immortales, homini homo quid praestat! stulto
  intellegens
quid interest! *Id., 232*

Sine Cerere et Libero friget Venus. *Id., 732*

Novi ingenium mulierum:
nolunt ubi velis, ubi nolis cupiunt ultro.

Id., 813

Quam inique comparatumst, ei qui minus habent
ut semper aliquid addant ditioribus! *Phormio, 41*

Ut nunc sunt mores, adeo res redit:
si quis quid reddit, magna habendast gratia.

Id., 56

Quot homines tot sententiae: suos quoique mos.
Id., 454

Senectus ipsa morbus est. *Id., 575*

Quid has metuis fores?
conclusam hic habeo uxorem saevam. *Id., 744*

Uxor, si cesses, aut te amare cogitat
aut tete amari aut potare atque animo obsequi,
et tibi bene esse soli, sibi quom sit male.

Adelphoe, 32

All these inconveniences are part of love: reproaches, suspicions, quarrels, reconciliations, war, then peace again. To try to turn these uncertainties into certainties, to treat them rationally, is like trying to go mad by rules of reason.

Immortal gods, how superior can one man be to another! What a difference between a wise man and a fool!

Without Ceres and Bacchus, Venus grows cold.

I know women's ways: they won't when you will, and when you won't they're dying for it.

How unfair that poor people should always be adding to the wealth of the rich!

The way things are today, you have to act very grateful when someone pays back what he owes you.

There are as many opinions as men: each has his own character.

Old age itself is a sickness.

Q. What terrifies you so about the door?
A. My shrew of a wife is right behind it.

When you're late, your wife gets ideas: you've picked up some girl or a girl picked you up, you're drinking and having a good time, and while you're having a good time, she's miserable.

Errat longe mea quidem sententia,
qui imperium credat gravius esse et stabilius
vi quod fit quam illud quod amicitia adiungitur.

Id., 65

Hoc patriumst, potius consuefacere filium
sua sponte recte facere quam alieno metu:
hoc pater ac dominus interest.   *Id.*, 74

Ego spem pretio non emo.   *Id.*, 219

Omnes, quibus res sunt minus secundae, magis sunt nescio
   quo modo
suspiciosi: ad contumeliam omnia accipiunt magis:
propter suam inpotentiam se semper credunt ludier.

Id., 605

Virginem vitiasti quam te non ius fuerat tangere.
iam id peccatum magnum, magnum, at humanum tamen:
fecere alii saepe item boni.   *Id.*, 686

Ita vitast hominum quasi quom ludas tesseris:
si illud quod maxume opus est iactu non cadit,
illud quod cecidit forte, id arte ut corrigas.   *Id.*, 739

Ad omnia alia aetate sapimus rectius;
solum unum hoc vitium adfert senectus hominibus:
adtentiores sumus ad rem omnes quam sat est.

Id., 832

As I see it, it is a great mistake to believe that authority founded on force carries more weight and is more enduring than authority allied with affection.

That's the way of a father, to accustom his son to do the right thing of his own accord rather than by fear of someone else: that's where a father differs from a master.

I am not one to put out good money merely on expectation.

People who are unsuccessful are all somehow inclined to be suspicious: they are prompt to take offense. Because of their poverty, they are always sure you are slighting them.

You assaulted a girl whom you had no right to touch. That alone is a great wrong, a very great wrong, but after all it is human. Many good men have done the same.

Human life is like shooting dice. If the dice don't turn up as you hoped, you have to make the most of how they did.

In every other respect wisdom grows with age. This sole vice comes with old age—we all try to make more money than we need.

GAIUS LUCILIUS

c. 180 – c. 102 B.C.

O curas hominum! O quantum est in rebus inane!

Vivite lurcones, comedones, vivite ventris!

Tristes difficiles sumus, fastidimus bonorum.

Ut pueri infantes credunt signa omnia aena
vivere et esse homines, sic isti somnia ficta
vera putant, credunt signis cor inesse in aenis.
Pergula pictorum, veri nil, omnia ficta.

Aurum vis hominemne? Habeas. "Hominem? quid ad
aurum?"

Publicanus vero ut Asiae fiam, ut scripturarius
pro Lucilio, id ego nolo et uno hoc non muto omnia.

Homini amico et familiari non est mentiri meum.

Ut Romanus populus victus vei, superatus proeliis
saepe est multis, bello vero numquam, in quo sunt omnia.

Hunc laborem sumas laudem qui tibi ac fructum ferat.

Paulo hoc melius quam mediocre, hoc minus malum quam
ut pessumum.

LUCILIUS

Lucilius came of a prominent family—Pompey the Great was his nephew. He was born at Suessa Aurunca (present-day Sessa) in Latium. He wrote thirty books of satires (about 1300 lines have survived), a genre of which, Horace says, Lucilius was the founder, "the first who dared to compose poems of this kind." Of independent character, he cared nothing for public office, and in his works spared neither leaders nor common people. Horace criticizes his loose style but often imitates him in his own *Satires*.

Ah, human cares! Ah, how much futility in the world!

Enjoy yourselves, gluttons and guzzlers, fill up your bellies!

We are disgruntled, hard to please, scornful of good things.

Like little children who believe that bronze statues are living men, so these people take dreams and fictions for real and suppose that bronze images possess a heart. Picture galleries, no truth, all fiction.

The man or his gold? Which will you take?—The man? When you could take the gold?

To be a tax collector in Asia, to gather pasture duties for the government instead of being Lucilius—never! I would not trade being myself for the whole world.

It is not my habit to lie to friends or family.

The Roman nation has been vanquished often by brute force, defeated in many battles, yet never lost a war. And that's the only thing that matters.

Accept tasks that bring praise and profit.

It's a little better than mediocre, a little less bad than the worst.

Cupiditas ex homine, cupido ex stulto numquam tollitur.

Accipiunt leges, populus quibus legibus exlex.

Nunc vero a mani ad noctem festo atque profesto
totus item pariterque die populusque patresque
iactare indu foro se omnes, decedere nusquam;
uni se atque eidem studio omnes dedere et arti—
verba dare ut caute possint, pugnare dolose,
blanditia certare, bonum simulare virum se,
insidias facere ut si hostes sint omnibus omnes.

LUCIUS ACCIUS

170 – c. 86 B.C.

Saepe ignavavit fortem ex spe expectatio.

Aeneadae

Muliebre ingenium, prolubium, occasio.

Andromeda

Virtuti sis par, dispar fortunis patris.

Armorum iudicium

Cuius sit vita indecoris mortem fugere turpem haut
convenit. *Athamas*

Oderint dum metuant. *Atreus*

A man can be cured of his lust, but never a fool of his greed.

They consent to laws which place the people beyond the pale of law. [*Criticism of anti-alien legislation, 126* B.C.]

Yet nowadays from morning to night, whether it's a holiday or not, the plebs and the senate alike flock to the Forum, and never think of leaving. They are all up to the same tricks, engaged in the same business: cheating each other cleverly, battling treacherously, outdoing one another in flattery, posing as respectable citizens, laying traps for each other—all of them acting as though each were the other's mortal enemy.

ACCIUS

Accius, son of a freedman, was born at ancient Pisaurum. He wrote fifty-two tragedies, several books of literary criticism, and a history of the Roman stage. For his vigor and dramatic brilliance he was still appreciated highly—by Ovid, for example—more than a century after his death.

Expectation based on hope has often disappointed courageous men.

A woman's nature—desire, opportunity.

Be like your father in courage, unlike him in fortune.

A man whose life has been dishonorable is not entitled to escape disgrace in death.

Let them hate me, just so long as they fear me.

Vigilandum est semper; multae insidiae sunt bonis.

Ibid.

Probae etsi in segetem sunt deteriorem datae
fruges, tamen ipsae suaptae natura enitent.   *Ibid.*

Laetum in Parnasso inter pines tripudiantem in circulis
ludere. . . . atque taedis fulgere.   *Bacchae*

Sapimus animo, fruimur anima; sine animo anima est
debilis.   *Epigoni*

Probis probatum potius quam multis fore.

Epinausimache

Is demum miser est, cuius nobilitas miserias nobilitat.

Telephus

Immo enim vero corpus Priamo reddidi, Hectora abstuli.

Ex incertis fabulis

LUCIUS AFRANIUS

b. c. 150 b.c.

Si possent homines delenimentis capi,
omnes haberent nunc amatores anus.
aetas et corpus tenerum et morigeratio,
haec sunt venena formosarum mulierum:
mala aetas nulla delenimenta invenit.   *Vopiscus*

One must always be on one's guard: there are many snares for the good.

A good seed, planted even in poor soil, will bear rich fruit by its own nature.

Joyous, on Parnassus, among the pines, leaping in a round, he plays. . . . and glistens under the light of torches.

We discern with the mind, enjoy with the heart; without the mind, the heart is feeble.

The praise of honorable men is worth more than that of the multitude.

Indeed, wretched the man whose fame makes his misfortunes famous.

Yes, I took Hector from Priam, I gave him back a corpse.

AFRANIUS

Almost nothing is known about the life of Afranius. Only a few fragments of his works have come down to us. According to Quintilian, he "excelled in the purely Roman comedy," and "defiled his plots by introducing indecent pederastic intrigues." Cicero calls him "a very witty man" (*homo perargutus*). The playwright himself proudly acknowledges his debt to Menander and to Terence. One of his plays, *Incendium,* was revived under Nero.

If men could be seduced by magic potions, all old women would have sweethearts today. Youth, a tender body, and compliance—these are the potions of pretty women. No magic has yet been found for unhappy old age.

Alius est Amor,
Alius Cupido.

Amabit sapiens, cupient caeteri.

Ista parentum est vita vilis liberis,
ubi malunt metui quam vereri se ab suis.

Consobrini

Usus me genuit, mater peperit Memoria.
Sophiam vocant me Graii, vos Sapientiam.   *Sella*

Formosa virgo est; dotis dimidium vocant
Isti, qui dotes neglegunt uxorias.

Fragmentum

MARCUS TERENTIUS VARRO

116–27 B.C.

Divina natura dedit agros, ars humana aedificavit urbes.

De Re Rustica, III, 1

Successum . . . fortuna, experientiam laus sequitur.

Antiquitates rerum humanarum et divinarum, XIV
(Aulus Gellius, I, 18)

Vitium uxoris aut tollendum aut ferendum est. Qui tollit
vitium,
uxorem commodiorem praestat; qui fert, sese meliorem
facit.   *Satirae Menippeae, De Officio mariti (Id., I, 17)*

Love is one thing, lust another.

The wise man loves, the others are merely lecherous.

Children hold cheap the life of parents who would rather be feared than respected.

Practice was my father, memory my mother. The Greeks call me *sophia*, you call me wisdom.

The girl is pretty; this is half a dowry, say men who aren't interested in a dowry.

VARRO

Born at Reate, educated in Rome, Varro studied philosophy in Athens. He was a partisan of Pompey and was proscribed by Antony, but he managed to survive. Under Augustus he held the post of librarian. He wrote more than five hundred books during his long life. These include plays, poems, satires, an encyclopedia of the liberal arts, and a number of treatises on diverse subjects. Of all this only *De Re Rustica,* about a quarter of *De Lingua Latina,* and about six hundred lines of his *Satirae Menippeae* survive, plus a few scattered fragments.

Divine nature gave us the country, human art built our cities.

Good fortune attends success, praise follows effort.

A wife's faults must either be corrected or put up with. Who corrects the faults, makes his wife more pleasant; who puts up with them, makes himself a better man.

[Dicit autem] convivarum numerum incipere oportere a
   Gratiarum numero
et progredi ad Musarum, id est proficisci a tribus et consistere in novem.

Id., Nescis quid vesper serus vehat (Id., XIII, 11)

Non videtis, unus ut
parvulus Amor ardifeta lampada arida
agat amantes aestuantes?
Et rex et misellus ille pauper amat
habetque intus ignem acrem.

Id., Gnoti seauton

Postremo nemo aegrotus quidquam somniat
tam infandum, quod non aliquis dicat philosophus.

Fragmenta

Ergo tum Romae parce pureque pudentes
   vixere in patria; nunc sumus in rutuba.   *Id.*

The number of guests at dinner should not be less than the number of the Graces nor exceed that of the Muses, *i.e.*, it should begin with three and stop at nine.

Can't you see little Cupid, all by himself with his tinder-dry torch, driving ardent lovers at his pleasure? Both king and poor man love, each carries the consuming fire within his heart.

In short, no sick man has ever dreamed of anything so absurd that one or another philosopher has not said it.

And so, in the Rome of those days, people were thrifty and modest. Theirs was a homeland, today we live in chaos.

MARCUS TULLIUS CICERO

106 – 43 B.C.

Cedant arma togae, concedat laurea linguae.

De Consulatu Suo

O fortunatam natam me consule Romam!   *Ibid.*

Vigilantem habemus consulem, Caninium,
Qui in consulatu somnum non vidit suo.

Epigramma

Dic, hospes, Spartae nos te hic vidisse iacentes,
Dum sanctis patriae legibus obsequimur.

(Translation from Simonides)

CICERO

Cicero's voluminous writings include poetry (both his own and translations from the Greek); orations (fifty-eight have survived, forty-eight are lost); treatises on rhetoric, philosophy, morals, and politics; and letters. Cicero himself thought that his best work was his verse, but no one else shared this judgment. Juvenal calls it ridiculous (*ridenda poemata*), and Tacitus observes that as a poet he was less lucky than Caesar and Brutus because the latters' verse never became widely known. Cicero is the greatest master of Latin prose, in a sense its creator; his subtly rhythmed style influenced countless writers in many languages. "For posterity," says Quintilian, "the name of Cicero has come to be regarded as the name of eloquence itself." His treatises are important historically because they contain much information on ancient thought. His letters, most of which were not written for publication, are the chief source for our knowledge of the period; in them the brilliant lawyer-statesman-philosopher reveals himself as all too human. His greatest achievement as a statesman, he believed, was saving the republic from Catiline. After Caesar's death he violently attacked Mark Antony in his celebrated *Philippics*. When the second triumvirate was formed, he was put on the list of the proscribed and was murdered by Antony's agents. He faced death with dignity; he may well have found life no longer worth living once the republic was destroyed. "If one balances his faults against his virtues," says Livy, "he was a man of greatness, energy, and distinction—a man, the complete exposition of whose merits would demand Cicero himself as eulogist."

Let arms yield to the toga, let the [victor's] laurel yield to the [orator's] tongue.

O fortunate Rome born in my consulship!

We have a vigilant consul, Caninius, who never slept once during his entire term of office! [His term lasted but a day.]

Stranger, tell the Spartans that you saw where we lie buried, for having obeyed the sacred laws of our homeland.

Innocens si accusatus sit, absolvi potest; nocens, nisi accusatus fuerit, condemnari non potest. Utilius est autem absolvi innocentem quam nocentem causam non dicere.

Pro Roscio Amerino, 56

L. Cassius . . . in causis quaerere solebat, "cui bono" fuisset. Sic vita hominum est, ut ad maleficium nemo conetur sine spe atque emolumento accedere. *Id., 84*

Non ingenerantur hominibus mores tam a stirpe generis ac seminis quam ex iis rebus, quae ab ipsa natura nobis ad vitae consuetudinem suppeditantur, quibus alimur et vivimus. *De Lege Agraria, II, 95*

Nihil tam munitum quod non expugnari pecunia possit.

In Verrem, I, ii, 4

Illa vox et imploratio "Civis Romanus sum," quae saepe multis in ultimis terris opem inter barbaros et salutem tulit.

In Verrem II, v, 147

Facinus est vincire civem Romanum, scelus verberare, prope parricidium necare: quid dicam in crucem tollere? Verbo satis digno tam nefaria res nullo modo appellari potest. *Ibid., 170*

Quo usque tandem abutere, Catilina, patientia nostra? Quam diu etiam furor iste tuus nos eludet?

In Catilinam, I, 1

O tempora, o mores! Senatus haec intellegit, consul videt; hic tamen vivit. *Ibid.*

Cum tacent, clamant. *Id., I, 21*

Abiit, excessit, evasit, erupit. *Id., II, 1*

Nam neque turpis mors forti viro potest accidere neque immatura consulari nec misera sapienti. *Id., IV, 3*

An innocent man, if accused, can be acquitted; a guilty man, unless accused, cannot be condemned. It is, however, more advantageous to absolve an innocent than not to prosecute a guilty man.

When trying a case [the famous judge] L. Cassius never failed to inquire, "Who gained by it?" Man's character is such that no one undertakes crimes without hope of gain.

Our character is not so much the product of race and heredity as of those circumstances by which nature forms our habits, by which we are nourished and live.

No place is so strongly fortified that money could not capture it.

"I am a Roman citizen"—that appeal has often helped and even saved many a man among barbarians in the remotest lands.

It is a crime to put a Roman citizen in chains, it is an enormity to flog one, sheer murder to slay one: what, then, shall I say of crucifixion? It is impossible to find the word for such an abomination.

How long, then, Catiline, will you abuse our patience? How long is this madness of yours to make sport of us?

What times! What manners! The Senate knows these things, the consul sees them, and yet this man lives.

Their very silence is a loud cry.

He has gone, departed, escaped, broken away.

For a courageous man cannot die dishonorably, a man who has attained the consulship cannot die before his time, a philosopher cannot die wretchedly.

53

Duae sunt artes igitur quae possunt locare homines in amplissimo gradu dignitatis, una imperatoris, altera oratoris boni. Ab hoc enim pacis ornamenta retinentur, ab illo belli pericula repelluntur. *Pro Murena, 30*

Nihil est incertius vulgo, nihil obscurius voluntate hominum, nihil fallacius ratione tota comitiorum. *Id., 36*

Cui placet obliviscitur, cui dolet meminit. *Id., 42*

Odit populus Romanus privatam luxuriam, publicam magnificentiam diligit. *Id., 76*

Ingenita levitas et erudita vanitas.
Pro Flacco (fragment)

Pleni sunt omnes libri, plenae sapientium voces, plena exemplorum vetustas: quae iacerent in tenebris omnia, nisi litterarum lumen accederet. *Pro Archia Poeta, 14*

Haec studia adolescentiam acuunt, senectutem oblectant, secundas res ornant, adversis perfugium ac solacium praebent, delectant domi, non impediunt foris, pernoctant nobiscum, peregrinantur, rusticantur. *Id., 16*

Trahimur omnes studio laudis et optimus quisque maxime gloria ducitur. Ipsi illi philosophi etiam illis libellis, quos de contemnenda gloria scribunt, nomen suum inscribunt.
Id., 26

Nihil tam proprium hominis existimo quam non modo beneficio, sed etiam benevolentiae significatione alligari: nihil porro tam inhumanum, tam immane, tam ferum quam committere ut beneficio non dicam indignus, sed victus esse videare. *Pro Plancio, xxxiii, 81*

There are two professions which lead a man to the highest rank of office, that of general, and that of good orator. For the latter secures for us the blessings of peace, the former averts the dangers of war.

Nothing is more unreliable than the populace, nothing more obscure than human intentions, nothing more deceptive than the whole electoral system.

We forget our pleasures, we remember our sufferings.

The Romans hate private luxury but love public magnificence.

Frivolity is inborn, conceit acquired by education.

The countless inspiring examples which we find in our books, our philosophy, our history would all have been buried in darkness had not the light of literature fallen upon them.

These studies stimulate the young, divert the old, are an ornament in prosperity and a refuge and comfort in adversity; they delight us at home, are no impediment in public life, keep us company at night, in our travels, and whenever we retire to the country.

We are eager for praise, even the noblest men are strongly motivated by the desire for fame. On the very books in which philosophers tell us to despise fame, they inscribe their names.

I believe that no characteristic is so distinctively human as the sense of indebtedness we feel, not necessarily for a favor received, but even for the slightest evidence of kindness; and there is nothing so boorish, savage, inhuman as to appear to be overwhelmed by a favor, let alone unworthy of it.

Videbar videre alios intrantes, alios autem exeuntes, quosdam ex vino vacillantes, quosdam hesterna ex potatione oscitantes. Humus erat immunda, lutulenta vino, coronis languidulis et spinis cooperta piscium.

Pro Gallio, fragmenta

Quod enim est ius civile? Quod neque inflecti gratia, neque perfringi potentia, neque adulterari pecunia possit; quod si non modo oppressum, sed etiam desertum aut negligentius asservatum erit, nihil est quod quisquam sese habere certum, aut a patre accepturum, aut relicturum liberis arbitretur. *Pro Caecina, 73*

Sapientissimum esse dicunt eum, cui quod opus sit ipsi veniat in mentem: proxime accedere illum, qui alterius bene inventis obtemperet. In stultitia contra est. Minus enim stultus est is, cui nihil in mentem venit, quam ille, qui, quod stulte alteri venit in mentem, comprobat.

Pro Cluentio, 84

Quid est igitur propositum his rei publicae gubernatoribus, quod intueri et quo cursum suum derigere debeant? It quod est praestantissimum maximeque optabile omnibus sanis et bonis et beatis, cum dignitate otium.

Pro Sestio, 98

Silent leges inter arma. *Pro Milone, 11*

Homines enim ad deos nulla re propius accedunt quam salutem hominibus dando. *Pro Ligario, 38*

Et nomen pacis dulce est et ipsa res salutaris, sed inter pacem et servitutem plurimum interest. Pax est tranquilla libertas, servitus postremum malorum omnium non modo bello, sed morte etiam repellendum. *Philippica II, 113*

I thought I saw some people entering, others leaving, some reeling drunkenly, others yawning from last night's tippling; the floor was filthy, stained with wine, covered with withered wreaths and fishbones.

Just what is the civil law? What neither influence can affect, nor power break, nor money corrupt: were it to be suppressed or even merely ignored or inadequately observed, no one could feel safe about anything, whether his own possessions, or the inheritance he expects from his father, or the bequests he makes to his children.

It is said that that man is wisest who can decide for himself what needs to be done; next comes the man who acts on another's good ideas. In the case of folly the opposite obtains. For the man to whose mind nothing ever occurs is less foolish than he who approves others' foolish ideas.

What then is the objective of those who are at the helm of government, which they should never lose sight of, toward which they ought to set their course? It is what is best and most desirable for all good, sound, prosperous citizens: namely, peace with dignity.

In time of war the laws are silent.

In nothing are men more like gods than in coming to the rescue of their fellow men.

The name of peace is sweet, and the thing itself is beneficial, but there is a great difference between peace and servitude. Peace is freedom in tranquillity, servitude is the worst of all evils, to be resisted not only by war, but even by death.

Populum Romanum servire fas non est, quem di immortales omnibus gentibus imperare voluerunt. . . .
Aliae nationes servitutem pati possunt, populi Romani est propria libertas.   *Philippica VI, vii, 19*

Cuisvis hominis est errare, nullius nisi insipientis in errore perseverare.   *Id., XII, ii, 5*

O miser cum re, tum hoc ipso, quod non sentis, quam miser sis!   *Id., XIII, xvii, 34*

O fortunata mors, quae naturae debita pro patria est potissimum reddita!   *Id., XIV, xii, 31*

Quid esse potest in otio aut iucundius, aut magis proprium humanitatis, quam sermo facetus ac nulla in res rudis? Hoc enim uno praestamus vel maxime feris, quod colloquimur inter nos, et quod exprimere dicendo sensa possumus.
                    De Oratore, I, 32

Nihil in hominum genere rarius perfecto oratore inveniri potest.   *Ibid., 128*

Nihil est . . . tam insigne, nec tam ad diuturnitatem memoriae stabile, quam id, in quo aliquid offenderis.
                    Ibid., 129

It is contrary to divine law that the Roman people should be enslaved, for the immortal gods have willed that Rome should have dominion over all nations. . . . Other nations may be able to put up with slavery, but freedom is the distinguishing attribute of the Roman people.

Any man is liable to err, only a fool persists in error.

O wretched man, wretched not just because of what you are, but also because you do not know how wretched you are!

How fortunate in death [those who fell for their country], of all the ways of paying this common debt to nature, the most to be desired!

(Tr. E. W. Sutton and H. Rackham)

What in hours of ease can be a pleasanter thing or one more characteristic of culture, than discourse that is graceful and nowhere uninstructed? For the one point in which we have our greatest advantage over the brute creation is that we converse with one another, and can reproduce our thought in words.

No rarer thing than a finished orator can be discovered among the sons of men.

Nothing stands out so conspicuously, or remains so firmly fixed in the memory, as something in which you have blundered.

Quis nescit, primam esse historiae legem, ne quid falsi dicere audeat? Deinde ne quid veri non audeat? Ne qua suspicio gratiae sit in scribendo? Ne qua simultatis?

De Oratore, II, 62

Tardi ingenii est rivulos consectari, fontis rerum non videre. *Id., 117*

Plura . . . multo homines iudicant odio aut amore aut cupiditate aut iracundia aut dolore aut laetitia aut spe aut timore aut errore aut aliqua permotione mentis, quam veritate aut prescripto aut iuris norma aliqua aut iudicii formula aut legibus. *Id., 178*

Omnibus in rebus voluptatibus maximis fastidium finitimum est. *Id., III, 100*

Cito enim arescit lacrima, praesertim in alienis malis.

De partitione oratoria, 57

Nescire autem quid ante quam natus sis acciderit, id est semper esse puerum. Quid enim est aetas hominis, nisi ea memoria rerum veterum cum superiorum aetate contexitur? *Orator, 120*

Ne in maximis quidem rebus quicquam adhuc inveni firmius, quod tenerem aut quo iudicium meum dirigerem, quam id quodcumque mihi quam simillimum veri videretur, cum ipsum illud verum tamen in occulto lateret.

Id., 237

Who does not know history's first law to be that an author must not dare to tell anything but the truth? And its second that he must make bold to tell the whole truth? That there must be no suggestion of partiality anywhere in his writings? Nor of malice?

It is a symptom of congenital dullness to follow up the tiny rills, but fail to discern the sources of things.

Men decide far more problems by hate, love, lust, rage, sorrow, joy, hope, fear, illusion, or some other inward emotion, than by reality, authority, any legal standard, judicial precedent, or statute.

The greatest pleasures are only narrowly separated from disgust.

For a tear is quickly dried, especially when shed for the misfortunes of others.

(Tr. G. L. Hendrickson and H. M. Hubbell)

To be ignorant of what occurred before you were born is to remain always a child. For what is the worth of human life, unless it is woven into the life of our ancestors by the records of history?

Even in the most important subjects, I have never found anything more substantial to hold to or use in forming my opinions, than what seemed like the truth; the truth itself is hidden in obscurity.

Etsi ars quidem, cum ea non utare, scientia tamen ipsa teneri potest, virtus in usu sui tota posita est; usus autem eius est maximus civitatis gubernatio. *De re publica, I, 2*

Nullus interitus est rei publicae naturalis ut hominis, in quo mors non modo necessaria est, verum etiam optanda persaepe. *Id., III, 34*

Illa iniusta bella sunt, quae sunt sine causa suscepta. nam extra ulciscendi aut propulsandorum hostium causam bellum geri iustum nullum potest. *Ibid., 35*

Vult plane virtus honorem, nec est virtutis ulla alia merces . . . quam tamen illa accipit facile, exigit non acerbe.

Ibid., 40

Sic habeto, non esse te mortalem, sed corpus hoc; nec enim tu is es, quem forma ista declarat, sed mens cuiusque is est quisque, non ea figura, quae digito demonstrari potest. *Id., VI, xxiv, 26*

Lex est ratio summa insita in natura, quae iubet ea, quae facienda sunt, prohibetque contraria. *De legibus, I, vi, 18*

Universus hic mundus sit una civitas communis deorum atque hominum existimanda. *Ibid., vii, 23*

Ut enim magistratibus leges, ita populo praesunt magistratus, vereque dici potest magistratum legem esse loquentem, legem autem mutum magistratum.

Id., III, i, 2

Though it is true that an art, even if you never use it, can still remain in your possession by the very fact of your knowledge of it, yet the existence of virtue depends entirely upon its use; and its noblest use is the government of the state.

Death is not natural for a state as it is for a human being, for whom death is not only necessary, but frequently even desirable.

Those wars are unjust which are undertaken without provocation. For only a war waged for revenge or defense can be just.

Virtue clearly desires honor, and has no other reward . . . yet though she receives it gladly, she does not exact it rigorously.

Be sure that it is not you that is mortal, but only your body. For that man whom your outward form reveals is not yourself; the spirit is the true self, not that physical figure which can be pointed out by your finger.

Law is the highest reason implanted in Nature, which commands what ought to be done and forbids the opposite.

We must conceive of this whole universe as one commonwealth of which both gods and men are members.

As the laws govern the magistrates, so the magistrates govern the people, and it can truly be said that the magistrate is a speaking law, and the law a silent magistrate.

Gratulemurque nobis, quoniam mors aut meliorem, quam qui est in vita, aut certe non deteriorem adlatura est statum; nam sine corpore animo vigente divina vita est, sensu carente nihil profecto est mali. *Id., fragmenta*

In omni autem honesto de quo loquimur nihil est tam illustre ne quod latius pateat quam coniunctio inter homines . . . et ipsa caritas generis humani, quae nata a primo satu . . . serpit sensim foras, cognationibus primum . . . deinde totius complexu gentis humanae; quae animi affectio suum cuique tribuens . . . iustitia dicitur.

De Finibus, V, xxiii, 65

Honos alit artes omnesque incenduntur ad studia gloria iacentque ea semper, quae apud quosque improbantur.

Tusculanae Disputationes, I, ii, 4

Mandare quemquam litteris cogitationes suas, qui eas nec disponere nec illustrare possit nec delectatione aliqua adlicere lectorem, hominis est intemperanter abutentis et otio et litteris. *Ibid., 6*

Firmissimum hoc adferri videtur, cur deos esse credamus, quod nulla gens tam fera, nemo omnium tam est immanis, cuius mentem non imbuerit deorum opinio. *Ibid., 30*

Natura inest in mentibus nostris insatiabilis quaedam cupiditas veri videndi. *Ibid., 44*

Nemo parum diu vixit, qui virtutis perfectae perfecto functus est munere. *Ibid., 109*

Let us deem ourselves happy that death will grant us either a better existence than our life on earth, or at least a condition that is no worse. For a life in which the mind is free from the body and yet retains its own powers is godlike; on the other hand, if we have no consciousness, no evil can befall us.

(Tr. H. Rackham)

In the whole moral sphere of which we are speaking there is nothing more glorious nor of wider range than the solidarity of mankind . . . and that actual affection which exists between man and man, which, coming into existence immediately upon our birth . . . gradually spreads its influence beyond the home, first by blood relationships . . . and lastly by embracing the whole of the human race. This sentiment assigning each his own . . . is termed justice.

(Tr. J. E. King)

Public esteem is the nurse of the arts, and all men are fired to application by fame, whilst those pursuits which meet with general disapproval always lie neglected.

To commit one's reflections to writing, without being able to arrange or express them clearly or to attract the reader by some sort of charm, indicates a man who makes an unpardonable misuse of leisure and his pen.

This seems to be advanced as the surest basis for our belief in the existence of gods, that there is no race so uncivilized, no one in the world so barbarous that his mind has no inkling of a belief in gods.

Nature has planted in our minds an insatiable longing to see the truth.

No one has lived too short a life who has discharged the perfect work of perfect virtue.

Quod autem omnibus necesse est, idne miserum uni potest?
Ibid., 119

Sunt enim ingeniis nostris semina innata virtutum, quae si adolescere liceret, ipsa nos ad beatam vitam natura perduceret. . . . Cum vero parentibus redditi, dein magistris traditi sumus, tum ita variis imbuimur erroribus, ut vanitati veritas et opinioni confirmatae natura ipsa cedat.
Id., III, 2

Totus vero iste, qui vulgo appellatur amor—nec hercule invenio quo nomine alio possit appellari—tantae levitatis est, ut nihil videam quod putem conferendum. *Id., IV, 68*

Quid est enim dulcius otio literato? iis dico litteris, quibus infinitatem rerum atque naturae et in hoc ipso mundo caelum, terras, maria cognoscimus. *Id., V, 105*

Nihil est tam incredibile quod non dicendo fiat probabile, nihil tam horridum tam incultum quod non splendescat oratione et tamquam excolatur.
Paradoxa Stoicorum, 3

An tu civem ab hoste natura ac loco, non animo factisque distinguis? *Ibid., 29*

Non intelligunt homines quam magnum vectigal sit parsimonia. *Ibid., 49*

Haud scio an pietate adversus deos sublata fides etiam et societas generi humani et una excellentissima virtus iustitia tollatur. *De Natura Deorum, I, 4*

But can that which is necessary for all be wretched for one alone? [death]

The seeds of virtue are inborn in our dispositions and, if they were allowed to ripen, nature's own hand would lead us on to happiness of life . . . but when we leave the nursery to be with parents and later on are handed over to teachers, we become imbued with deceptions so varied that truth gives way to unreality and the voice of nature to ready-made opinions.

In fact the whole passion ordinarily termed love (and heaven help me if I can think of any other term to apply to it) is of such exceeding triviality that I see nothing that I think comparable with it.

What is more delightful than leisure devoted to literature? That literature I mean which gives us the knowledge of the infinite greatness of nature, and, in this actual world of ours, of the sky, the lands, the sea.

(*Tr. H. Rackham*)

Nothing is so difficult to believe that oratory cannot make it acceptable, nothing so rough and uncultured as not to gain brilliance and refinement from eloquence.

Do you distinguish a citizen from an enemy by race and by locality, not by character and conduct?

Cannot people realize how large an income is thrift?

In all probability the disappearance of piety toward the gods will entail the disappearance of loyalty and social union among men as well and of justice itself, the queen of all the virtues.

Utinam tam facile vera invenire possem quam falsa convincere. *Ibid., 91*

Horum enim sententiae omnium non modo superstitionem tollunt in qua inest timor inanis deorum, sed etiam religionem quae deorum cultu pio continetur. *Ibid., 117*

Sunt enim ex terra homines non ut incolae atque habitatores sed quasi spectatores superarum rerum atque caelestium, quarum spectaculum ad nullum aliud genus animalium pertinet. *Id., II, 140*

Magna di curant, parva neglegunt. *Ibid., 167*

Mala enim et impia consuetudo est contra deos disputandi, sive ex animo id fit sive simulate. *Ibid., 168*

Iudicium hoc omnium mortalium est, fortunam a deo petendam, a se ipso sumendam esse sapientiam.
Id., III, 88

Nemo enim est tam senex qui se annum non putet posse vivere. *De Senectute, 24*

Avaritia vero senilis quid sibi velit, non intellego. Potest enim quicquam esse absurdius quam, quo viae minus restet, eo plus viatici quaerere? *Ibid., 65/66*

Quod si in hoc erro, qui animos hominum immortalis esse credam, libenter erro nec mihi hunc errorem, quo delector, dum vivo, extorqueri volo. *Ibid., 85*

I only wish I could discover the truth as easily as I can expose falsehood.

The doctrines of all these thinkers abolish not only superstition, which implies a groundless fear of the gods, but also religion, which consists in piously worshiping them.

For men are sprung from the earth, not as its inhabitants and denizens, but to be as it were the spectators of things supernal and heavenly, in the contemplation whereof no other animal participates.

The gods attend to great matters, they neglect small ones.

The habit of arguing in support of atheism, whether it be done from conviction or in pretense, is a wicked and impious practice.

It is the considered belief of all mankind that they must pray to God for fortune but obtain wisdom for themselves.

(Tr. W. A. Falconer)

No one is so old as to think he cannot live one more year.

As for avarice in the old, what purpose it can serve I cannot understand. For can anything be more absurd in the traveler than to increase his luggage as he nears his journey's end?

If I err in belief that the souls of men are immortal, I gladly err, nor do I wish this error which gives me pleasure to be wrested from me while I live.

Est enim amicitia nihil aliud nisi omnium divinarum humanarumque rerum cum benevolentia et caritate consensio, qua quidem haud scio an excepta sapientia nil quicquam melius homini sit a dis immortalibus datum.

De Amicitia, 20

Et secundas res splendidiores facit amicitia, et adversas, partiens communicansque, leviores. *Ibid., 22*

Ipse enim se quisque diligit, non ut aliquam a se ipse mercedem exigat caritatis suae, sed quod per se quisque sibi carus est; quod nisi idem in amicitiam transferetur, verus amicus numquam reperetur: est enim is qui est tamquam alter idem. *Ibid., 80*

Amare autem nihil est, nisi eum ipsum diligere quem ames, nulla indigentia, nulla utilitate quaesita. *Ibid., 100*

Vetus illud Catonis admodum scitum est, qui mirari se aiebat quod non rideret haruspex haruspicem cum vidisset. *De Divinatione, II, 51*

Summum ius summa iniuria. *De Officiis, I, 33*

Omnium autem rerum, ex quibus aliquid acquiritur, nihil est agri cultura melius, nihil uberius, nihil dulcius, nihil homini libero dignius. *Ibid., 151*

Cognitio contemplatioque naturae manca quodam modo atque inchoata sit, si nulla actio rerum consequatur.

Ibid., 153

Quo quis versutior et callidior, hoc invisior et suspectior est detracta opinione probitatis. *Id., II, 34*

Friendship is nothing else than an accord in all things, human and divine, conjoined with mutual goodwill and affection, and I am inclined to think that, with the exception of wisdom, no better thing has been given to man by the immortal gods.

Friendship adds a brighter radiance to prosperity and lightens the burden of adversity by dividing and sharing it.

Everyone loves himself, not with a view of acquiring some profit for himself from his self-love, but because he is dear to himself on his own account; and unless this same thing were transferred to friendship, the real friend would never be found; for he is, as it were, another self.

Love is nothing other than the great esteem and affection felt for him who inspires that sentiment, and it is not sought because of material need or for the sake of material gain.

The well-known old remark of Cato, who used to wonder how two soothsayers could look one another in the face without laughing.

(*Tr. W. Miller*)

More law, less justice.

Of all the occupations in which gain is secured, none is better than agriculture, none more profitable, none more delightful, none more becoming to a freeman.

The study and knowledge of the universe would somehow be lame and defective were no practical results to follow.

Take from a man his reputation for probity, and the more shrewd and clever he is, the more hated and mistrusted he becomes.

Conveniet . . . a litibus . . . quantum liceat et nescio an paulo plus etiam, quam liceat, abhorrentem. Est enim non modo liberale paulum non numquam de suo iure decedere, sed interdum etiam fructuosum.   *Ibid., 64*

Nulla est enim societas nobis cum tyrannis, et potius summa distractio est, neque est contra naturam spoliare eum, si possis, quem est honestum necare, atque hoc omne genus pestiferum atque impium ex hominum communitate extermindandum est.   *Id., III, 32*

Non defendi homines sine vituperatione fortasse posse, neglegenter defendi sine scelere non posse.
                    (Quoted by Ammianus Marcellinus, XXX, 4, 7)

Numquam . . . praestantibus in re publica gubernanda viris laudata est in una sententia perpetua permansio.
                              Epistulae ad Familiares, I, 9, 21

Estque animi ingenui, cui multum debeas, eidem plurimum velle debere.   *Id., II, 6, 2*

Nihil est . . . quod studio et benevolentia vel amore potius effici non potest.   *Id., III, 9, 1*

Nunc vero nec locus tibi ullus dulcior esse debet patria nec eam minus diligere debes, quod deformior est, sed misereri potius.   *Id., IV, 9, 3*

Epistola . . . non erubescit.   *Id., V, 12, 1*

Nihil est . . . aptius ad delectationem lectoris quam temporum varietatem fortunaeque vicissitudines. Quae etsi optabiles in experiendo non fuerunt, in legendo tamen erunt iucundae; habet enim praeteriti doloris secura recordatio delectationem.   *Ibid., 4*

It will befit a gentleman . . . to keep out of litigation . . . as far as his interests will permit and perhaps even a little farther. For it is not only generous occasionally to share a little of one's own rightful claims, but it is sometimes even advantageous.

We have no tie of fellowship with a tyrant, but rather the bitterest feud; and it is not opposed to nature to rob, if one can, a man whom it is morally right to kill—nay, all that pestilent and abominable race should be exterminated from human society.

It might be pardonable to refuse to defend some men, but to defend them negligently is nothing short of criminal.

Persistence in a single view has never been regarded as a merit in political leaders.

It shows nobility to be willing to increase your debt to a man to whom you already owe much.

Nothing is . . . impossible for devotion and kindness or rather love.

No place should be dearer to you than your homeland, nor should you love it less because it has grown uglier, but rather pity it the more.

A letter . . . does not blush.

Nothing is . . . more likely to delight a reader than variety of circumstances and the vicissitudes of fortune. Even though we found no pleasure in experiencing them, we enjoy reading about them: there is something delectable in calm remembrance of a past sorrow.

Nihil esse praecipue cuiquam dolendum in eo, quod accidat universis.   *Id., VI, 2, 2*

Quae potest homini esse polito delectatio, cum aut homo imbecillus a valentissima bestia laniatur aut praeclara bestia venabulo transverberatur? quae tamen, si videnda sunt, saepe vidisti; neque nos, qui haec spectamus, quicquam novi vidimus. Extremus elephantorum dies fuit. In quo admiratio magna vulgi atquae turbae, delectatio nulla exstitit; quin etiam misericordia quaedam consecuta est atque opinio eius modi, esse quamdam illi beluae cum genere humano societatem.   *Id., VII, 1, 3*

Mortem mihi cur consciscerem causa non visa est, cur optarem multae causae. Vetus est enim, "ubi non sis qui fueris, non esse cur velis vivere." Sed tamen vacare culpa magnum est solacium, praesertim cum habeam duas res, quibus me sustentem, optimarum artium scientiam et maximarum rerum gloriam; quarum altera mihi vivo numquam eripietur, altera ne mortuo quidem.   *Ibid., 3, 4*

Nihil est quod adventum nostrum extimescas: non multi cibi hospitem accipies, multi ioci.   *Id., IX, 26, 4*

Laudandum adulescentem, ornandum, tollendum.
Id., XI, 20, 1

Ut quisque est vir optimus, ita difficillime esse alios improbos suspicatur.   *Ad Quintum fratrem, I, 4, 12*

Ubi nihil erit quod scribas, it ipsum scribito.
Epistulae at Atticum, IV, 8, 4

No one has the right to be sorry for himself for a misfortune that strikes everyone.

What pleasure can it give a cultivated man to watch some poor fellow being torn to pieces by a powerful beast or a superb beast being pierced with a hunting spear? Even were such things worth looking at, you've seen them many times, and we saw nothing new this time. The last day was devoted to the elephants. The vulgar populace was enthusiastic, but there was no pleasure in it; indeed, the show provoked some sort of compassion, a feeling that there is some kinship between this great beast and humankind.

I found no reason for killing myself, but many reasons why I should wish I were dead. For there is an old proverb, "When you are no longer what you were, there is no reason left to live." However, it is a great comfort to be without guilt, the more so because I am sustained by two things: practice of the noble arts and the fame of my great deeds. The former will never be taken away from me so long as I live, and the latter not even after my death.

Absolutely no reason why you should be apprehensive of my visit: you'll receive a guest who is a small eater but a big joker.

Let's praise the young man [Octavian], let's honor him, let's elevate [or eliminate] him. [*From a letter addressed to Cicero by D. Brutus. Brutus informs him that Octavian has been angered by this phrase with its double meaning, which has been attributed to Cicero.*]

The nobler a man is, the harder for him to suspect baseness in others.

Even if you have nothing to write, write and say so.

Ubi est autem dignitas nisi ubi honestas? *Id., VII, 11, 1*

Nihil . . . de maerore minuendo scriptum ab ullo est, quod ego non domi tuae legerim. Sed omnem consolationem vincit dolor. Quin etiam feci quod profecto ante me nemo, ut ipse me per litteras consolarer. Quem librum ad te mittam, si descripserint librarii. Adfirmo tibi nullam consolationem esse talem. Totos dies scribo, non quo proficiam quid, sed tantisper impedior; non equidem satis (vis enim urget), sed relaxor tamen omniaque nitor non ad animum, set ad vultum ipsum, si queam, reficiendum idque faciens interdum mihi peccare videor, interdum peccaturus esse, nisi faciam. *Id., XII, 14, 3*

Longumque illud tempus cum non ero magis me movet quam hoc exiguum, quod mihi tamen longum videtur.
Ibid., 18, 1

Mea mihi conscientia pluris est quam omnium sermo.
Ibid., 28, 2

Nemo umquam neque poeta neque orator fuit, qui quemquam meliorem quam se arbitraretur. *Id., XIV, 20, 3*

Nemo doctus umquam . . . mutationem consilii inconstantiam dixit esse. *Id., XVI, 7, 3*

What is dignity without honesty?

Nothing . . . ever written on how to allay grief did I
fail to read while I was staying in your house. But suffering
gets the better of any consolation. Why, I even did something that surely no one has ever done before me—I wrote
a letter of consolation to myself! I'll send it to you as soon
as my scribes have copied it. I assure you it is not like any
other consolation. I write all day long, not that I get any
profit from it, but at least it keeps me busy; not enough,
to be sure, for my grief is great, still it relaxes me. I do
everything to compose—not my mind, but as far as I can,
my face. And as I do it, I sometimes feel I am doing wrong
and sometimes that I would be doing wrong if I didn't do
it.

That long time to come when I shall not exist has more
effect on me than this short present time, which nevertheless seems endless.

My own conscience is more to me than what the world
says.

No poet or orator has ever existed who believed there was
another better than himself.

No thinker has ever . . . said that a change of mind was
inconsistency.

DECIMUS LABERIUS

c. 105 – 43 B.C.

Quem nulla ambitio, nulla unquam largitio,
nullus timor, vis nulla, nulla auctoritas
movere potuit in iuventa de statu,
ecce in senecta ut facile labefecit loco
viri excellentis mente clemente edita,
summissa placide blandiloquens oratio!

Ut hedera serpens vires arboreas necat,
ita me vetustas amplexu annorum enecat.
sepulcri similis nihil nisi nomen retineo.

Porro, Quirites, libertatem perdimus.

Necesse est multos timeat quem multi timent.

Non possunt primi esse omnes omni in tempore.
summum ad gradum cum claritatis veneris,
consistes aegre et citius quam escendas cades;
ceci ego, cadet qui sequitur; laus est publica.
Fragments quoted in Macrobius, Saturnalia, II, 7

LABERIUS

Laberius, a Roman knight was, with Publilius Syrus, the most famous writer and actor of mimes in the first century B.C. In the year 45 B.C., when he was over sixty, he was persuaded by Caesar to compete publicly with Syrus, and the younger man was decided victor. Laberius' most important contribution was to transform the mime into a literary genre and a vehicle of social criticism. Hitherto it had been a kind of roustabout farce with stock characters—the faithless wife, the lover, etc.

Never, when I was younger, could any urging, any promise of reward, any threat, compulsion, or command from above persuade me to stoop below my rank. Now, in my old age, an illustrious man has readily induced me to do so, by soft and flattering words, uttered with kindness.

As ivy chokes the life of the tree it enlaces, so is old age killing me with the embrace of years. Like a tomb, I have been left with nothing but my name.

From now on, Romans, it's all over with our freedom.

He must fear many, whom many fear. [*A line said to have made the audience look at Caesar.*]

Not all can occupy the first rank forever. Once you have reached the highest pitch of fame, it is hard to hold onto it, and you fall down faster than you climbed. He who follows me will fall in turn; it is the public that confers renown.

C. IULIUS CAESAR

100 – 44 B.C.

Consuesse enim deos immortales, quo gravius homines ex commutatione rerum doleant, quos pro scelere eorum ulcisci velint, his secundiores interdum res et diutiurniorem impunitatem concedere.

Commentarii de bello Gallico, I, 14

Fere libenter homines id quod volunt credunt. *Id., III, 18*

Ut ad bella suscipienda Gallorum alacer ac promptus est animus, sic mollis ac minime resistens ad calamitates perferendas mens eorum est. *Ibid., 19*

Non esse consuetudinem populi Romani, ullam accipere ab hoste armato conditionem. *Id., V, 41*

Nemo est tam fortis quin rei novitate perturbetur.

Id., VI, 39

Omnia enim plerumque quae absunt vehementius hominum mentes perturbant. *Id., VII, 84*

Quae volumus et credimus libenter, et quae sentimus ipsi, reliquos sentire speramus.

Commentarii de bello civili, II, 27

Communi . . . fit vitio naturae, ut inusitatis atque incognitis rebus magis confidamus vehementiusque exterreamur. *Ibid., 4*

CAESAR

Besides the famous *Commentaries* on the Gallic and Civil wars (*Gallia est omnis divisa . . .*), in which he is his own historian and propagandist, and which are his only works to come down to us, the great general and statesman wrote a tragedy on Oedipus and treatises on grammar and astronomy; he also compiled a collection of aphorisms. However, his best-known remarks, which were widely quoted in his own lifetime, do not come from his writings. He was also a great orator who, Cicero says, yielded to none in brilliance, elegance, and nobility of style.

The immortal gods, when they intend to punish some men for their sins, sometimes grant them temporary prosperity and prolonged immunity to make them suffer more severely from a change of fortune.

Men readily believe what they want to believe.

While it is in the character of the Gauls to be quick and eager to go to war, their minds are weak and lacking in resistance to disaster.

It is not the custom of the Roman people to negotiate with an armed enemy.

No one is so courageous as not to be upset by an unexpected turn of events.

As a rule men's minds are more deeply disturbed by what they do not see.

What we desire we readily believe, and what we ourselves think we expect others to think.

By common defect of nature, the unusual and the unknown make us either overconfident or overly fearful.

Fortuna quae plurimum potest cum in reliquis rebus tam praecipue in bello parvis momentis magnas rerum commutationes efficit. *Id., III, 68*

Tamquam scopulum, sic fugias inauditum atque insolens verbum. *De Analogia, Aulus Gellius, I, x, 4*

Nam si violandum est ius, regnandi gratia violandum est: aliis rebus pietatem colas. *Cicero, De Officiis, III, 12*

Iacta alea esto. *Suetonius, I, 32*

Veni, vidi, vici. *Ibid., 37*

Meos tam suspicione quam crimine iudico carere oportere. *Ibid., 74*

Et tu Brute. *Ibid., 82*

Non tam sua quam reipublicae interesse uti salvus esset; se iampridem potentiae gloriaeque abunde adeptum, rempublicam, si quid sibi eveniret, neque quietam fore, et aliquanto deteriore conditione civilia bella subituram. *Ibid., 86*

Satis diu vel naturae vixi, vel gloriae. *Cicero, Pro Marcello, VIII, 25*

Chance, which means a great deal in all sorts of circumstances, but especially in war, can effect great changes with a very slight shift of the balance.

Avoid a strange and unfamiliar word as you would a dangerous reef.

If you must break the law, do it only to seize power: in all other cases observe it.

The die is cast. [*Said as he was about to cross the Rubicon.*]

I came, I saw, I conquered.

I feel that members of my family should never be suspected of breaking the law. [*"Caesar's wife should be above suspicion," is Plutarch's version.*]

You, too, Brutus. [*According to Suetonius, however, he spoke in Greek:* kai su teknon, *"You too, my son!"*]

[He said that] his safety mattered more to the republic than to himself; for he had long since acquired enough power and glory, whereas the republic, if anything happened to him, would not enjoy peace, and would be subjected to a much worse condition and torn by civil war.

I have lived long enough both in years and in accomplishment. [*Said two years before his death.*]

Recte auguraris de me (bene enim cognitus sum) nihil a me abesse longius crudelitate. Atque ego cum ex ipsa re magnam capio voluptatem tum meum factum probari abs te triumpho gaudio. Neque illud me movet quod ii qui a me dimissi sunt discessisse dicuntur ut mihi rursus bellum inferrent. Nihil enim malo quam et me mei similem esse et illos sui.   *Cicero, Epistulae ad Atticum, IX, 16, 2*

Quod ne facias pro iure nostrae amicitiae a te peto. Postremo quid viro bono et quieto et bono civi magis convenit quam abesse a civilibus controversiis?   *Id., X, 8*

CORNELIUS NEPOS

C. 100 – C. 25 B.C.

Huic maxime putamus malo fuisse nimiam opinionem ingenii atque virtutis.
          De excellentibus ducibus exterarum gentium,
          Alcibiades, 7

Matrem timidi flere non solere.   *Id., Thrasybulus, 2*

What you surmise about me is correct (for you know me well): nothing is more foreign to my nature than cruelty. And while I derive great pleasure from the thing itself, I am overjoyed when you approve of my conduct. Nor am I the slightest bit upset when I am told that men I have spared are deserting me and intend to make war upon me again. For there is nothing that pleases me more than that I should always be the way I am and they the way they are. [*From a letter to Cicero written in the spring of 49* B.C.]

In the name of our friendship I ask you not to do it. After all, what can be more becoming to a respectable man and a peace-loving citizen than to stay out of civil strife? [*From a letter Caesar addressed to Cicero upon hearing that the latter was planning to join Pompey; summer 49* B.C.]

CORNELIUS NEPOS

Cornelius Nepos was born in northern Italy (probably at Ticinum, today's Pavia) and spent most of his life in Rome. He held no public office and devoted himself entirely to writing. His works included light verse, a universal history, a collection of anecdotes, lives of Cato and of Cicero, a treatise on geography, and *De Viris Illustribus* (On Famous Men). All that survive are portions of the last-named (the lives of famous non-Roman generals) a biography of Atticus, two lives of Latin historians, and some fragments. While not the most elegant of writers, he is clear, concise, and edifying—as schoolmasters long since discovered, an ideal writer for the young.

We think that what harmed him [Alcibiades] most was his excessive opinion of his own gifts and merits.

The mother of a careful man seldom has reason to weep.

Miseranda vita, qui se metui, quam amari malunt.

Id., Dion, 9

Est enim hoc commune vitium in magnis liberisque civitatibus, ut invidia gloriae comes sit, et libenter de his detrahant, quos eminere videant altius: neque animo aequo pauperes alienam opulentium intuentur fortunam.

Id., Chabrias, 3

Magnos homines virtute metimur, non fortuna.

Id., Eumenes, 1

Sui cuique fingunt fortunam.   *T. Pomponii Attici vita, 11*

Plus salis, quam sumptus.   *Ibid., 13*

Elegans, non magnificus; splendidus, non sumptuosus, omni diligentia munditiam, non affluentiam, affectabat.

Ibid.

Tantum abest, ut ego magistram esse putem vitae philosophiam, beataeque vitae perfectricem, ut nullis magis existimem opus esse magistris vivendi, quam plerisque, qui in ea disputanda versantur. Video enim magnam partem eorum, qui in schola de pudore et continentia praecipiant argutissime, eosdem in omnium libidinum cupiditatibus vivere.   *Ad Ciceronem Epistulae fragmentum*

Pitiable is the life of those who prefer being feared to being loved.

It is a general failing in great and free states that envy should be a concomitant of distinction: people like to pull down those whom they see rising too high; nor do the poor look with equanimity on fortunes in which they have no share.

We measure great men by their virtue, not their fortune.

Character fashions fate.

More taste than expense.

[Atticus] was fastidious rather than magnificent; luxury-loving without extravagance, he aimed at elegance without ostentation.

I am far from holding that philosophy is a guide to life or that it furthers happiness; rather, I believe that no one is more in need of instruction in living than the majority of those engaged in teaching it. I have noticed that most of those who in schools formulate the subtlest precepts of moderation and self-mastery themselves indulge in every kind of unbridled passion.

TITUS LUCRETIUS CARUS

c. 99 – c. 55 B.C.

Aeneadum genetrix, hominum divomque voluptas,
alma Venus, caeli subter labentia signa
quae mare navigerum, quae terras frugiferentis
concelebras, per te quoniam genus omne animantum
concipitur visitque exortum lumina solis.

De Rerum Natura, I, 1

Humana ante oculos foede cum vita iaceret
in terris oppressa gravi sub religione
quae caput a caeli regionibus ostendebat
horribili super aspectu mortalibus instans,
primum Graius homo mortalis tollere contra
est oculos ausus primusque obsistere contra.

Ibid., 62

Ergo vivida vis animi pervicit, et extra
processit longe flammantia moenia mundi
atque omne immensum peragravit mente animoque.

Ibid., 72

Tantum religio potuit suadere malorum.

Ibid., 101

Nil igitur fieri de nilo posse fatendumst.

Ibid., 205

LUCRETIUS

Nothing certain is known about the life of this philosopher and poet. His single work, *De Rerum Natura,* was published posthumously by Cicero. Vergil studied it, Ovid admired it, Statius speaks of the *Docti furor arduus Lucreti* (*Silvae,* II, 10, 71), and many authors of didactic poems since have tried to imitate him. No one, however, has equaled his passionate sincerity, his fearless logic, his breadth of vision, his virile morality. He was not a popular poet; Quintilian, the educator, complained of his difficulty. He was not read during the Middle Ages, being wrongly believed to be atheistic and immoral. His present-day fame dates from the Renaissance.

(Tr. W. H. D. Rouse)

Mother of Aeneas and his race, darling of men and gods, nurturing Venus, who beneath the smooth-moving heavenly signs fillest with thyself the ship-bearing sea and the fertile earth, since through thee every generation of living things is conceived and rising up looks on the light of the sun.

When man's life lay for all to see foully groveling upon the ground, crushed beneath the weight of Religion, which displayed her head in the regions of heaven, threatening mortals from on high with horrible aspect, a man of Greece was the first that dared to uplift mortal eyes against her, the first to make stand against her.

Therefore the lively power of his mind prevailed, and forth he marched far beyond the flaming walls of the heavens, as he traversed the immeasurable universe in thought and imagination.

So potent was religion in persuading to evil deeds.

Therefore we must confess that nothing comes from nothing.

Omnia enim stolidi magis admirantur amantque,
inversis quae sub verbis latitantia cernunt,
veraque constituunt quae belle tangere possunt
auris et lepido quae sunt fucata sonore.   *Ibid., 641*

Iuvat integros accedere fontis
atque haurire, iuvatque novos decerpere flores
insignemque meo capiti petere inde coronam
unde prius nulli velarint tempora musae;
primum quod magnis doceo de rebus et artis
religionum animum nodis exsolvere pergo,
deinde quod obscura de re tam lucida pango
carmina, musaeo contingens cuncta lepore.
                                   Ibid., 927

Suave, mari magno turbantibus aequora ventis,
e terra magnum alterius spectare laborem;
non quia vexari quemquamst iucunda voluptas,
sed quibus ipse malis careas quia cernere suave est.
                                   Id., II, 1

Sed nil dulcius est, bene quam munita tenere
edita doctrina sapientum templa serena,
despicere unde queas alios passimque videre
errare atque viam palantis quaerere vitae. *Ibid., 7*

O miseras hominum mentes, o pectora caeca!
qualibus in tenebris vitae quantisque periclis
degitur hoc aevi quodcumquest!   *Ibid., 14*

Hunc igitur terrorem animi tenebrasque necessest
non radii solis neque lucida tela diei
discutiant, sed naturae species ratioque.   *Ibid., 59*

For dolts admire and love everything more which they see hidden amid distorted words, and set down as true whatever can prettily tickle the ears and all that is varnished over with fine-sounding phrases.

I love to approach virgin springs and there to drink: I love to pluck fresh flowers, and to seek an illustrious chaplet for my head from fields whence ere this the Muses have crowned the brows of none; first because my teaching is of high matters, and I proceed to unloose the mind from the close knots of religion; next because the subject is so dark and the lines I write so clear, as I touch all with the Muses' grace.

Pleasant it is, when over a great sea the winds trouble the waters, to gaze from shore upon another's great tribulation: not because any man's troubles are a delectable joy, but because to perceive you are free from them yourself is pleasant.

But nothing is more delightful than to possess well-fortified sanctuaries, serene, built up by the teachings of the wise, whence you may look down from the height upon others and behold them all astray, wandering abroad and seeking the path of life.

O pitiable minds of men, O blind intelligences! In what gloom of life, in how great perils is passed all your poor span of time!

This terror of the mind, therefore, and this gloom must be dispelled, not by the sun's rays nor the bright shafts of day, but by the aspect and law of nature.

Sic rerum summa novatur
semper, et inter se mortales mutua vivunt.
augescunt aliae gentes, aliae minuuntur,
inque brevi spatio mutantur saecla animantum
et quasi cursores vitai lampada tradunt.　　*Ibid.*, 75

Nequaquam nobis divinitus esse creatam
naturam mundi, quanta stat praedita culpa.
　　　　　　　　　　　　　　　　Ibid., 180

Subdola cum ridet placidi pellacia ponti.
　　　　　　　　　　　　　　　　Ibid., 559

Miscetur funere vagor
quem pueri tollunt visentis luminis oras;
nex nox ulla diem neque noctem aurora secutast
quae non audierit mixtos vagitibus aegris
ploratus mortis comites et funeris atri.　　*Ibid.*, 576

Omnis enim per se divom natura necessest
immortali aevo summa cum pace fruatur
semota ab nostris rebus seiunctaque longe;
nam privata dolore omni, privata periclis,
ipsa suis pollens opibus, nil indiga nostri,
nec bene promeritis capitur neque tangitur ira.
　　　　　　　　　　　　　　　　Ibid., 646

Iamque adeo fracta est aetas effetaque tellus
vix animalia parva creat quae cuncta creavit
saecla deditque ferarum ingentia corpora partu.
　　　　　　　　　　　　　　　　Ibid., 1150

Mortis formidine, vitae
percipit humanos odium lucisque videndae,
ut sibi consciscant maerenti pectore letum
obliti fontem curarum hunc esse timorem.
　　　　　　　　　　　　　　　　Id., III, 79

Thus the sum of things is ever being renewed, and mortal creatures live dependent one upon another. Some nations increase, others diminish, and in a short space the generations of living creatures are changed and like runners pass on the torch of life.

The nature of the universe has by no means been made through divine power, seeing how great are the faults that mar it.

When the calm sea shows her false, alluring smile.

With the funeral dirge is mingled the wail that children raise when they first see the light; and no night ever followed day, or dawn followed night, but has heard mingled with their sickly wailings the lamentations that attend upon death and the black funeral.

For the very nature of divinity must necessarily enjoy immortal life in the deepest peace, far removed and separated from our troubles; for without any pain, without danger, itself mighty by its own resources, needing us not at all, it is neither propitiated with services nor touched by wrath.

Even now the power of life is broken, and the earth exhausted scarce produces tiny creatures, she who once produced all kinds and gave birth to the huge bodies of wild beasts.

For fear of death men are seized by hatred of life and of seeing the light, so that with sorrowing heart they devise their own death, forgetting that this fear is the fountain of all care.

Quid tibi tanto operest, mortalis, quod nimis aegris
luctibus indulges? quid mortem congemis ac fles?
nam si grata fuit tibi vita anteacta priorque
et non omnia pertusum congesta quasi in vas
commoda perfluxere atque ingrata interiere:
cur non ut plenus vitae conviva recedis
aequo animoque capis securam, stulte, quietem?

Ibid., 933

Sic aliud ex alio numquam desistet oriri
vitaque mancipio nulli datur, omnibus usu.

Ibid., 970

Scipiadas, belli fulmen, Carthaginis horror,
ossa dedit terrae proinde ac famul infimus esset.

Ibid., 1035

Licet quot vis vivendo condere saecla;
mors aeterna tamen nilo minus illa manebit.

Ibid., 1090

Idque petit corpus, mens unde est saucia amore.

Id., IV, 1047

Nequiquam, quoniam medio de fonte leporum
surgit amari aliquid quod in ipsis floribus angat.

Ibid., 1133

Nec pietas ullast velatum saepe videri
vertier ad lapidem atque omnis accedere ad aras
nec procumbere humi prostratum et pandere palmas
ante deum delubra nec aras sanguine multo
spargere quadrupedum nec votis nectere vota,
sed mage pacata posse omnia mente tueri.

Id., V, 1198

What ails you, O mortal, to indulge overmuch in sickly lamentations? Why do you groan aloud and weep at death? For if your former life now past has been to your liking, if it is not true that all your blessings have been gathered, as it were, into a riddled jar, and have run through and been lost without gratification: why not like a banqueter full of life, withdraw with contentment and rest in peace, you fool?

So one thing will never cease to arise from another, and no man possesses life in freehold—all as tenants.

The son of the house of Scipio, thunderbolt of war, terror of Carthage, gave his bones to the earth as though he had been the humblest menial.

You may live to complete as many generations as you will, nevertheless that everlasting death will still be waiting.

The body seeks that which has wounded the mind with love.

All is vanity, since from the very fountain of enchantment rises a drop of bitterness to torment amongst all the flowers.

It is no piety to show oneself often with covered head, turning toward a stone and approaching every altar, none to fall prostrate upon the ground and to spread open the palms before shrines of the gods, none to sprinkle altars with the blood of beasts in showers and to link vow to vow; but rather to be able to survey all things with mind at peace.

C. SALLUSTIUS CRISPUS

86 – 35 B.C.

Omnis homines qui sese student praestare ceteris animalibus summa ope niti decet ne vitam silentio transeant veluti pecora, quae natura prona atque ventri oboedientia finxit.   *Bellum Catilinae, I, 1*

Divitiarum et formae gloria fluxa et fragilis est, virtus clara aeternaque habetur.   *Ibid., 4*

Verum enimvero is demum mihi vivere atque frui anima videtur, qui aliquo negotio intentus praeclari facinoris aut artis bonae famam quaerit.   *Id., II, 9*

Pulchrum est bene facere rei publicae, etiam bene dicere haud absurdum est.   *Id., III, 1*

Idem velle atque idem nolle, ea demum firma amicitia est.   *Id., XX, 4*

SALLUST

Born at Amiternum, Sallust was the first of the greater Roman historians. He was tribune of the plebs of 52 B.C. and was expelled from the senate on a charge of immorality in 50. However, in 49, Caesar appointed him quaestor, and later, in recognition of his services during a military campaign, made him proconsul of Numidia. Sallust returned an extremely wealthy man; he was tried for extortion but was acquitted through Caesar's influence. After Caesar's death he retired from politics and devoted his remaining years to the writing of history, because, as he said, he became disgusted with the politics and morals of Rome, and because he regarded history as the most useful intellectual pursuit. He developed a style of his own marked by archaisms and short, abrupt sentences, which was much admired in antiquity. He believed that men would control fate rather than be controlled by it if they did not all too often yield to base desires; hence his preoccupation with human character. He produced three monographs that are literary masterpieces—a history of the war with Catiline, a history of the war with Iugurtha, and a work entitled *Historiae,* of which only fragments have come down to us. Like Thucydides, Sallust (and later Livy) composed the speeches for his historical figures.

All men who would surpass the other animals should do their utmost not to go through life in silence like the brutes whom nature made to face the ground, obedient to their bellies.

The fame that goes with wealth and beauty is fleeting and fragile; intellectual superiority is a possession glorious and eternal.

As I see it, only that man lives and enjoys life who is eager for achievement, who sets out to become famous by some glorious exploit or a noble career.

It is honorable to serve one's country well; even to serve it by speaking well is not unpraiseworthy.

To have the same likes and dislikes—this, after all, is what defines solid friendship.

Omnis homines . . . qui de rebus dubiis consultant, ab odio, amicitia, ira atque misericordia vacuos esse decet.

Id., LI, 1

Neque cuiquam mortalium iniuriae suae parvae videntur; multi eas gravius aequo habuere. *Ibid., 11*

Omnia mala exempla ex rebus bonis orta sunt. *Ibid., 27*

Non votis neque suppliciis muliebribus auxilia deorum parantur; vigilando, agundo, bene consulundo prospera omnia cedunt. *Id., LII, 29*

Esse quam videri bonus malebat; ita quo minus petebat gloriam, eo magis illum sequebatur. *Id., LIV, 6*

Semper in proelio eis maxumum est periculum qui maxume timent, audacia pro muro habetur. *Id., LVIII, 17*

Pro patria, pro liberis, pro aris atque focis suis certare.

Id., LIX, 5

Falso queritur de natura sua genus humanum, quod imbecilla atque aevi brevis forte potius quam virtute regatur. Nam contra reputando neque maius aliud neque praestabilius invenias. *Bellum Iugurthinum, I, 1*

Corporis et fortunae bonorum ut initium sic finis est, omniaque orta occidunt et aucta senescunt; animus incorruptus, aeternus, rector humani generis agit atque habet cuncta neque ipse habetur. *Id., II, 3*

Quod difficillumum inter mortalis est, gloria invidiam vicisti. *Id., X, 2*

Men who deliberate on controversial matters should be free from hatred, friendship, anger, and pity. [*Caesar*]

No man underestimates the wrongs he suffers; many take them more seriously than is right. [*Caesar*]

Every bad precedent originated as a justifiable measure. [*Caesar*]

Not by vows nor by womanish prayers is the help of the gods obtained; success comes through vigilance, energy, wise counsel. [*Cato*]

Rather than *seem* good he chose to *be* good, and so, the less he strove for fame, the closer it dogged his footsteps.

In battle it is always those who are most afraid who are exposed to the greatest dangers; courage acts as a protecting wall.

To fight for our country, for our children, for our altars, for our hearths.

Men are wrong to complain about their nature, alleging that it is weak, and that their lives are short and governed by chance rather than by virtue. Actually, if you think about it you will find nothing greater or more exalted.

The goods of the body and of fortune have an end just as they have a beginning: they rise and fall, they prosper and decline; but the mind, incorrupt, eternal, ruler of the human race, is the master of all things, while it is itself free.

[You have achieved] what is hardest for men to do: by your fame you have vanquished envy.

Urbem venalem et mature periturum, si emptorem in-
venerit. *Id., XXXV, 10*

Bono vinci satius est quam malo more iniuriam vincere.
Id., XLII, 3

Res humanae ita sese habent: in victoria vel ignavis gloriari licet, adversae res etiam bonos detrectant. *Id., LIII, 8*

Omne bellum sumi facile, ceterum aegerrume desinere
. . . incipere cuivis, etiam ignavo licere, deponi, cum vic-
tores velint. *Id., LXXXIII, 1*

Homini potentiam quaerenti egentissumus quisque oppor-
tunissumus. *Id., LXXXVI, 3*

Ante Carthaginem deletam populus et senatus Romanus
placide modesteque inter se rem publicam tractabant,
neque gloriae neque dominationis certamen inter civis erat;
metus hostilis in bonis artibus civitatem retinebat. Sed ubi
illa formido mentibus decessit, scilicet ea quae res secundae amant, lascivia atque superbia incessere. Id quod
in advorsis rebus optaverant otium postquam adepti sunt,
asperius acerbiusque fuit. Namque coepere nobilitas digni-
tatem, populus libertatem in lubidinam vortere, sibi
quisque ducere, trahere, rapere. *Id., XLI, 2*

Contemnunt novitatem meam, ego illorum ignaviam; mihi
fortuna, illis probra obiectantur. Quamquam ego naturam
unam et communem omnium existumo, sed fortissimum
quemque generosissimum. *Id., LXXXV, 14*

A venal city destined to perish as soon as it finds a buyer.

A good man would rather suffer defeat than defeat injustice by foul means.

This is how it is with human affairs: in victory even cowards boast, whereas in defeat even the brave are discredited.

War is always easy to start, but very hard to end . . . anyone, even a coward, may take up arms, but only the victors can say when they are to be laid down.

To someone seeking power, the poorest man is the most useful.

Before the destruction of Carthage the Roman people and senate together governed the commonwealth peacefully and moderately, nor was there rivalry among citizens for glory and power; fear of the enemy kept the state on the path of justice. But when the minds were freed from that fear, immorality and arrogance, which are encouraged by prosperity, entered them. Thus the peace which they had desired proved all the more cruel and harsh after they got it. For the nobles began to turn their dignity, and the people their liberty into license, and every man took, robbed, and pillaged for himself.

They [the patricians] despise me as an upstart, I despise their worthlessness. However, I believe that all men are equal and alike by nature, and that the bravest man is the noblest. [Marius]

Sordidum me et incultis moribus aiunt, quia parum scite convivium exorno neque histrionem ullum neque pluris pretii cocum quam vilicum habeo. Quae mihi lubet confiteri, Quirites. Nam ex parente meo et ex aliis sanctis viris ita accepi: munditias mulieribus, laborem viris convenire, omnibusque bonis oportere plus gloriae quam divitiarum esse. *Id., LXXXV, 39*

PUBLILIUS SYRUS

c. 85–43 B.C.

Alienum est omne quicquid optando evenit.

Amor animi arbitrio sumitur, non ponitur.

Aut amat aut odit mulier: nihil est tertium.

Absentem laedit cum ebrio qui litigat.

Amans iratus multa mentitur sibi.

Aperte mala cum est mulier, tum demum est bona.

Amoris vulnus idem sanat qui facit.

Amori finem tempus, non animus facit.

Beneficium accipere libertatem est vendere.

Brevis ipsa vita est sed malis fit longior.

They say that I am vulgar and have bad manners because I do not give elegant dinners and have no actor or cook more expensive than a farm overseer. I gladly admit this, fellow citizens. For I learned from my father and other good men that elegance behooves women and exertions men, that to all good men glory is more becoming than riches. [*Marius*]

SYRUS

Like Laberius (see page 79) Syrus was a celebrated mime. He was of Syrian origin, brought to Rome as a slave and later manumitted. The collection of his maxims, allegedly taken from his plays, was probably composed long after his death and may contain sayings of others as well.

What we obtain merely by asking is not really our own.

We choose to love, we do not choose to cease loving.

Woman either loves or hates: nothing in between.

To quarrel with a drunk is to wrong a man who isn't really there.

An angry lover tells himself many lies.

Only when a woman is openly bad is she really good.

Love's wounds are cured by love itself.

It is time, not the mind, that puts an end to love.

To accept a favor is to sell one's freedom.

Life is short but misfortunes make it longer.

Cum ames non sapias aut cum sapias non ames.

De inimico non loquaris male sed cogites.

Fortunam citius reperias quam retineas.

Fortuna vitrea est: tum cum splendet frangitur.

Homo totiens moritur quotiens amittit suos.

Heredis fletus sub persona risus est.

Inopiae desunt multa, avaritiae omnia.

Lucrum sine damno alterius fieri non potest.

Malo in consilio feminae vincunt viros.

Male facere qui vult numquam non causam invenit.

Mors infanti felix, iuvenis acerba, nimis sera est seni.

Pudor doceri non potest, nasci potest.

Pecunia regimen est rerum omnium.

Peccare pauci nolunt, nulli nesciunt.

Paratae lacrimae insidias non fletum indicant.

Stultum facit fortuna quem vult perdere.

When you are in love you are not wise, or rather, when you are wise you don't fall in love.

Don't *speak* ill of your enemy: plot it.

It is easier to meet with good fortune than to hold onto it.

Fortune is like glass: it is most breakable when it shines brightest.

A man dies as many times as he loses a dear one.

The tears of an heir are laughter under a vizard.   [*Bacon*]

Poverty is a lack of many things, avarice of everything.

There is no profit without another's loss.

Women surpass men at scheming evil.

Those who mean to do ill never fail to find a reason.

Death is fortunate for the child, bitter to the young man, too late for the old.

Modesty may be innate, it cannot be learned.

Money rules all.

Few are unwilling to do wrong, all know how.

Ready tears are a sign of treachery, not of grief.

Whom Fortune would ruin she deprives of good sense. [*The better-known* Quos Deus vult perdere prius dementat (*Whom God would ruin he first deprives of reason*) *is a Latin translation of a line from Euripides.*]

Satis est superare inimicum, nimium est perdere.

Ubi innocens damnatur, pars patriae exsulat.

C. HELVIUS CINNA

c. 84 – 44 B.C.

Te matutinus flentem conspexit Eous
et flentem paulo vidit post Hesperus idem.
Zmyrna

At scelus incesto Zmyrnae crescebat in alvo.   *Id.*

It is enough to defeat an enemy, too much to ruin him.

When an innocent man is convicted, part of his country is exiled.

CINNA

Cinna was much admired by his contemporaries for his epic poem *Zmyrna*. Zmyrna is the maiden of mythology whose incestuous love for her father produced Adonis. The author also of epigrams and erotic verses, Cinna was lynched the day of Caesar's funeral ("I am Cinna the poet, I am Cinna the poet," Shakespeare, *Julius Caesar*, III, 3). His works earned the praises of Catullus and Vergil. Of *Zmyrna* only three lines have survived, and a handful of fragments from other poems.

Eos saw you weeping in the early morning, and at sunset Hesperus found you still weeping.

The heinous design was gaining strength in Zmyrna's incestuous bosom.

GAIUS VALERIUS CATULLUS

c. 84 – 54 B.C.

Lugete, o Veneres Cupidinesque,
et quantumst hominum venustiorum.
passer mortuus est meae puellae,
passer, deliciae meae puellae,
quem plus oculis suis amabat.

Catulli Veronensis liber, III, 1

Qui nunc it per iter tenebricosum
illuc, unde negant redire quemquam.
at vobis male sit, malae tenebrae
Orci, quae omnia bella devoratis.   *Ibid.,* 11

Vivamus, mea Lesbia, atque amemus,
rumoresque senum severiorum
omnes unius aestimemus assis.
soles occidere et redire possunt:
nobis cum semel occidit brevis lux,
nox est perpetua una dormienda.
da mihi basia mille, deinde centum,
deinde mille altera, deinde secunda centum . . .

Id., V, 1

CATULLUS

Catullus, the first and greatest Latin lyric poet, was born at Verona and came to Rome when he was twenty-two. There he fell in love with "Lesbia," who was probably the notorious Clodia. Most of his poems relate the vicissitudes of this passionate affair in a language of unequaled spontaneity and directness—*his* Latin is certainly not "dead." In his odes he anticipated Horace, in his elegies Propertius and Tibullus, and his epic style (in *Attis,* for example) equals and perhaps surpasses Vergil.

(Tr. R. Ellis)

Weep each heavenly Venus, all the Cupids,
Weep all men that have any grace about ye,
Dead the sparrow, in whom my love delighted,
The dead sparrow, in whom my love delighted.
Yea, most precious, above her eyes, she held him . . .

Now he wendeth along the murky pathway,
Whence, they tell us, is hopeless all returning.
Evil on ye, the shades of evil Orcus,
Shades all beauteous happy things devouring.

(Tr. Richard Crashaw)

Come and let us live, my dear,
Let us love and never fear
What the sourest fathers say:
Brightest Sol that dies today
Lives again as blithe tomorrow;
But if we dark sons of sorrow
Set, O then, how long a night
Shuts the eyes of our short light!
Then let amorous kisses dwell
On our lips, begin and tell
A thousand, and a hundred score,
An hundred and a thousand more . . .

Miser Catulle, desinas ineptire,
et quod vides perisse perditum ducas.

Id., VIII, 1

Nunc iam illa non vult: tu quoque, impotens, noli,
nec quae fugit sectare, nec miser vive,
sed obstinata mente perfer, obdura.   *Ibid., 9*

Nam castum esse decet pium poetam
ipsum, versiculos nihil necesse est,
qui tum denique habent salem ac leporem,
si sunt molliculi ac parum pudici
et quod pruriat incitare possunt,
non dico pueris, sed his pilosis
qui duros nequeunt movere lumbos.   *Id., XVI, 5*

O saeclum insapiens et infacetum!

Id., XLIII, 8

Ille mi par esse deo videtur
ille, si fas est, superare divos,
qui sedens adversus identidem te spectat et audit
dulce ridentem, misero quod omnis
eripit sensus mihi.   *Id., LI, 1*

Otium, Catulle, tibi molestumst:
otio exultas nimiumque gestis.
otium et reges prius et beatas
      perdidit urbes.   *Id., LI-a*

(Tr. F. W. Cornish)

Poor Catullus, 'tis time you should cease your folly, and account as lost what you see is lost.

Now she desires no more—no more should you desire, poor madman, nor follow her who flies, nor live in misery, but with resolved mind endure, be firm.

(Tr. N.G.)

For a poet respectful of the Muses should himself be chaste, but his little verses need not be so. All their salt and elegance comes from being licentious, immodest, suggestive of prurient thoughts—not indeed in children but in hairy old men unable to bestir their numbed loins.

Oh this dull coarse age!

(Tr. W. E. Gladstone)

> Him rival to the gods I place
> Him loftier yet, if loftier be,
> Who, Lesbia, sits before thy face,
> Who listens and who looks on thee;
> Thee smiling soft. Yet this delight
> Doth all my sense consign to death.

(Tr. F. W. Cornish)

Idleness, Catullus, does you harm: you riot in your idleness and wanton too much. Idleness ere now has ruined both kings and wealthy cities.

Caeli, Lesbia nostra, Lesbia illa,
illa Lesbia, quam Catullus unam
plus quam se atque suos amavit omnes,
nunc in quadriviis et angiportis
glubit magnanimi Remi nepotes.   *Id., LVIII*

Super alta vectus Attis celeri rate maria
Phrygium ut nemus citato cupide pede tetigit
adiitque opaca silvis redimita loca deae,
stimulatus ibi furenti rabie, vagus animi,
devolvit ili acuto sibi pondera silice.   *Id., LXIII, 1*

Nulli se dicit mulier mea nubere malle
   quam mihi, non si se Iuppiter ipse petat.
dicit: sed mulier cupido quod dicit amanti
   in vento et rapida scribere oportet aqua.

                                    Id., LXX

Huc est mens deducta tua, mea Lesbia, culpa,
   atque ita se officio perdidit ipsa suo,
ut iam nec bene velle queat tibi, si optima fias,
   nec desistere amare, omnia si facias.   *Id., LXXV*

Quare cum te iam amplius excrucies?
   quin tu animum offirmas atque istinc teque reducis
et dis invitis desinis esse miser?
   Difficilest longum subito deponere amorem.

                                Id., LXXVI, 10

O, Caelius, my Lesbia, that Lesbia, Lesbia whom Catullus alone loved more than himself and all his own, now in the crossroads and alleys serves the filthy lusts of the descendants of lordly-minded Remus.

(Tr. Leigh Hunt)

Atys o'er the distant waters, driving in rapid bark,
Soon with foot of wild impatience touched the Phrygian
    forest dark,
Where amid the awful shades possessed by mighty Cybele,
In his zealous frenzy blind,
And wand'ring in his hapless mind,
With flinty knife he gave to earth the weights that stamp
    virility.

(Tr. Theodore Martin)

> My mistress says, there's not a man
>   Of all the many that she knows,
> She'd rather wed than me, not one,
>   Though Jove himself were to propose.
> She says so: but what woman says
>   To him who fancies he has caught her,
> 'Tis only fit it should be writ
>   In air or in the running water.

(Tr. F. W. Cornish)

To this point is my mind reduced by your fault, my Lesbia, and has so ruined itself by its own devotion, that now it can neither wish you well though you should become the best of women, nor cease to love you though you do the worst that can be done.

Why should you torment yourself any more? Why do you not settle your mind firmly, and draw back, and cease to be miserable, in spite of the gods? It is difficult suddenly to lay aside a long-cherished love.

O di, si vestrumst misereri, aut si quibus umquam
    extremam iam ipsa in morte tulistis opem,
me miserum aspicite et, si vitam puriter egi,
    eripite hanc pestem perniciemque mihi.   *Ibid.*, *17*

Odi et amo. quare id faciam, fortasse requiris.
    Nescio, sed fieri sentior et excrucior.

Id., LXXXV

Nulla potest mulier tantum se dicere amatam
    vere, quantum a me Lesbia amata mea's.
nulla fides ullo fuit umquam foedere tanta,
    quanta in amore tuo ex parte reperta meast.

Id., LXXXVII

Lesbia mi dicit semper male nec tacet umquam
    de me: Lesbia me dispeream nisi amat.
quo signo? quia sunt totidem mea: deprecor illam
    assidue, verum dispeream nisi amo.   *Id., XCII*

Multas per gentes et multa per aequora vectus
    advenio has miseras, frater, ad inferias,
ut te postremo donarem munere mortis
    et mutam nequiquam alloquerer cinerem.

Id., CI, 1

Ye, gods, if mercy is your attribute, or if ye ever brought aid to any at the very moment of death, look upon me in my trouble, and if I have led a pure life, take away this plague and ruin from me.

I hate and love. Why I do so, perhaps you ask. I know not, but I feel it, and I am in torment.

(Tr. Walter Savage Landor)

> None could ever say that she,
> Lesbia! was so loved by me.
> Never all the world around
> Faith so true as mine was found.

(Tr. Jonathan Swift)

> Lesbia for ever on me rails
> To talk of me she never fails.
> Now, hang me, but for all her art,
> I find that I have gained her heart.
> My proof is this: I plainly see
> The case is just the same with me;
> I curse her every hour sincerely,
> Yet, hang me, but I love her dearly.

(Tr. Aubrey Beardsley)

> By ways remote and distant waters sped,
> Brother, to thy sad grave-side am I come,
> That I may give the last gifts to the dead,
> And vainly parley with thine ashes dumb.

· · · ·

Nunc tamen interea haec, prisco quae more parentum
　　tradita sunt tristi munere ad inferias,
accipe fraterno multum manantia fletu,
　　atque in perpetuum, frater, ave atque vale.　　*Ibid.,* 7

At non effugies meos iambos.

Fragmenta, 1

C. LICINIUS CALVUS

82 – 47 B.C.

A! virgo infelix, herbis pasceris amaris!　　　*Io*

Cum iam fulva cinis fuero . . .

Lilium, vaga candido
nympha quod secet ungui.

But lo! these gifts, the heirlooms of past years,
Are made sad things to grace thy coffin shell;
Take them, all drenched with a brother's tears,
And brother, for all time, hail and farewell!

(*Tr. F. W. Cornish*)

But you shall not escape my iambics.

CALVUS

Calvus was a celebrated orator, one of the leaders of the so-called Attic school, opposed to the Ciceronian school, and a poet of great talent to whom Horace, Propertius, and Ovid grant equal rank with Catullus. Only meager fragments have survived of his works, which included a brief epic, *Io*, epigrams, and an elegy on the death of his wife.

Unfortunate maiden, you will have to graze on bitter herbs.

When I will be nothing but a heap of golden ashes . . .

A lily that a wandering nymph will cut with her shiny fingernail.

L. VARIUS RUFUS

74 – 14 B.C.

Tene magis salvum populus velit an populum tu?
servet in ambiguo, qui consulit et tibi et Urbi,
Iuppiter.   *Panegyricus Augusti*

PUBLIUS VERGILIUS MARO

70 – 19 B.C.

Tityre, tu patulae recubans sub tegmine fagi
silvestrem tenui musam meditaris avena:
nos patriae finis et dulcia linquimus arva.
                                     Ecloga, I, 1

VARIUS

Varius, a close friend of Horace and Vergil, came of a well-known plebeian family. His works, of which almost nothing has survived, included an epic on Julius Caesar, a panegyric on Augustus, and a tragedy *Thyestes,* which was praised in the highest terms by Quintilian and Tacitus.

Is your life dearer to the people than the people's life to you? May Jupiter, who keeps watch over you and Rome, leave the answer in doubt.

VERGIL

Born at Andes (probably the modern Virgilio) near Mantua, Vergil studied rhetoric, history, medicine, mathematics, and philosophy. As a result of the proscriptions of 42 B.C. he lost his estate, but, thanks to Pollio and Maecenas, it was restored to him. Out of gratitude to his patrons he wrote the ten eclogues known as *Bucolics.* At the suggestion of Maecenas he wrote the *Georgics,* a didactic poem on agriculture that Montaigne, Dryden, and others praise as his greatest work. The last ten or twelve years of his life he spent working on the famous *Aeneid,* also at the suggestion of Maecenas. He left it unfinished. Apparently he was dissatisfied with it, for he instructed his friend Varius to burn it after his death. However, by order of Augustus, Varius published it.

Vergil has enjoyed an uninterrupted fame down to our own day; the two-thousandth anniversary of his death was officially celebrated at Rome. His works were used in schools almost at once; throughout the Middle Ages and later he was revered as a magician and prophet; Dante chose him as guide through the infernal regions; lines from his poems were used as mottoes by writers in all ages. A line from the *Aeneid* (VII, 312) appears on the title page of Sigmund Freud's *Interpretation of Dreams.*

(*Tr. C. D. Lewis*)

Tityrus, here you loll, your slim reed-pipe serenading
The woodland spirit beneath a spread of sheltering beech,
While I must leave my home place, the fields so dear to me.

Non equidem invideo, miror magis.   *Ibid.*, 11

Et penitus toto divisos orbe Britannos.
Ibid., 66

Et iam summa procul villarum culmina fumant,
maioresque cadunt altis de montibus umbrae.
Ibid., 82

Formosum pastor Corydon ardebat Alexim,
delicias domini.   *Id.*, II, 1

O formose puer, nimium ne crede colori!
Ibid., 17

Torva leaena lupum sequitur, lupus ipse capellam,
florentem cytisum sequitur lasciva capella,
te Corydon, o Alexi: trahit sua quemque voluptas.
Ibid., 63

Aspice, aratra iugo referunt suspensa iuvenci,
et sol crescentis decedens duplicat umbras:
me tamen urit amor: quis enim modus adsit amori?
Ibid., 66

Malo me Galatea petit, lasciva puella,
et fugit ad salices et se cupit ante videri.
Id., III, 64

Qui legitis flores et humi nascentia fraga,
frigidus, o pueri, fugite hinc, latet anguis in herba.
Ibid., 93

Well, I don't grudge you that: but it does amaze me.

Even to Britain—that place cut off at the very world's end.

Look over there—smoke rises already from the rooftops
And longer fall the shadows cast by the mountain heights.

A shepherd, Corydon, burned with love for his master's
favorite,
Handsome Alexis.

Don't bank too much on your complexion, lovely boy!

Fierce lioness goes after wolf, wolf after goat,
The wanton goat goes after the flowering clover, and I
Go after you, Alexis—each towed by his own fancy.

Look, ploughs feather the ground as the ox-teams draw
them home,
And a declining sun enlarges the lengthening shadows:
Yet love still scorches me—love has no lull, no limit.

Now Galatea throws at me an apple—she's a wanton maid:
Off to the sally trees she do run wishing I spy whereto
she's fled.

Oh children dear, who gather flowers,
who gather flowers and wild strawberries near,
Run away quick—away from that grass,
a cold cold snake is lurking there.

Ultima Cumaei venit iam carminis aetas;
magnus ab integro saeclorum nascitur ordo.
iam redit et Virgo, redeunt Saturnia regna,
iam nova progenies caelo demittitur alto.

Id., IV, 4

Incipe, parve puer: qui non risere parenti,
nec deus hunc mensa, dea nec dignata cubili est.

Ibid., 62

Ambo florentes aetatibus, Arcades ambo,
et cantare pares et respondere parati. *Id., VII, 4*

Nunc scio quid sit Amor. *Id., VIII, 43*

Non omnia possumus omnes. *Ibid., 63*

Numero deus impare gaudet. *Ibid., 75*

Credimus? an, qui amant, ipsi sibi somnia fingunt?

Ibid., 108

Et me fecere poetam
Pierides, sunt et mihi carmina, me quoque dicunt
vatem pastores; sed non ego credulus illis.
nam neque adhuc Vario videor nec dicere Cinna
digna, sed argutos inter strepere anser olores.

Id., IX, 32

Omnia fert aetas, animum quoque. *Ibid., 51*

Non canimus surdis, respondent omnia silvae.

Id., X, 8

Omnia vincit amor, et nos cedamus amori.

Ibid., 69

Ours is the crowning era foretold in prophecy:
Born of Time, a great new cycle of centuries
Begins. Justice returns to earth, the Golden Age
Returns, and its first-born comes down from heaven above.

Begin, dear babe. The boy who does not smile at his
   mother
Will never deserve to sup with a god or sleep with a
   goddess.

They were both in the flower of their youth, Arcadians,
Both ready to sing at the drop of a hat, or to take a tune up.

I know what Love is—too well I know him.

We cannot all do all things.

Odd numbers bring luck.

Is it true, or the dream of a lover's desire?

      The Muses made me
A poet too. There are songs of mine. The shepherd folk
Call me their bard—though I'm not deluded by what *they*
   say:
I know I cannot be mentioned in the same breath with
   Cinna
Or Varius—a honking goose with silver-throated swans.

Time bears all away, even memory.

Not to deaf ears I sing, for the woods echo my singing.

All-conquering is Love—no use to fight against him.

Deucalion vacuum lapides iactavit in orbem,
unde homines nati, durum genus. *Georgica, I, 62*

Labor omnia vicit
improbus et duris urgens in rebus egestas.

Ibid., 145

Inopi metuens formica senectae.   *Ibid., 186*

Tot bella per orbem,
tam multae scelerum facies, non ullus aratro
dignus honos, squalent abductis arva colonis
et curvae rigidum falces conflantur in ensem.
hinc movet Euphrates, illinc Germania bellum;
vicinae ruptis inter se legibus urbes
arma ferunt; saevit toto Mars impius orbe.

Ibid., 505

Salve, magna parens frugum, Saturnia tellus,
magna virum.   *Id., II, 173*

O fortunatos nimium, sua si bona norint,
agricolas! quibus ipsa procul discordibus armis
fundit humo facilem victum iustissima tellus.

Ibid., 458

At secura quies et nescia fallere vita,
dives opum variarum, ac latis otia fundis,
speluncae vivique lacus et frigida Tempe
mugitusque boum mollesque sub arbore somni
non absunt.   *Ibid., 467*

Rura mihi et rigui placeant in vallibus amnes,
flumina amem silvasque inglorius.   *Ibid., 485*

Deucalion cast over a tenantless world the stones
From which arose mankind, that dour race.

Yes, unremitting labor
And harsh necessity's hand will master anything.

The ant that insures against a destitute old age.

There's so much war in the world,
Evil has so many faces, the plough so little
honor, the laborers are taken, the fields untended,
And the curving sickle is beaten into the sword that yields
    not.
There the East is in arms, here Germany marches:
Neighbor cities, breaking their treaties, attack each other:
The wicked War-god runs amok through all the world.

Hail, great mother of harvests! O land of Saturn, hail!
Mother of men!

Oh, too lucky for words, if only he knew his luck,
Is the countryman who far from the clash of armaments
Lives, and rewarding earth is lavish of all he needs!

But calm security and a life that will not cheat you,
Rich in its own rewards, are here: the broad ease of the
    farmlands,
Caves, living lakes, and combes that are cool even at mid-
    summer
Mooing of herds, and slumber mild in the trees' shade.

Then let the country charm me, the rivers that channel its
    valleys,
Then may I love its forest and stream, and let fame go
    hang.

Felix qui potuit rerum cognoscere causas,
atque metus omnis et inexorabile fatum
subiecit pedibus strepitumque Acherontis avari.
fortunatus et ille deos qui novit agrestis
Panaque Silvanumque senem Nymphasque sorores.

Ibid., 490

Temptanda via est, qua me quoque possim
tollere humo victorque virum volitare per ora.

Id., III, 8

Optima quaeque dies miseris mortalibus aevi
prima fugit: subeunt morbi tristique senectus
et labor, et durae rapit inclementia mortis.

Ibid., 66

Omne adeo genus in terris hominumque ferarumque
et genus aequoreum, pecudes pictaeque volucres,
in furias ignemque ruunt: amor omnibus idem.

Ibid., 242

Sed fugit interea, fugit inreparabile tempus.

Ibid., 284

Primus vere rosam atque autumno carpere poma.

Id., IV, 134

Agmine facto
ignavum fucos pecus a praesepibus arcent.

Ibid., 167

Eurydicen vox ipsa et frigida lingua
a miseram Eurydicen! anima fugiente vocabat.

Ibid., 525

Lucky is he who can learn the roots of the universe,
Has mastered all his fears and fate's intransigence
And the hungry clamor of hell.
But fortunate too the man who is friends with the country
  gods—
Pan and old Silvanus and the sisterhood of nymphs.

I must venture a theme will exalt me
From earth and give me wings and a triumph on every
  tongue.

Of the measure of days allowed to piteous mortals, the
  best days
Are first to leave: illness and sorry old age loom up,
Suffering and death's untender mercies take all away.

All manner of life on earth—men, fauna of land and sea,
Cattle and colored birds—
Run to this fiery madness: love is alike for all.

But time is on the move still, time that will not return.

His the first rose of spring, the earliest apples in autumn.

Closing ranks
[they] shoo the drones—that work-shy gang—away from the
  bee-folds.

That cold, cold tongue cried out "Eurydice!"
Cried "Poor Eurydice!" as the soul of the singer fled.

Arma virumque cano, Troiae qui primus ab oris
Italiam fato profugus Laviniaque venit
litora—multum ille et terris iactatus et alto
vi superum, saevae memorem Iunonis ob iram.

Aeneis, I, 1

Tantaene animis caelestibus irae? *Ibid., 11*

Manet alta mente repostum
iudicium Paridis spretaeque iniuria formae.

Ibid., 26

Tantae molis erat Romanam condere gentem.

Ibid., 33

O terque quaterque beati,
quis ante ora patrum Troiae sub moenibus altis
contigit oppetere! *Ibid., 94*

Apparent rari nantes in gurgite vasto.

Ibid., 118

O socii (neque enim ignari sumus ante malorum)
o passi graviora, dabit deus his quoque finem.

Ibid., 198

Revocate animos maestumque timorem
mittite; forsan et haec olim meminisse iuvabit.

Ibid., 202

Dixit et avertens rosea cervice refulsit,
ambrosiaeque comae divinum vertice odorem
spiravere; pedes vestis defluxit ad imos;
et vera incessu patuit dea. *Ibid., 402*

I tell about war and the hero who first from Troy's frontier
Displaced by destiny, came to the Lavinian shores,
To Italy—a man much travailed on sea and land
By the powers above, because of the brooding anger of
  Juno.

Can a divine being be so persevering in anger?

    Deep in her mind rankles
The judgment of Paris, the insult of having her beauty
  scorned.

So massive a task it was to found the Roman race.

    Oh, thrice and four times blessèd you
Whose luck it was to fall before your fathers' eyes
Under Troy's battlements!

A man or two can be seen swimming the huge maelstrom.

Comrades, we're well acquainted with evils, then and now.
Worse than this you have suffered. God will end all this too.

Take heart again, oh, put your dismal fears away!
One day—who knows?—even these will be grand things to
  look back on.

She spoke. She turned away; and as she turned, her neck
Glowed to a rose-flush, her crown of ambrosial hair
  breathed out
A heavenly fragrance, her robe flowed down, down to her
  feet,
And in gait she was all a goddess.

Sunt lacrimae rerum et mentem mortalia tangunt.

Ibid., 462

Non ignara mali miseris succurrere disco.

Ibid., 630

Nec non et vario nocte sermone trahebat
Infelix Dido longumque bibebat amorem.

Ibid., 747

Infandum, regina, iubes renovare dolorem,
Troianas ut opes et lamentabile regnum
eruerint Danai, quaeque ipse miserrima vidi
et quorum pars magna fui.   *Id., II, 3*

Et iam nox umida caelo
praecipitat suadentque cadentia sidera somnos.

Ibid., 8

Equo ne credite, Teucri.
Quidquid id est, timeo Danaos et dona ferentes.

Ibid., 48

Horresco referens.   *Ibid., 204*

Tempus erat quo prima quies mortalibus aegris
incipit et dono divum gratissima serpit.   *Ibid., 268*

Una salus victis nullam sperare salutem.

Ibid., 354

Heu nihil invitis fas quemquam fidere divis!

Ibid., 402

Dextrae se parvus Iulus
implicuit sequiturque patrem non passibus aequis.

Ibid., 723

Tears in the nature of things, hearts touched by human
  transience.

Being acquainted with grief, I am learning to help the unlucky.

Yes, and ill-starred Dido talked on into the small hours,
Talked over many things as she drank deep of love.

O queen, the griefs you bid me reopen are inexpressible—
The tale of Troy, a rich and a most tragic empire
Erased by the Greeks; most piteous events I saw with my
  own eyes
And played no minor part in.

    The dewy night drops fast
From heaven, and the declining stars invite to sleep.

    No, you must never feel safe with the horse, Trojans.
Whatever it is, I distrust the Greeks, even when they are
  generous.

Telling it makes me shudder.

It was the hour when worn-out men begin to get
Some rest, and by god's grace genial sleep steals over them.

Losers have one salvation—to give up all hope of salvation.

Ah well, there's no trusting the gods for anything, once
  they're against you!

    Ascanius twined his fingers
In mine, hurrying to keep with his father's longer stride.

Infelix simulacrum atque ipsius umbra Creusae
visa mihi ante oculos et nota maior imago.

Ibid., 772

Heu fuge crudelis terras, fuge litus avarum.

Id., III, 44

Quid non mortalia cogis,
auri sacra fames?

Ibid., 56

Anna soror, quae me suspensam somnia terrent!

Id., IV, 9

Degeneres animos timor arguit.   *Ibid., 13*

Agnosco veteris vestigia flammae.   *Ibid., 23*

Neque enim specie famave movetur
nec iam furtivum Dido meditatur amorem:
coniugium vocat, hoc praetexit nomine culpam.

Ibid., 170

Fama, malum qua non aliud velocius ullum:
mobilitate viget virisque adquirit eundo,
parva metu primo, mox sese attollit in auras
ingrediturque solo et caput inter nubila condit.

Ibid., 173

Quis fallere possit amantem?   *Ibid., 296*

Cui me moribundam deseris, hospes
(hoc solum nomen quoniam de coniuge restat)?

Ibid., 323

There appeared before my eyes a piteous phantom, yes,
The very ghost of Creusa—a figure larger than life.

Get away from this cruel land, from these hard-fisted
shores!

What lengths is the heart of man driven to
By this cursed craving for gold!

Anna, sister, why do these nerve-racking dreams haunt
me?

Mean souls convict themselves by cowardice.

I feel once more the scars of the old flame.

Dido recked nothing for appearance or reputation:
The love she brooded on now was a secret love no longer;
Marriage, she called it, drawing the word to veil her sin.

Rumor, the swiftest traveler of all the ills on earth,
Thriving on movement, gathering strength as it goes; at the
start
A small and cowardly thing, it soon puffs itself up,
And walking upon the ground, buries its head in the cloud-
base.

But who can ever hoodwink a woman in love?

To what, my guest, are you leaving me?
"Guest"—that is all I may call you now, who have called
you husband.

Qui tibi tum, Dido, cernenti talia sensus,
quosve dabas gemitus, cum litora fervere late
prospiceres arce ex summa, totumque videres
misceri ante oculos tantis clamoribus aequor!

Ibid., 408

Mens immota manet, lacrimae volvuntur inanes.

Ibid., 449

Varium et mutabile semper
femina.

Ibid., 569

Exoriare aliquis nostris ex ossibus ultor.

Ibid., 625

Duri magno sed amore dolores
polluto, notumque furens quid femina possit.

Id., V, 5

Possunt, quia posse videntur.   *Ibid., 231*

Sternitur exanimisque tremens procumbit humi bos.

Ibid., 481

Quo fata trahunt retrahuntque sequamur;
quidquid erit, superanda omnis fortuna ferendo est.

Ibid., 709

Tu ne cede malis, sed contra audentior ito
qua tua te fortuna sinet.   *Id., VI, 95*

Facilis descensus Averno:
noctes atque dies patet atri ianua Ditis;
sed revocare gradum superasque evadere ad auras,
hoc opus, hic labor est.   *Ibid., 126*

Ah, Dido, what did you feel when you saw these things
    going forward?
What moans you gave when, looking forth from your high
    rooftop,
You beheld the whole length of the beach aswarm with
    men, and the sea's face
Alive with the sound and fury of preparations for sailing!

Resolute, though, was his mind; unavailingly rolled her
    tears.

    Woman was ever
A veering, weathercock creature.

Rise up from my dead bones, avenger!

    Knowing what a woman is capable of
When insane with the grief of having her love cruelly
    dishonored.

They could do it because they believed they could do it.

Sprawling, quivering, lifeless, down on the ground the brute
    fell.

    Let us follow our destiny, ebb or flow.
Whatever may happen, we master fortune by fully accept-
    ing it.

Never give way to those evils: face them all the more
    boldly
Using what methods your luck allows you.

    The way to Avernus is easy;
Night and day lie open the gates of death's dark kingdom:
But to retrace your steps, to find the way back to day-
    light—
That is the task, the hard thing.

Primo avulso non deficit alter
aureus, et simili frondescit virga metallo.

Ibid., 143

Vestibulum ante ipsum primis in faucibus Orci
Luctus et ultrices posuere cubilia Curae;
pallentesque habitant Morbi tristisque Senectus,
et Metus et malesuada Fames ac turpis Egestas,
terribiles visu formae, Letumque Labosque;
tum consanguineus Leti Sopor et mala mentis
Gaudia, mortiferumque adverso in limine Bellum,
ferreique Eumenidum thalami et Discordia demens.

Ibid., 273

Hic manus ob patriam pugnando vulnera passi,
quique sacerdotes casti, dum vita manebat,
quique pii vates et Phoebo digna locuti,
inventas aut qui vitam excoluere per artis,
quique sui memores alios fecere merendo.

Ibid., 660

Principio caelum ac terram camposque liquentis
lucentemque globum lunae Titaniaque astra
spiritus intus alit, totamque infusa per artus
mens agitat molem et magno se corpore miscet.

Ibid., 724

When a bough is torn away, another
Gold one grows in its place with leaves of the same metal.

At the very porch and entrance way to Orcus
Grief and ever-haunting Anxiety make their bed;
Here dwell pallid Diseases, here morose Old Age,
With Fear, ill-prompting Hunger, and squalid Indigence,
Shapes horrible to look at, Death and Agony;
Sleep, too, which is the cousin of Death; and Guilty Joys,
And there, against the threshold, War, the bringer of
    Death:
Here are the iron cells of the Furies, and lunatic Strife.

Here were assembled those who had suffered wounds in
    defense of
Their country; those who had lived pure lives as priests;
    and poets
Who had not disgraced Apollo, poets of true integrity;
Men who civilized life by the skills they discovered, and
    men whose
Kindness to other people has kept their memory green.

First, you must know that the heavens, the earth, the
    watery plains
Of the sea, the moon's bright globe, the sun and the stars
    are all
Sustained by a spirit within; for immanent mind, flowing
Through all its parts and leavening its mass, makes the
    universe work.

Excudent alii spirantia mollius aera
(credo equidem), vivos ducent de marmore vultus,
orabunt causas melius, caelique meatus
describent radio et surgentia sidera dicent:
tu regere imperio populos, Romane, memento
(hae tibi erunt artes), pacisque imponere morem,
parcere subiectis et debellare superbos.   *Ibid., 847*

Heu, miserande puer, si qua fata aspera rumpas,
tu Marcellus eris.   *Ibid., 882*

Sunt geminae Somni portae, quarum altera fertur
cornea, qua veris facilis datur exitus umbris,
altera candenti perfecta nitens elephanto,
sed falsa ad caelum mittunt insomnia manes.

Ibid., 893

Flectere si nequeo superos, Acheronta movebo.

Id., VII, 312

Aude, hospes, contemnere opes et te quoque dignum
finge deo, rebusque veni non asper egenis.

Id., VIII, 364

Ea verba locutus
optatos dedit amplexus placidumque petivit
coniugis infusus gremio per membra soporem.

Ibid., 404

O mihi praeteritos referat si Iuppiter annos.

Ibid., 560

Let others fashion from bronze more lifelike, breathing images—
For so they shall—and evoke living faces from marble;
Others excel as orators, others track with their instruments
The planets circling in heaven and predict when stars will appear.
But, Romans, never forget that government is your medium!
Be this your art:—to practise men in the habit of peace,
Generosity to the conquered, and firmness against aggressors.

Alas, poor youth! If only you could escape your harsh fate!
Marcellus you shall be.

There are two gates of Sleep: the one is made of horn,
They say, and affords the outlet for genuine apparitions;
The other's a gate of brightly-shining ivory: this way
The Shades send up to earth false dreams that impose upon us.

If the gods above are no use to me, then I'll move all hell.

Have the courage, my guest, to despise possessions; train yourself,
As he, to be worthy of godhead: don't be intolerant of poverty.

    Thus saying,
He gave his wife the love he was aching to give her; then he
Sank into soothing sleep, relaxed upon her breast.

If Jupiter would only restore those bygone years.

It clamor, et agmine facto
quadripedante putrem sonitu quatit ungula campum.

Ibid., 595

Peccare fuisset
ante satis, penitus modo non genus omne perosos
femineum. *Id., IX,* 140

Macte nova virtute, puer, sic itur ad astra.

Ibid., 641

Audentis Fortuna iuvat. *Id., X,* 284

Stat sua cuique dies, breve et inreparabile tempus
omnibus est vitae; sed famam extendere factis,
hoc virtutis opus. *Ibid.,* 467

Nescia mens hominum fati sortisque futurae
et servare modum rebus sublata secundis!

Ibid., 501

Arma manu trepidi poscunt, fremit arma iuventus,
flent maesti mussantque patres. *Id., XI,* 453

Disce, puer, virtutem ex me verumque laborem,
fortunam ex aliis. *Id., XII,* 435

Aestuat ingens
uno in corde pudor mixtoque insania luctu
et furiis agitatus amor et conscia virtus. *Ibid.,* 666

Non me tua fervida terrent
dicta, ferox; di me terrent et Iuppiter hostis.

Ibid., 894

Then loud shouts are heard as, all in a body,
With clatter of hammering hooves they go galloping over
the dry flats.

It should be enough to have sinned once and then to loathe
well nigh all
The feminine sex.

More power to your young valor, my son! You're going the
right way
To starry fame.

Fortune always fights for the bold.

Every man's hour is appointed. Brief and unalterable
For all, the span of life. To enlarge his fame by deeds
Is what the brave man must aim at.

Ah, mind of man, so ignorant of fate, of what shall befall
him,
So weak to preserve moderation when riding the crest of
good fortune!

"To arms!" the young men shout;
While the senators gloomily weep and mutter.

From me you may learn courage and what real effort is;
From others, the meaning of fortune.

His heart in a violent conflict,
Torn by humiliation, by grief shot through with madness,
By love's tormenting jealousy and a sense of his own
courage.

It's the gods and Jupiter's
Enmity frighten me, not your sneers or your bloodthirsty
speeches.

QUINTUS HORATIUS FLACCUS

December 8, 65 – November 27, 8 B.C.

Beatus ille qui procul negotiis,
ut prisca gens mortalium,
paterna rura bobus exercet suis
solutus omni faenore.   *Iambi, ii,* **1**

Nox erat et caelo fulgebat luna sereno
inter minora sidera.   *Id., xv,* **1**

Arva, beata
petamus arva divites et insulas,
reddit ubi Cererem tellus inarata quotannis
et imputata floret usque vinea.   *Id., xvi,* **41**

Qui fit, Maecenas, ut nemo, quam sibi sortem
seu ratio dederit seu fors obiecerit, illa
contentus vivat, laudet diversa sequentes?
          Satirae, I, i, **1**

HORACE

Horace, certainly the Latin poet most quoted in English, is praised for his inimitable grace, urbanity, and mellow outlook, but his smiling philosophy was the product of turbulent years. He was born at Venosa, the son of an ex-slave. His father gave him a good education, sending him when he was twelve to Rome, and later to Athens, where he studied under the most reputed rhetoricians and philosophers. He was twenty-two when Caesar was assassinated and the civil war broke out. Brutus came to Athens, and Horace enlisted in his army. After its defeat at Philippi, Horace returned to Rome; impoverished as a result of the penalties imposed on republican veterans, he took a post as clerk. About that time he began to write poetry. Vergil and Varius introduced him to Maecenas, who in turn introduced him to Augustus, and soon Horace was able to devote himself entirely to writing. All his works seem to have come down to us—nearly ten thousand lines, composed over thirty-five years. Their technical perfection has been admired down to this day, though Petronius' well-known judgment, *"Horatii curiosa felicitas"* (Horace's "studied" or "painstaking" felicity), seems to imply a criticism.

(Tr. E. C. Wickham)

Happy the man who far from schemes of business, like the early generations of mankind, ploughs and ploughs again his ancestral land with oxen of his own breeding, with no yoke of usury on his neck!

'Twas night and the moon was shining in a cloudless sky amid the host of lesser stars.

Let us look for the land, the happy land, the islands of wealth; where the soil unploughed gives its corn crop year by year, and the vineyard ever blooms unpruned.

How comes it, Maecenas, that, whether it be self-chosen or flung to him by chance, everyone is discontented with his own lot and keeps his praises for those who tread some other path?

Quamquam ridentem dicere verum
quid vetat? ut pueris dant crustula blandi
doctores, elementa velint ut discere prima.

Ibid., 24

Nil obstet tibi, dum ne sit te ditior alter.

Ibid., 40

Populus me sibilat, at mihi plaudo
ipse domi, simul ac nummos contemplor in arca.

Ibid., 66

Quid rides? Mutato nomine, de te
fabula narratur.   *Ibid.*, 69

Miraris, cum tu argento post omnia ponas,
si nemo praestet quem non merearis amorem?

Ibid., 86

Est modus in rebus, sunt certi denique fines,
quos ultra citraque nequit consistere rectum.

Ibid., 106

Inde fit, ut raro, qui se vixisse beatum
dicat et exacto contentus tempore vita
cedat uti conviva satur, reperire queamus.

Ibid., 117

Dum vitant stulti vitia, in contraria currunt.

Id., *ii*, 24

Pastillos Rufillus olet, Gargonius hircum.

Ibid., 27

Omnibus hoc vitium est cantoribus, inter amicos
ut numquam inducant animum cantare rogati,
iniussi numquam desistant.   *Id.*, *iii*, 1

Why may not one be telling truth while one laughs, as teachers sometimes give little boys cakes to coax them into learning their letters?

Nothing stops you, if only there may be no rival richer than yourself.

The people hisses me, but I applaud myself, as often as I gaze on the moneys in my chest.

Why do you smile? Change but the name, and it is of yourself that the tale is told.

Can you wonder, when you rank everything after your money, that no one renders you the love which you do not earn?

There are fixed limits beyond which and short of which right cannot find resting place.

This is how it comes to pass that we can seldom find one to confess that he has had a happy life, and rise contented, when his time is up, like a satisfied guest from his banquet.

Fools in avoiding a vice run into its opposite.

Rufillus smells of perfumery, Gargonius of the goat.

All singers have this fault: when they are begged to sing in a party of friends they can never persuade themselves to do it; when they are not asked they never leave off.

At ingenium ingens
inculto latet hoc sub corpore. *Ibid.*, 33

At pater ut gnati, sic nos debemus amici
si quod sit vitium non fastidire. *Ibid.*, 43

Quam temere in nosmet legem sancimus iniquam!
nam vitiis nemo sine nascitur; optimus ille est,
qui minimis urgetur. *Ibid.*, 67

Qui ne tuberibus propriis offendat amicum
postulat, ignoscet verrucis illius; aequum est
peccatis veniam poscentem reddere rursus.
Ibid., 73

Iura inventa metu iniusti fateare necesse est,
tempora si fastosque velis evolvere mundi.
Ibid., 111

Faenum habet in cornu: longe fuge! dummodo risum
excutiat sibi, non hic cuiquam parcet amico.
Id., *iv*, 34

Neque si quis scribat uti nos
sermoni propiora, putes hunc esse poetam.
ingenium cui sit, cui mens divinior atque os
magna sonaturum, des nominis huius honorem.
Ibid., 41

Non satis est puris versum perscribere verbis.
Ibid., 54

Under that uncouth outside are hidden vast gifts of mind.

But at least we might do for a friend what a father does for his son—not be disgusted for a single blemish.

How rashly do we give our sanction to a harsh law which will recoil upon ourselves! For none in this world is without failings: he is best who labors under the smallest ones.

He who expects his friend not to be annoyed at his wens will excuse the other's warts. It is only fair that one who asks indulgence for shortcomings should give it in return.

If you examine the dates of the world's history you will have to confess that the source of justice was the fear of injustice.

He carries hay on his horns [*i.e.*, he is dangerous], give him a wide berth: provided he can raise a laugh he will spare neither himself nor any friend.

Nor [must you] give a man the name of poet while he writes, as I do, in the style of common talk. Who has the native gift, who has the inspired soul and tongue of lofty utterance, to him you may give the honor of that name.

It is not enough to make up your verse of plain words.

His, ego quae nunc,
olim quae scripsit Lucilius, eripias si
tempora certa modosque, et quod prius ordine verbum est,
posterius facias, praeponens ultima primis,
Non, ut si solvas "Postquam Discordia taetra
belli ferratos postis portasque refregit,"
invenias etiam disiecti membra poetae.   *Ibid., 56*

Absentem qui rodit amicum,
qui non defendit alio culpante, solutos
qui captat risus hominum famamque dicacis,
fingere qui non visa potest, commissa tacere
qui nequit: hic niger est, hunc tu, Romane, caveto.
                                          Ibid., 81

Nil ego contulerim iucundo sanus amico.
                                          Id., v, 44

Credat Iudaeus Apella,
non ego: namque deos didici securum agere aevum,
nec, si quid miri faciat natura, deos id
tristis ex alto caeli demittere tecto.   *Ibid., 100*

Fulgente trahit constrictos Gloria curru
non minus ignotos generosis.   *Id., vi, 23*

Magnum hoc ego duco,
quod placui tibi, qui turpi secernis honestum
non patre praeclaro, sed vita et pectore puro.
                                          Ibid., 62

Nil sine magno
vita labore dedit mortalibus.   *Id., ix, 59*

Est brevitate opus, ut currat sententia neu se
impediat verbis lassas onerantibus auris.   *Id., x, 9*

With the verses which I write, or which Lucilius in old days wrote, if you took away the regularity of quantity and rhythm, and altered the order of the words, you would not, as you would if you decomposed such lines as
     "When foul Discord's jar
Had burst the steel-clad doors and oped the gates of war [by Ennius]," recognize, even in his dismembered state, the limbs of a poet.

The man who backbites an absent friend, nay, who does not stand up for him when another blames him, the man who angles for bursts of laughter and for the repute of a wit, who can invent what he never saw, who cannot keep a secret—that man is black at heart: mark and avoid him, if you are a Roman.

Never while I keep my senses shall I compare anything to the delight of a friend.

Apella the Jew must believe it, not I; for I have learnt the lesson that gods live in careless ease, and that if Nature works some marvel it is not something sent down from the vault of heaven by gods out of humor.

Glory drags bound at the wheels of her triumphal chariot the unknown no less than the well-born.

I am proud to think that I pleased one who draws as you do the line between honor and disgrace, not by a father's renown but by the blamelessness of my own life and heart.

The prizes of life are never to be had without trouble.

There must be the power of terse expression, that the thoughts may flow on unimpeded by the verbiage, which only tires the overladen ears.

Ridiculum acri
fortius et melius magnas plerumque secat res.

Ibid., 14

Quot capitum vivunt, totidem studiorum
milia.   *Id., II, i, 26*

Nec meus hic sermo est, sed quae praecepit Ofellus
rusticus, abnormis sapiens crassaque Minerva.

Id., ii, 2

Male verum examinat omnis
corruptus iudex.   *Ibid., 8*

Ieiunus raro stomachus volgaria temnit.

Ibid., 38

Vivite fortes
fortiaque adversis opponite pectora rebus.

Ibid., 135

Vitanda est improba Siren
desidia, aut quidquid vita meliore parasti
ponendum aequo animo.   *Id., iii, 14*

Omnis enim res,
virtus, fama, decus, divina humanaque pulchris
divitiis parent; quas qui construxerit, ille
clarus erit, fortis, iustus. "sapiensne?" etiam, et rex
et quidquid volet.   *Ibid., 94*

Nil agit exemplum, litem quod lite resolvit.

Ibid., 103

Et genus et virtus, nisi cum re, vilior alga est.

Id., v, 8

Humor very often cuts the knot of serious questions more trenchantly and successfully than severity.

For every thousand souls there are a thousand tastes.

This is no talk of my own, but the teaching of Ofellus, the countryman, a philosopher, though not from the schools, but of homespun wit.

A bribed judge weighs truth in false scales.

Contempt for things common belongs to the stomach which seldom feels real hunger.

Live as brave men; and if fortune is adverse, front its blows with brave hearts.

You must avoid the shameless Siren, idleness, or else be content to give up all that in your better hours you have earned.

Riches, you know, are the beautiful things: everything else, worth, repute, honor, things divine and things human, bow down to them. Any one who has gathered a pile of them will be famous, gallant, just. "And wise too?" Certainly— and a king and anything else he could wish.

An instance carries us no further which settles one quarrel only by opening another.

Without substance, blood and valor are more valueless than seaweed.

Hoc erat in votis: modus agri non ita magnus,
hortus ubi et tecto vicinus iugis aquae fons
et paulum silvae super his foret. *Id., vi, 1*

O si angulus ille
proximus accedat, qui nunc denormat agellum!
Ibid., 8

O rus, quando ego te aspiciam! quandoque licebit
nunc veterum libris, nunc somno et inertibus horis,
ducere sollicitae iucunda oblivia vitae! *Ibid., 60*

O noctes cenaeque deum! *Ibid., 65*

Dum licet, in rebus iucundus vive beatus;
vive memor, quam sis aevi brevis. *Ibid., 96*

Pars hominum vitiis gaudet constanter et urget
propositum; pars multa natat, modo recte capessens,
interdum pravis obnoxia. *Id., vii, 6*

Romae rus optas; absentem rusticus urbem
tollis ad astra levis. *Ibid., 28*

Quisnam igitur liber? sapiens, sibi qui imperiosus,
quem neque pauperies neque mors neque vincula terrent,
responsare cupidinibus, contemnere honores
fortis, et in se ipso totus, teres atque rotundus. *Ibid., 83*

Non horam tecum esse potes, non otia recte
ponere, teque ipsum vitas fugitivus et erro,
iam vino quaerens, iam somno fallere Curam;
frustra: nam comes atra premit sequiturque fugacem.
Ibid., 112

This used to be among my prayers—a portion of land not so very large, but which should contain a garden, and near the homestead a spring of ever-flowing water, and a bit of forest to complete it.

O, if I could throw in that adjoining corner that spoils the shape of my little farm!

O country home, when shall I look on you again! when shall I be allowed, between my library of classics and sleep and hours of idleness, to drink the sweet draughts that make us forget the troubles of life!

O nights and suppers of gods!

Live whilst you may in the enjoyment of what is pleasant; live, and remember how short the time is!

A part of the world finds its pleasure consistently in vice and keeps steady to its purpose. Another and a larger part wavers, at one moment setting its hand to what is right, at another giving way to evil.

At Rome you are all for the country: in the country you extol to the stars the distant town.

Who then is free? The wise man alone, who is a stern master to himself, whom neither poverty nor death nor bonds affright, who has the courage to say "no" again and again to desires, to despise the objects of ambition, who is a whole in himself, smoothed and rounded.

You cannot bear your own company for an hour together, you cannot employ leisure wisely, you would give yourself the slip, a runaway and a vagrant, seeking now with wine, now with sleep, to cheat Care. In vain: fast as you run, black Care is at your side or at your heels.

Aut insanit homo aut versus facit.   *Ibid., 117*

Heu, Fortuna, quis est crudelior in nos
te deus? ut semper gaudes illudere rebus
humanis!   *Id., viii, 61*

Maecenas atavis edite regibus
o et praesidium et dulce decus meum.
                                Carmina, I, i, 1

            Bellaque matribus
        detestata.   *Ibid., 24*

Me doctarum hederae praemia frontium
dis miscent superis.   *Ibid., 29*

        Quodsi me lyricis vatibus inseres,
        sublimi feriam sidera vertice.   *Ibid., 36*

        Audiet pugnas, vitio parentum
            rara iuventus.   *Id., ii, 23*

    Illi robur et aes triplex
        circa pectus erat, qui fragilem truci
    commisit pelago ratem
        primus.   *Id., iii, 9*

    Audax omnia perpeti
    Gens humana ruit per vetitum nefas.   *Ibid., 25*

        Nil mortalibus ardui est.   *Ibid., 37*

Pallida Mors aequo pulsat pede pauperum tabernas
    regumque turres.   *Id., iv, 13*

Vitae summa brevis spem nos vetat inchoare longam.
                                Ibid., 15

Why, if the man isn't raving, he is composing verses!

Ah Fortune, what divine power is more cruel towards us than thou! How thou delightest ever to make sport of human affairs!

Maecenas, in lineage the child of kings, but oh! to me my protector, pride, and joy.

And the wars which mothers abhor.

For me, the ivy crown which rewards the poet's brow admits me to the company of gods.

If you will give me a place among the bards of the lyre, I shall lift my head till it strikes the stars.

How they fought shall be told to a young generation scant in number for their parents' crimes.

His heart was mailed in oak and triple brass who was the first to commit a frail bark to the rough seas.

In its boldness to bear and to dare all things, the race of man rushes headlong into sin, despite of law.

No height is too arduous for mortal men.

Pale death with impartial foot knocks at the doors of poor men's hovels and king's palaces.

Life's short span forbids us to enter on far-reaching hopes.

Quis multa gracilis te puer in rosa
perfusus liquidis urget odoribus
    grato, Pyrrha, sub antro?
        cui flavam religas comam,
simplex munditiis?   *Id., v, 1*

    Tiburni lucus, et uda
mobilibus pomaria rivis.   *Id., vii, 13*

O fortes peioraque passi
mecum saepe viri, nunc vino pellite curas:
    cras ingens iterabimus aequor.   *Ibid., 30*

Quid sit futurum cras, fuge quaerere et
quem Fors dierum cumque dabit, lucro
    appone nec dulces amores
        sperne puer neque tu choreas,
donec virenti canities abest
morosa.   *Id., ix, 13*

        Latentis proditor intimo
    gratus puellae risus ab angulo.   *Ibid., 21*

Tu ne quaesieris—scire nefas—quem mihi, quem tibi
finem di dederint, Leuconoë, nec Babylonios
temptaris numeros. ut melius, quicquid erit, pati!
                                      Id., xi, 1

Carpe diem, quam minimum credula postero.
                                      Ibid., 8

    Felices ter et amplius
        quos inrupta tenet copula nec malis
    divulsus querimoniis
        suprema citius solvet amor die.   *Id., xiii, 17*

(Tr. John Milton, "Rendered almost word for word without Rhyme according to the Latin Measure, as near as the Language will permit.")

What slender youth bedewed with liquid odours
Courts thee on roses in some pleasant cave,
Pyrrha, for whom bindst thou
In wreaths thy golden hair,
Plain in thy neatness?

(Tr. E. C. Wickham)

The grove of Tiburnus, and the apple orchards wet with streamlets never still.

Brave hearts, heroes who have weathered with me worse storms than this, today chase your cares with wine: tomorrow we set out once more upon the boundless sea.

What shall be tomorrow, think not of asking. Each day that Fortune gives you, be it what it may, set down for gain; nor refuse sweet loves while boyhood is yours, nor the dance, so long as youth is green and testy old age is far off.

The sweet tell-tale laughter from the secret corner which betrays the hiding girl.

Pray, ask not, Leuconoe—such knowledge is not for us— what end for me, for you, the gods ordain, nor tamper with the Chaldaeans' tables. How much better, whatever it is to be, to bear it!

Snatch the sleeve of today, and trust as little as you may to tomorrow.

Thrice happy they, and more than thrice, to whom an unbroken bond holds fast, and whom love, never torn asunder by foolish quarrelings, will not loose till life's last day!

Et tollens vacuum plus nimio Gloria verticem.

Id., xviii, 15

Integer vitae scelerisque purus.   *Id., xxii, 1*

Dulce ridentem Lalagen amabo,
   dulce loquentem.   *Ibid., 23*

Quis desiderio sit pudor aut modus
tam cari capitis?   *Id., xxiv, 1*

Cui Pudor, et Iustitiae soror,
incorrupta Fides, nudaque Veritas,
   quando ullum inveniet parem?   *Ibid., 6*

Durum: sed levius fit patientia,
   quidquid corrigere est nefas.   *Ibid., 19*

Parcus deorum cultor et infrequens,
insanientis dum sapientiae
   consultus erro.   *Id., xxxiv, 1*

Nunc est bibendum, nunc pede libera
pulsanda tellus.   *Id., xxxvii, 1*

Persicos odi, puer, apparatus,
   displicent nexae philyra coronae;
mitte sectari, rosa quo locorum
   sera moretur.   *Id., xxxviii, 1*

Quae caret ora cruore nostro?

Id., II, i, 36

Nullus argento color est avaris
abdito terris.   *Id., ii, 1*

Aequam memento rebus in arduis
servare mentem.   *Id., iii, 1*

Vainglory, lifting far too high her empty head.

He that is unstained in life and pure from guilt.

I shall love Lalage and her sweet laughter, Lalage and her sweet prattle.

What shame or measure should there be in grief for one so dear?

When shall Modesty find again his peer, and stainless Faith, own sister to Justice, and naked Truth?

'Tis hard. But what may not be altered is made lighter by patience.

A grudging and infrequent worshipper of the gods, whilst I strayed, the professor of a wisdom that is folly.

Now we must drink, now beat the earth with free step.

Persian luxury, boy, I hate. I have no taste for garlands twined with linden bark. Cease your efforts to find where the last rose lingers.

What shore is clean from blood of ours?

Silver has no shine while it is hidden in the miserly earth.

Remember when life's path is steep to keep your mind even.

Rectius vives, Licini, neque altum
semper urgendo neque, dum procellas
cautus horrescis, nimium premendo
litus iniquum.   *Id., x, 1*

Auream quisquis mediocritatem
diligit, tutus caret obsoleti
sordibus tecti, caret invidenda
sobrius alta.   *Ibid., 5*

Sperat infestis, metuit secundis
alteram sortem bene praeparatum
pectus.   *Ibid., 13*

Eheu fugaces, Postume, Postume,
labuntur anni, nec pietas moram
rugis et instanti senectae
adferet indomitaeque morti.   *Id., xiv, 1*

Linquenda tellus et domus et placens
uxor, neque harum, quas colis, arborum
te praeter invisas cupressos
ulla brevem dominum sequetur.   *Ibid., 21*

Quid brevi fortes iaculamur aevo
multa? quid terras alio calentes
sole mutamus? patriae quis exsul
se quoque fugit?   *Id., xvi, 17*

Nihil est ab omni
parte beatum.   *Ibid., 27*

Odi profanum vulgus et arceo;
favete linguis. carmina non prius
audita Musarum sacerdos
virginibus puerisque canto.

Id., III, i, 1

You will live a happier life, Licinius, by neither steering always for the deep sea nor in cautious dread of storms hugging too close a dangerous shore.

Whoso loves well the golden mean avoids the squalor of a ruinous hovel and is safe, is sober and avoids the palace that attracts envy.

The heart that is well forearmed hopes when times are adverse, and when they are favorable fears a change of fortune.

Ah me, Postumus, Postumus, the fleeting years are slipping by, nor will piety give a moment's stay to wrinkles and hurrying old age and death the unconquerable.

The earth we needs must leave, and house and wife of our choice; nor of the trees which you tend shall any save the hated cypresses go along with their short-lived master.

Why, with our short years, are we so bold to aim our shafts at many marks? Why change our home for lands warm with another sun? What exile from his country finds that he has left himself also behind?

No lot is happy on all sides.

I hate the uninitiate crowd and bid them avaunt. Listen all in silence! Strains unheard before I, the Muses' hierophant, now chant to maidens and to boys.

Aequa lege Necessitas
sortitur insignes et imos:
omne capax movet urna nomen.   *Ibid.,* 14

Dulce et decorum est pro patria mori.
mors et fugacem persequitur virum,
nec parcit imbellis iuventae
poplitibus timidove tergo.   *Id., ii,* 13

Est et fideli tuta silentio
merces.   *Ibid.,* 25

Raro antecedentem scelestum
deseruit pede Poena claudo.   *Ibid.,* 31

Iustum et tenacem propositi virum
non civium ardor prava iubentium,
non vultus instantis tyranni
mente quatit solida.   *Id., iii,* 1

Si fractus inlabatur orbis,
impavidum ferient ruinae.   *Ibid.,* 7

Vis consili expers mole ruit sua.   *Id., iv,* 65

Damnosa quid non imminuit dies?
aetas parentum, peior avis, tulit
nos nequiores, mox daturos
progeniem vitiosiorem.   *Id., vi,* 45

Hic dies anno redeunte festus
corticem adstrictum pice demovebit
amphorae fumum bibere institutae
consule Tullo.   *Id., viii,* 9

By one and the same impartial law Doom assigns the lot of highest and humblest: every name alike is shaken in her roomy urn.

To die for the fatherland is a sweet thing and becoming. Death is at the heels even of the runaway, nor spares the haunches and back of the coward and malingerer.

Loyal reticence too has its reward secure.

Rarely has Punishment, though halt of foot, left the track of the criminal in the way before her.

The just man and firm of purpose not the heat of fellow citizens clamoring for what is wrong, nor presence of threatening tyrant can shake in his rock-like soul.

If the round sky should crack and fall upon him, the wreck will strike him fearless still.

Force without mind falls by its own weight.

Destroying time! what does it not make worse! Our sires' age was worse than our grandsires'. We their sons are more worthless than they; so in our turn we shall give the world a progeny yet more corrupt.

This day, as each year comes round, will be a holiday. It will remove the pitch-covered cork from a jar which first was taught to drink the smoke when Tullus was consul.

Donec gratus eram tibi
  nec quisquam potior bracchia candidae
cervici iuvenis dabat,
  Persarum vigui rege beatior.   *Id., ix,* 1

Tecum vivere amem, tecum obeam libens!
                                        Ibid., 24

  Una de multis, face nuptiali
  digna periurum fuit in parentem
  splendide mendax et in omne virgo
      nobilis aevum.   *Id., xi,* 33

  O fons Bandusiae, splendidior vitro.
                                        Id., xiii, 1

  Crescentem sequitur cura pecuniam
  maiorumque fames.   *Id., xvi,* 17

          Magnas inter opes inops.   *Ibid.,* 28

      Multa petentibus
  desunt multa: bene est cui deus obtulit
      parca quod satis est manu.   *Ibid.,* 42

  O nata mecum consule Manlio,
  seu tu querellas sive geris iocos
      seu rixam et insanos amores
          seu facilem, pia testa, somnum.

                                        Id., xxi, 1

          Narratur et prisci Catonis
              saepe mero caluisse virtus. *Ibid.,* 11

  Virtutem incolumem odimus,
      sublatam ex oculis quaerimus, invidi.
                                        Id., xxiv, 31

> Whilst, Lydia, I was lov'd of thee,
> And ('bout thy Ivory neck) no youth did fling
>   His arms more acceptable free,
> I thought me richer than the Persian King.

(*Tr. E. C. Wickham*)

Yet would I wish to love, live, die with thee.

One only of the number worthy of the marriage torch, with glorious falsehood met her sire, a maid famous to all time.

O spring of Bandusia, more brilliant than glass.

As money grows, care follows it and the hunger for more.

A pauper in the midst of wealth.

Who asks for much always wants much. Well for him to whom God has given with sparing hand, but enough!

O born with me when Manlius was consul, whether what you bring us be voice of complaint or of mirth, whether strife and blind passionate love, or rather, my gentle wine-jar, sleep that comes at will.

They say that even old Cato, for all his virtue, warmed his heart many a time with good wine.

Worth, while still safely ours, we hate, when lifted from our sight (such is envy) we seek for it in vain.

Quid leges sine moribus
vanae proficiunt? *Ibid.*, 35

Vixi puellis nuper idoneus
et militavi non sine gloria. *Id., xxvi*, 1

Festo quid potius die
Neptuni faciam? prome reconditum,
Lyde, strenua Caecubum
munitaeque adhibe vim sapientiae.
Id., xxviii, 1

Omitte mirari beatae
fumum et opes strepitumque Romae.
Id., xxix, 11

Ille potens sui
laetusque deget, cui licet in diem
dixisse "vixi: cras vel atra
nube polum pater occupato
vel sole puro; non tamen irritum,
quodcumque retro est, efficiet, neque
diffinget infectumque reddet,
quod fugiens semel hora vixit." *Ibid.*, 41

Exegi monumentum aere perennius
regalique situ pyramidum altius,
quod non imber edax, non Aquilo impotens
possit diruere aut innumerabilis
annorum series et fuga temporum.
non omnis moriar multaque pars mei
vitabit Libitinam. *Id., xxx*, 1

What profit laws, which without lives are empty?

Though that life is past, I was but now still meet for ladies' love, and fought my battles not without glory.

What better could I do on Neptune's holiday? Quick, Lyde, bring out from its secret bin the Caecuban, and push the siege of our deep-entrenched seriousness.

Abate for a time your admiration for the smoke and the grandeur and the noise which make the happiness of Rome.

He will through life be master of himself and a happy man who from day to day can have said, "I have lived: tomorrow the Sire may fill the sky with black clouds or with cloudless sunshine; he will not undo aught that is left behind me, nor change or make as though it had not been aught that the hour, fast as it flies, has once brought."

My work is done, the memorial more enduring than brass and loftier than the kingly building of the pyramids—something that neither the corroding rain nor the wild rage of Aquilo can ever destroy, nor the numberless succession of years and flight of ages. I shall not die: a large part of me will escape the Funeral-queen.

Intermissa, Venus, diu
  rursus bella moves. parce, precor, precor.
non sum qualis eram bonae
  sub regno Cinarae. desine, dulcium
mater saeva Cupidinum,
  circa lustra decem flectere mollibus
iam durum imperiis.   *Id., IV, i,* 1

    Pindarum quisquis studet aemulari,
    Iule, ceratis ope Daedalea
    nititur pinnis vitreo daturus
        nomina ponto.   *Id., ii,* 1

        Ego apis Matinae
        more modoque
    grata carpentis thyma per laborem
    plurimum circa nemus uvidique
    Tiburis ripas operosa parvus
        carmina fingo.   *Ibid.,* 27

Totum muneris hoc tui est,
  quod monstror digito praetereuntium
Romanae fidicen lyrae:
  quod spiro et placeo, si placeo, tuum est.
                                             Id., iii, 21

    Fortes creantur fortibus et bonis.   *Id., iv,* 29

    Doctrina sed vim promovet insitam,
    rectique cultus pectora roborant;
        utcumque defecere mores
            indecorant bene nata culpae.   *Ibid.,* 33

(*Tr. Ben Jonson*)

> Venus, again thou mov'st a war
>   Long intermitted; pray thee, pray thee spare!
> I am not such, as in the reign
>   Of the good Cynara I was: refrain
> Sour mother of sweet loves, forbear
>   To bend a man, now at his fiftieth year
> Too stubborn for commands so slack.

(*Tr. E. C. Wickham*)

Whoso would rival Pindar, Iulus, is poising himself on wings that some Daedalus has fastened for him with wax, and will give his name to some glassy sea.

For me, after the fashion of a Matine bee, that through incessant toil makes boot upon the fragrant thyme about the woods and river-banks of streaming Tibur, I humbly build my laborious verse.

It is all of thy free gift that the finger of the passer-by points me out as the tuner of a Roman lyre. Breath of song and power to please, if please I may, are alike of thee.

Gallant sons spring from the gallant and good.

But teaching quickens the native power and right training fortifies the heart. If ever it be that the public manners fail, faults discredit even the nobly born.

Duris ut ilex tonsa bipennibus
nigrae feraci frondis in Algido
per damna, per caedes ab ipso
ducit opes animumque ferro.   *Ibid.,* 57

Merses profundo, pulchrior evenit.   *Ibid.,* 65

Diffugere nives, redeunt iam gramina campis
arboribusque comae.   *Id., vii,* 1

Immortalia ne speres, monet annus et almum
quae rapit hora diem.   *Ibid.,* 7

Quis scit an adiciant hodiernae crastina summae
tempora di superi?   *Ibid.,* 17

Digno laude virum Musa vetat mori.
caelo Musa beat.   *Id., viii,* 28

Vixere fortes ante Agamemnona
multi: sed omnes inlacrimabiles
urgentur ignotique longa
nocte, carent quia vate sacro.   *Id., ix,* 25

Iudex honestum praetulit utili,
reiecit alto dona nocentium
vultu.   *Ibid.,* 41

Non possidentem multa vocaveris
recte beatum; rectius occupat
nomen beati, qui deorum
muneribus sapienter uti
duramque callet pauperiem pati
peiusque leto flagitium timet,
non ille pro caris amicis
aut patria timidus perire.   *Ibid.,* 45

Like the holm-oak shorn by ruthless axes on Algidus where black leaves grow thick, through loss, through havoc, from the very edge of the steel [the Roman race] draws new strength and heart.

Plunge it in the depth—it comes forth the fairer.

The snows have scattered and fled; already the grass comes again in the fields and the leaves on the trees.

That you hope for nothing to last forever, is the lesson of the revolving year and of the flight of time which snatches from us the sunny days.

Who knows whether the gods' will be to add tomorrow's hours to the sum as it stands today.

The hero who is worthy of her praise the Muse will not let die—the Muse makes happy in heaven.

Gallant heroes lived before Agamemnon, not a few: but on all alike, unwept and unknown, eternal night lies heavy because they lack a sacred poet.

On a judgment seat, generous and leal he has set honor before expediency, has flung back with lofty mien the gifts of the guilty.

It is not the possessor of many things whom you will rightly call happy. The name of the happy man is claimed more justly by him who has learnt the art wisely to use what the gods give, and who can endure the hardships of poverty, who dreads disgrace as something worse than death. He will not fear to die for the friends he loves, or for his country.

Misce stultitiam consiliis brevem;
dulce est desipere in loco.   *Id., xii, 27*

Solve senescentem mature sanus equum, ne
peccet ad extremum ridendus et ilia ducat.
                                     Epistulae, I, i, 8

Nullius addictus iurare in verba magistri,
quo me cumque rapit tempestas, deferor hospes.
                                            Ibid., 14

Et mihi res, non me rebus, subiungere conor.
                                            Ibid., 19

Virtus est vitium fugere et sapientia prima
stultitia caruisse.   *Ibid., 41*

Vilius argentum est auro, virtutibus aurum.
                                            Ibid., 52

"O cives, cives, quaerenda pecunia primum est;
virtus post nummos!"   *Ibid., 53*

Hic murus aeneus esto,
nil conscire sibi, nulla pallescere culpa.
                                            Ibid., 60

Isne tibi melius suadet, qui "rem facias, rem,
si possis recte, si non, quocumque mode, rem"?
                                            Ibid., 65

Olim quod volpes aegroto cauta leoni
respondit referam: "Quia me vestigia terrent,
omnia te adversum spectantia, nulla retrorsum."
                                            Ibid., 73

Ad summam: sapiens uno minor est Iove, dives,
liber, honoratus, pulcher, rex denique regum,
praecipue sanus, nisi cum pituita molesta est.
                                            Ibid., 106

Mix with your sage counsels some brief folly. In due place to forget one's wisdom is sweet.

Be wise in time and turn your horse out to grass when he shows signs of age, lest he end in a ludicrous breakdown with straining flanks.

I am not bound over to swear allegiance to any master: where the wind carries me, I put into port and make myself at home.

I try to suit life to myself, not myself to life.

To flee vice is the beginning of virtue, and the beginning of wisdom is to have got rid of folly.

As gold is worth more than silver, so is virtue than gold.

"O fellow citizens, fellow citizens, money is the first thing to see: virtue after money."

Be this your wall of brass, to have no guilty secrets, no wrong-doing that makes you turn pale.

Does he advise you better who bids you make "money, money by right means if you can, if not, by any means money"?

I shall answer as the wary fox in the fable answered the sick lion: "Because I am frightened at seeing that all the footprints point towards your den and none the other way."

The sum of it all is, the wise man ranks only second to Jove. He is rich, free, honored, beautiful, king (in fine) of kings—above all, he is sound, except when the phlegm troubles him.

Qui quid sit pulchrum, quid turpe, quid utile, quid non,
planius ac melius Chrysippo et Crantore dicit.   *Id., ii, 3*

Quidquid delirant reges, plectuntur Achivi.
seditione, dolis, scelere atque libidine et ira
Iliacos intra muros peccatur et extra.   *Ibid., 14*

Rursus, quid virtus et quid sapientia possit,
utile proposuit nobis exemplar Ulixen.   *Ibid., 17*

Nos numerus sumus et fruges consumere nati.
     Ibid., 27

Ut iugulent hominem, surgunt de nocte latrones;
ut te ipsum serves, non expergisceris?   *Ibid., 32*

Dimidium facti qui coepit habet; sapere aude;
incipe! Qui recte vivendi prorogat horam,
rusticus exspectat dum defluat amnis; at ille
labitur et labetur in omne volubilis aevum.
     Ibid., 40

Sincerum est nisi vas, quodcumque infundis acescit.
     Ibid., 54

Semper avarus eget; certum voto pete finem.
     Ibid., 56

Invidus alterius macrescit rebus opimis;
invidia Siculi non invenere tyranni
maius tormentum.   *Ibid., 58*

Ira furor brevis est.   *Ibid., 62*

[Homer] shows us what is fair, what is foul, what is profitable, what not, more plainly and better than a Chrysippus or a Crantor.

For every folly of their princes the Greeks feel the scourge. Faction, craft, wickedness, and the lust and anger from which it springs—these are the sources of wrong-doing within the walls of Troy and without them.

Again, of the power of virtue and of wisdom he has given us a profitable example in Ulysses.

We are the ciphers, fit for nothing but to eat our share of earth's fruits.

To cut men's throats, robbers rise in the night. To save yourself alive, can you not wake?

He who has begun his task has half done it. Have the courage to be wise. Begin! He who keeps putting off the moment of reform is like the countryman waiting for the river to run by. But the river slides and rolls, and will slide and roll on to all time.

Unless the vessel is clean, everything you pour into it turns sour.

The covetous is a beggar always. Try to find a definite limit to your wishing.

The envious man grows lean because his neighbor thrives. The tyrants of Sicily never invented a torture worse than envy.

Anger is a short madness.

Inter spem curamque, timores et iras
omnem crede diem tibi diluxisse supremum.
grata superveniet, quae non sperabitur hora.

Id., iv, 14

Quo mihi fortunam, si non conceditur uti?

Id., v, 12

Quid non ebrietas dissignat? operta recludit,
spes iubet esse ratas, ad proelia trudit inertem,
sollicitis animis onus eximit, addocet artes.
fecundi calices quem non fecere disertum?
contracta quem non in paupertate solutum?

Ibid., 16

Nil admirari prope res est una, Numici,
solaque quae possit facere et servare beatum.

Id., vi, 1

Insani sapiens nomen ferat, aequus iniqui,
ultra quam satis est Virtutem si petat ipsam.

Ibid., 15

Scilicet uxorem cum dote fidemque et amicos
et genus et formam regina Pecunia donat,
ac bene nummatum decorat Suadela Venusque.

Ibid., 36

Prodigus et stultus donat quae spernit et odit;
haec seges ingratos tulit et feret omnibus annis.

Id., vii, 20

Nec somnum plebis laudo satur altilium nec
otia divitiis Arabum liberrima muto.   *Ibid., 35*

In a world of hope and care, of fears and angry passions, hold for yourself the belief that each day that dawns is your last: the hour to which you do not look forward will be a pleasant surprise.

What is fortune to me, if I may not enjoy it?

What changes are not wrought by good drinking! It unlocks secrets, bids hopes be certainties, thrusts the coward into the fray, takes their load from anxious hearts, teaches new accomplishments. The life-giving winecup, whom has it not made eloquent, whom has it not made free even in the pinch of poverty!

Nought to admire is perhaps the one and only thing, Numicius, that can make a man happy and keep him so.

The wise man would deserve the name of madman, the just of unjust, if they were to pursue even Virtue herself too far.

Of course, you know, a wife and dower, credit and friends, even birth and beauty, are all in the gift of Queen Money: the goddess of persuasion and the goddess of love both honor the well-moneyed man.

The prodigal and fool gives what he despises and hates: seed so sown has always produced, and will always produce, a crop of ingratitude.

And do not think that I praise the sleep of the humble while my own belly is with fat capon lined. I have no mind to exchange my ease and freedom for the riches of the Arabs.

Parvum parva decent: mihi iam non regia Roma
sed vacuum Tibur placet aut imbelle Tarentum.

Ibid., *44*

Metiri se quemque suo modulo ac pede verum est.

Ibid., *98*

Naturam expelles furca, tamen usque recurret.

Id., *x*, *24*

Quem res plus nimio delectavere secundae,
mutatae quatient. *Ibid.*, *30*

Fuge magna: licet sub paupere tecto
reges et regum vita praecurrere amicos. *Ibid.*, *32*

Cui non conveniet sua res, ut calceus olim,
si pede maior erit, subvertet, si minor, uret.

Ibid., *42*

Tamen illic vivere vellem
oblitusque meorum, obliviscendus et illis.

Id., *xi*, *8*

Caelum, non animum, mutant, qui trans mare currunt.
strenua nos exercet inertia: navibus atque
quadrigis petimus bene vivere. quod petis hic est,
est Ulubris, animus si te non deficit aequus. *Ibid.*, *27*

Rerum concordia discors. *Id.*, *xii*, *36*

Nec lusisse pudet, sed non incidere ludum.

Id., *xiv*, *36*

Stultorum incurata pudor malus ulcera celat.

Id., *xvi*, *38*

Small things beseem the small. My pleasure now is not in queenly Rome, but in leisurely Tibur or peaceful Tarentum.

The true course is that each should measure himself with the foot-rule which belongs to him.

If you drive nature out with a pitchfork, she will soon find a way back.

Whom prosperity has charmed too much, adversity will shatter.

Flee grandeur: under a humble roof you may live a far happier life than kings and kings' friends.

Like the shoe in the fable, when a man's circumstances do not fit him, if they are too large for his foot they will trip him up, if too small they will gall it.

Yet I could find it in my heart to live there, and, forgetting my friends and forgotten by them . . .

They change their sky, not their soul, who run across the sea. We work hard at doing nothing: we seek happiness in yachts and four-horse coaches. What you seek is here —is at Ulubrae—if an even soul does not fail you.

Nature's harmony in discord.

Shame is not in having played, but in not knowing where to break off the play.

It is a false shame which makes fools hide wounds instead of healing them.

Vir bonus est quis?
"qui consulta patrum, qui leges iuraque servat,
quo multae magnaeque secantur iudice lites,
quo res sponsore et quo causae teste tenentur."
sed videt hunc omnis domus et vicinia tota
introrsum turpem, speciosum pelle decora. *Ibid., 40*

Qui cupiet, metuet quoque; porro
qui metuens vivet, liber mihi non erit umquam.
perdidit arma, locum Virtutis deseruit, qui
semper in augenda festinat et obruitur re. *Ibid., 65*

Mors ultima linea rerum est. *Ibid., 79*

Principibus placuisse viris non ultima laus est.
non cuivis homini contigit adire Corinthum.
                                    Id., xvii, 35

Virtus est medium vitiorum et utrimque reductum.
                                    Id., xviii, 9

Percontatorem fugito: nam garrulus idem est,
nec retinent patulae commissa fideliter aures,
et semel emissum volat irrevocabile verbum.
                                    Ibid., 69

Nam tua res agitur, paries cum proximus ardet.
                                    Ibid., 84

Dulcis inexpertis cultura potentis amici:
expertus metuit. tu, dum tua navis in alto est,
hoc age, ne mutata retrorsum te ferat aura.
oderunt hilarem tristes tristemque iocosi,
sedatum celeres, agilem navumque remissi.
                                    Ibid., 86

Who is your "good man"? You answer, "one who observes the decrees of the senate, statutes, and laws; one who is set as arbitrator to decide quarrels many and grave; money is safe when he is the security, a cause when he is the witness." Yet this very man all his household and all his neighbors see to be base within, beneath the fair-looking skin of respectability.

He who shall have desires will have fears too; and again he who shall live in fear will never, in my judgment, be a free man. One who is always in a hurry, always over head and ears in the amassing of wealth, has lost his shield, has run away from Virtue's post.

Death is the limit that ends everything.

To have found favor with leaders of mankind is not the meanest of glories. It is not everyone that can get to Corinth.

True Virtue is the mean between vices, as far from one extreme as from the other.

Fly from a questioner; he is sure to be a babbler also. Open ears never keep faithfully the secrets whispered to them; and meanwhile a word once let out of the cage cannot be whistled back.

It is your own interest that is at stake when your next neighbor's wall is ablaze.

Making up to a powerful friend seems a pleasant thing to those who have not tried: who has tried will dread it. For yourself, my friend, while your bark is on the sea, give all heed lest the breeze shift and turn your course back again. The gloomy hate the cheerful, the mirthful the gloomy, the hasty the man of calm, the indolent the man of action.

Secretum iter et fallentis semita vitae.

Ibid., 103

Sit mihi quod nunc est, etiam minus, et mihi vivam
quod superest aevi, si quid superesse volunt di;
sit bona librorum et provisae frugis in annum
copia, neu fluitem dubiae spe pendulus horae.
Sed satis est orare Iovem, qui ponit et aufert,
det vitam, det opes; aequum mi animum ipse parabo.

Ibid., 107

Nulla placere diu nec vivere carmina possunt
quae scribuntur aquae potoribus.   *Id.*, *xix*, 2

O imitatores, servum pecus, ut mihi saepe
bilem, saepe iocum vestri movere tumultus!

Ibid., 19

Non ego ventosae plebis suffragia venor
impensis cenarum et tritae munere vestis.

Ibid., 37

Adeo sanctum est vetus omne poema.

Id., *II*, *i*, 54

Interdum volgus rectum videt, est ubi peccat.

Ibid., 63

Indignor quicquam reprehendi, non quia crasse
compositum illepideve putetur, sed quia nuper,
nec veniam antiquis, sed honorem et praemia posci.

Ibid., 76

Quod si tam Graecis novitas invisa fuisset
quam nobis, quid nunc esset vetus?   *Ibid.*, 90

A quiet journey in the untrodden paths of life.

Give me what I have, or even less; and therewith let me live to myself for what remains of life, if the gods will that anything remain. Let me have a generous supply of books and of food stored a year ahead; nor let me hang and tremble on the hope of the uncertain hour. Nay, it is enough to ask Jove, who gives them and takes them away, that he grant life and subsistence; a balanced mind I will find for myself.

No poems can please long, nor live, which are written by water drinkers.

O imitators, you slavish herd! How often have your false alarms stirred my wrath, how often my mirth!

I am not the man to hunt the suffrages of the windy crowd at the cost of suppers and by the gift of worn raiment.

So sacred a thing is any ancient poem.

At times the world sees straight: there are occasions when it goes wrong.

I feel how unjust it is that anything should be criticized not because its composition is thought coarse or out of taste but because it is modern, and that men should claim for ancient writings not indulgence but honor and all the prizes.

Now if novelty had been viewed as grudgingly by the Greeks as it is by us, what in these times would be ancient?

Mutavit mentem populus levis et calet uno
scribendi studio; pueri patresque severi
fronde comas vincti cenant et carmina dictant.

Ibid., 108

Quod medicorum est
promittunt medici; tractant fabrilia fabri;
scribimus indocti doctique poemata passim.

Ibid., 115

Os tenerum pueri balbumque poeta figurat,
torquet ab obscenis iam nunc sermonibus aurem,
mox etiam pectus praeceptis format amicis,
asperitatis et invidiae corrector et irae.   *Ibid., 126*

Graecia capta ferum victorem cepit et artes
intulit agresti Latio.   *Ibid., 156*

Si foret in terris, rideret Democritus.

Ibid., 194

Discit enim citius meminitque libentius illud
quod quis deridet, quam quod probat et veneratur.

Ibid., 262

Atque inter silvas Academi quaerere verum.

Id., ii, 45

Singula de nobis anni praedantur euntes;
eripuere iocos, Venerem, convivia, ludum;
tendunt extorquere poemata: quid faciam vis?

Ibid., 55

Multa fero, ut placem genus irritabile vatum,
cum scribo et supplex populi suffragia capto.

Ibid., 102

The fickle populace has changed its taste, and nowadays is fevered with a universal passion for writing. Boys and grave fathers alike sit at supper with their brows crowned with leaves and have an amanuensis to take down their poetry.

Doctors undertake what belongs to doctors; carpenters handle carpenters' tools. Poetry we all write, those who have learnt and those who have not, without distinction.

It is the poet that gives form to the child's utterance while it is still tender and lisping. He gives the ear a bias from the first against coarse ways of speaking. Presently he molds the heart also with kindly teaching, correcting roughness and envy and anger.

When Greece had been enslaved she made a slave of her rough conqueror, and introduced the arts into Latium, still rude.

If he were on earth, Democritus would laugh.

For men learn more quickly and remember more readily what they laugh at than what they approve and look up to.

And seek for truth in the garden of Academus.

Years as they pass plunder us of one thing after another. They have snatched from me mirth, love, banquets, play. They are on the way to wrench poetry from my grasp. What would you have me do?

So long as I am writing and wooing on my knees the people's suffrages, I have to submit to much in order to pacify the sensitive race of poets.

Ridentur mala qui componunt carmina; verum
gaudent scribentes et se venerantur et ultro,
si taceas, laudant quidquid scripsere beati.
at qui legitimum cupiet fecisse poema,
cum tabulis animum censoris sumet honesti.

Ibid., 106

Obscurata diu populo bonus eruet atque
proferet in lucem speciosa vocabula rerum,
quae priscis memorata Catonibus atque Cethegis
nunc situs informis premit et deserta vetustas.

Ibid., 115

Perpetuus nulli datur usus, et heres
heredem alterius velut unda supervenit undam.

Ibid., 175

Quid te exempta iuvat spinis de pluribus una?
vivere si recte nescis, decede peritis.
lusisti satis, edisti satis atque bibisti:
tempus abire tibi est, ne potum largius aequo
rideat et pulset lasciva decentius aetas.   *Ibid., 212*

"Pictoribus atque poetis
quidlibet audendi semper fuit aequa potestas."
scimus, et hanc veniam petimusque damusque vicissim;
sed non ut placidis coeant immitia, non ut
serpentes avibus geminentur, tigribus agni.

De Art Poetica, 9

Inceptis gravibus plerumque et magna professis
purpureus, late qui splendeat, unus et alter
adsuitur pannus.   *Ibid., 14*

Amphora coepit
institui: currente rota cur urceus exit?

Ibid., 21

Those who write bad verses get laughed at; but yet they enjoy writing them and pay reverence to themselves, and if you should hold your tongue, take the lead in praising their own composition, be it what it may—happy people! But the man who shall desire to leave behind him a poem true to the laws of art, when he takes his tablets to write will take also the spirit of an honest censor.

Phrases of beauty that have been lost to popular view he will kindly disinter and bring into the light, phrases which, though they were on the lips of a Cato and a Cethegus of old time, now lie uncouth because out of fashion, and disused because old.

No one is given perpetual occupation—heir follows heir as wave follows wave.

How does it relieve you to pluck out one thorn out of many? If you do not know how to live aright, make way for those who do. You have played enough, have eaten and drunk enough. It is time for you to leave the scene; lest, when you have drunk more than your fair share, you be laughed at and driven away by an age to which play is more becoming.

"Poets and painters," you say, "have always had an equal license in daring invention." We know it: this liberty we claim for ourselves and give again to others; but it does not go to the extent that savage should mate with tame, that serpents should couple with birds, or lambs with tigers.

Often on a work of grave purpose and high promises is tacked a purple patch or two to give an effect of color.

It was a wine jar that was to be molded: as the wheel runs round why does it come out a pitcher?

Brevis esse laboro
obscurus fio.   *Ibid.*, 25

In vitium ducit culpae fuga, si caret arte.
                                                 Ibid., 31

Cui lecta potenter erit res,
nec facundia deseret hunc nec lucidus ordo.
                                                 Ibid., 40

Dixeris egregie, notum si callida verbum
reddiderit iunctura novum.   *Ibid.*, 47

Multa renascentur quae iam cecidere, cadentque
quae nunc sunt in honore vocabula, si volet usus.
                                                 Ibid., 70

Grammatici certant et adhuc sub iudice lis est.
                                                 Ibid., 78

Proicit ampullas et sesquipedalia verba
si curat cor spectantis tetigisse querella.
                                                 Ibid., 97

Non satis est pulchra esse poemata; dulcia sunto
et quocumque volent animum auditoris agunto.
                                                 Ibid., 99

Si vis me flere, dolendum est
primum ipsi tibi.   *Ibid.*, 102

Difficile est proprie communia dicere.
                                                 Ibid., 128

Parturiunt montes, nascetur ridiculus mus.
                                                 Ibid., 139

Non fumum ex fulgore, sed ex fumo dare lucem.
                                                 Ibid., 143

It is when I am struggling to be brief that I become unintelligible.

Effort to avoid a fault may lead astray, if it be not guided by art.

If a man's subject be chosen effectively, neither ready speech will fail him nor clearness of order.

You may gain the finest effects in language by the skillful setting which makes a well-known word new.

Many a term which has fallen from use shall have a second birth, and those shall fall that are now in high honor, if so Usage shall will it.

Scholars dispute, and the case is still before the court.

[The tragic hero] throws aside his paint pots and his words a foot and a half long, if he cares that his sorrows should go home to the spectator's heart.

It is not enough that poems should have beauty of form: they must have charm, and draw the hearer's feelings which way they will.

If you wish to draw tears from me, you must first feel pain yourself.

It is a hard task to treat what is common in a way of your own.

Mountains will be in labor, the birth will be a single laughable mouse.

Not to give flame first and then smoke, but from smoke to let light break out.

Semper ad eventum festinat, et in medias res
non secus ac notas auditorem rapit.   *Ibid.,* 148

Difficilis, querulus, laudator temporis acti
se puero, castigator censorque minorum.
multa ferunt anni venientes commoda secum,
multa recedentes adimunt.   *Ibid.,* 173

Ne pueros coram populo Medea trucidet.
                                             Ibid., 185

Quodcumque ostendis mihi sic, incredulus odi.
                                             Ibid., 188

Nec deus intersit, nisi dignus vindice nodus
inciderit.   *Ibid.,* 191

Tantum series iuncturaque pollet,
tantum de medio sumptis accedit honoris.
                                             Ibid., 242

Vitavi denique culpam,
non laudem merui.   *Ibid.,* 267

Vos exemplaria Graeca
nocturna versate manu, versate diurna.
                                             Ibid., 268

Scribendi recte sapere est et principium et fons.
                                             Ibid., 309

Verbaque provisam rem non invita sequentur.
                                             Ibid., 311

Grais ingenium, Grais dedit ore rotundo
Musa loqui, praeter laudem nullius avaris.
Romani pueri longis rationibus assem
discunt in partis centum diducere.   *Ibid.,* 324

He ever hastens to the issue, and hurries his hearers into the midst of the story, just as if they knew it before.

Testy, a grumbler, inclined to praise the way the world went when he was a boy, to play the critic and censor of the new generation. The tide of years as it rises brings many conveniences, as it ebbs carries many away.

You will not let Medea slay her boys before the audience.

Anything that you thus thrust upon my sight I discredit and revolt at.

Neither should a god intervene, unless a knot befalls worthy of his interference.

Such is the potency of order and arrangement, with such dignity may things of common life be clothed.

After all I have saved myself from blame, I have not earned praise.

For yourselves, do ye thumb well by night and day Greek models.

Of writing well the source and fountainhead is wise thinking.

And when the matter is first found, the words will not be slow to follow.

It was the Greeks who had at the Muse's hand the native gift, the Greeks who had the utterance of finished grace; for their sole greediness was for glory. Romans learn in their schoolboy days to divide the *as* by long sums into a hundred parts.

Aut prodesse volunt aut delectare poetae
aut simul et iucunda et idonea dicere vitae.
quidquid praecipies, esto brevis, ut cito dicta
percipiant animi dociles teneantque fideles:
omne supervacuum pleno de pectore manat.

Ibid., 333

Omne tulit punctum qui miscuit utile dulci,
lectorem delectando pariterque monendo.

Ibid., 343

Nec semper feriet quodcumque minabitur arcus.

Ibid., 350

Indignor quandoque bonus dormitat Homerus,
verum operi longo fas est obrepere somnum.

Ibid., 359

Ut pictura poesis: erit quae, si propius stes,
te capiat magis, et quaedam, si longius abstes.

Ibid., 361

Mediocribus esse poetis
non homines, non di, non concessere columnae.

Ibid., 372

Tu nihil invita dices faciesve Minerva.

Ibid., 385

Nonumque prematur in annum,
membranis intus positis: delere licebit
quod non edideris; nescit vox missa reverti.

Ibid., 388

Natura fieret laudabile carmen an arte,
quaesitum est: ego nec studium sine divite vena,
nec rude quid possit video ingenium.   *Ibid.*, 408

The aim of the poet is either to benefit, or to amuse, or to make his words at once please and give lessons of life. When you wish to instruct, be brief; that men's minds take in quickly what you say, learn its lesson, and retain it faithfully. Every word that is unnecessary only pours over the side of the brimming mind.

He has gained every vote who has mingled profit with pleasure by delighting the reader at once and instructing him.

Nor will the bow always hit what it threatens to hit.

If Homer, usually good, nods for a moment, I think it shame; and yet it may well be that over a work of great length one should grow drowsy now and then.

As with the painter's work, so with the poet's: one piece will take you more if you stand close to it, another at a greater distance.

To poets to be second-rate is a privilege which neither men nor gods nor bookstalls ever allowed.

You will say nothing, do nothing, unless Minerva pleases.

And then put the parchments in the cupboard, and let them be kept quiet till the ninth year. What you have not published you will be able to destroy. The word once uncaged never comes home again.

It is an old question whether a praiseworthy poem be the creation of Nature or of Art. For my part I do not see what study can do without a rich vein of native gift, nor what the native gift can do without culture.

Vesanum tetigisse timent fugiuntque poetam
qui sapiunt. *Ibid., 455*

Sit ius liceatque perire poetis:
invitum qui servat, idem facit occidenti.
Ibid., 466

TITUS LIVIUS

59 B.C. — A.D. 17

Ab exiguis profecta initiis eo creverit ut iam magnitudine
laboret sua. *Ab Urbe condita, Praefatio, 4*

Nec vitia nostra nec remedia pati possumus. *Ibid., 9*

Hoc illud est praecipue in cognitione rerum salubre ac
frugiferum, omnis te exempli documenta in inlustri posita
monumento intueri. *Ibid., 10*

Romani veteres . . . regnari omnes volebant libertatis
dulcetudine nondum experta. *Id., I, 17*

Omnium primum, rem ad multitudinem imperitam et illis
saeculis rudem efficacissimam, deorum metum iniciendum
ratus est. Qui cum descendere ad animos sine aliquo com-
mento miraculi non posset, simulat sibi cum dea Egeria
congressos nocturnos esse. *Ibid., 19*

The rapt poet is the terror of all sensible people: they fly at his approach.

Poets should have the right and the power if they choose to destroy themselves. To save a man against his will is as bad as to murder him.

LIVY

The celebrated historian was born in Padua. He composed philosophical treatises and dialogues (now lost) dedicated to Augustus, who appointed him tutor to Claudius. His history of Rome, entitled *Ab Urbe condita*, which he began around 26 B.C. and on which he worked for twenty-one years, soon brought him fame. Of its original 140 books only the first ten and Books 21 to 45 have come down to us; brief summaries of the rest are extant, plus some fragments. His purpose was to build a monument to Roman glory, to extol the virtues of her great men, and to trace the causes of the murderous internecine conflicts that preceded the empire.

Rome has grown so since its humble beginnings that it is now overwhelmed by its own greatness.

We can endure neither our vices nor the remedies for them.

This above all makes history useful and desirable: it unfolds before our eyes a glorious record of exemplary actions.

The old Romans all wished to have a king over them because they had not yet tasted the sweetness of freedom.

Before anything else [Numa] decided that he must instill in his subjects the fear of the gods, this being the most effective measure with an ignorant, and at that time uncultured, people. And since he could not influence their minds without inventing some fairytale, he pretended that he had conversations with the goddess Egeria at night.

Ego nisi peperissem, Roma non oppugnaretur; nisi filium
haberem, libera in libera patria mortua essem.   *Id., II, 40*

Intoleranda Romanis vox, Vae victis.   *Id., V, 48*

Vincere scis, Hannibal, victoria uti nescis.   *Id., XXII, 51*

Ea natura multitudinis est: aut servit humiliter, aut
superbe dominatur; libertatem, quae media est, nec
suscipere modice nec habere sciunt.   *Id., XXIV, 25*

In bello nihil tam leve est quod non magnae interdum rei
momentum faciat.   *Id., XXV, 28*

Ad id quod ne timeatur fortuna facit minime tuti sunt
homines.   *Ibid.*

In rebus asperis et tenui spe fortissima quaeque consilia
tutissima sunt.   *Ibid.*

Multitudo omnis sicut natura maris per se immobilia est;
at venti et aurae cient.   *Id., XXVIII, 27*

Nullum scelum rationem habet.   *Ibid., 28*

Non semper temeritas est felix.   *Ibid., 42*

Segnius homines bona quam mala sentire.   *Id., XXX, 21*

Maximae cuique fortunae minime credendum est.
Ibid., 30

Melior tutiorque est certa pax quam sperata victoria; haec
in tua, illa in deorum manu est.   *Ibid.*

Had I not become a mother, Rome would not be besieged; had I not a son, I should have died a free woman in a free land. [*From the plea of Coriolanus' mother.*]

"Woe to the conquered," a saying intolerable to Roman ears.

You know how to vanquish, Hannibal, but you do not know how to profit from victory.

Such is the nature of crowds: either they are humble and servile or arrogant and dominating. They are incapable of making moderate use of freedom, which is the middle course, or of keeping it.

In war nothing is so light that it may not carry great weight in the end.

Men are least safe from what success induces them not to fear.

In difficult and hopeless circumstances the boldest plans are the safest.

Every crowd is in itself motionless, as the sea is naturally, but winds and breezes ruffle it.

No crime is rational.

Temerity is not always successful.

Men are slower to become aware of blessings than of evils.

The greatest good fortune is the least to be trusted.

Better and safer is an assured peace than a victory hoped for. The one is in your own power, the other is in the hands of the gods.

Tantum nimirum ex publicis malis sentimus quantum ad privatas res pertinet, nec in iis quicquam acrius quam pecuniae damnum stimulat. Itaque cum spolia victae Carthagini detrahebantur . . . nemo ingemuit; nunc, quia tributum ex privato conferendum est, tamquam in publico funere comploratis.   *Ibid., 44*

Nihil tam incertum nec tam inaestimabile est quam animi multitudinis.   *Id., XXXI, 34*

Nulla lex satis commoda omnibus est.   *Id., XXXIV, 3*

Amicitiae immortales, mortales inimicitias debere esse.
                    Id., XL, 46

Apparently we are affected by public misfortunes only to the extent that they involve our private interests, and in these nothing hurts us more than loss of money. This is why no one groaned when the spoils of defeated Carthage were being carted off; now that we must collect tribute money from private sources, you lament as at a public funeral. [*Hannibal upbraiding the Carthaginian senate for weeping over the magnitude of war reparations.*]

Nothing is so uncertain or so incalculable as the disposition of a crowd.

No law is sufficiently convenient to all.

Our friendships should be immortal, our enmities mortal.

LUCIUS (or MARCUS)
ANNAEUS SENECA

c. 55 B.C. — A.D. 37

Perierat totus orbis, nisi iram finiret misericordia.

Controversiae, I, 1, 6 (Fuscus Arellius)

Quaedam iura non scripta, sed omnibus scriptis certiora sunt. *Ibid., 14 (Gallio)*

Iniquum est collapsis manum non porrigere: commune hoc ius generis humani est. *Ibid. (Gallio)*

Facilius in amore finem impetres quam modum. Tu hoc obtinebis, ut terminos, quos approbaveris, custodiant, ut nihil faciant nisi considerate, nihil promittant nisi ut iure pacturi, omnia verba ratione et fide ponderent? Senes sic amant. *Id., II, 2, 10 (Ovidius)*

Bibamus, moriendum est. *Ibid., 6, 3 (Vibius Gallus)*

SENECA THE ELDER

Seneca was born at Córdoba, Spain, and came to Rome when he was about fifteen. Around 13 B.C. he returned to Spain, where he married and where his three sons were born: Annaeus Novatus, who is mentioned in Acts XVIII as Gallio, as proconsul of Achaea; Seneca the Philosopher, and Annaeus Mela, father of the poet Lucan. In about A.D. 2, Seneca the Elder was back in Rome.

He wrote a history that was highly esteemed in antiquity but has not come down to us. His only surviving work is a collection of exercises of the kind practiced in schools of rhetoric. They include *Controversiae* (trials of fictitious cases) and *Suasoriae* (advisory speeches addressed to historical figures hesitating between two courses). Prominent orators and lawyers, who after the empire was founded enjoyed much leisure time, took part in them; occasionally writers participated in the discussion (Ovid spoke in a case involving a suicide pact between husband and wife). The lawyers sometimes ventured interpretations based on the humane notion of equity rather than codified law, and welcomed the opportunity to express republican opinions with impunity. Seneca attended many of these exercises and recorded them years later at the request of his sons. He was endowed with a phenomenal memory.

The whole world would perish if pity did not put an end to anger.

Some laws, though unwritten, are more firmly established than all written laws.

It is wrong not to stretch out your hand to the fallen: that is a common law of the human race.

It is easier to end love than to moderate it. How can you persuade [lovers] to observe the limits you set, to do nothing save on reflection, to promise nothing save in terms of legal contract, to weigh their every word on the scales of reason and honesty? That's how old men love.

Let's drink, death is inevitable.

Hoc habent scholasticorum studia; leviter tacta delectant, contrectata et propius admota fastidio sunt.

Id., X, Praefatio, 1

Aiunt fertiles in Oceano iacere terras ultraque Oceanum rursus alia litora, alium nasci orbem. . . . Facile ista finguntur, quia Oceanus navigari non potest.

Suasoriae, I, 1, 1

Magni pectoris est inter secunda moderatio (*Albucius Silius*). *Id., I, 3*

ALBIUS TIBULLUS

c. 60 – 19 B.C.

Divitias alius fulvo sibi congerat auro
    et teneat culti iugera multa soli,
quem labor adsiduus vicino terreat hoste,
    Martia cui somnos classica pulsa fugent:
me mea paupertas vita traducat inerti,
    dum meus adsiduo luceat igne focus.

Elegiae, I, 1, 1

It's like the things you study in school: they are a pleasure to skim over, but when you apply yourself to them, go into them deeply, they are boring.

They say that there are fertile lands somewhere in the Ocean, and that beyond the Ocean lie other shores, another world begins. . . . It is easy to imagine such things, for the Ocean is not navigable.

Moderation in prosperity is the mark of a great heart.

TIBULLUS

Tibullus was a native of Pedum. From the poem Horace dedicated to him (*Epistles,* I, 4) we learn that the gods gave him "beauty, wealth, and the art of enjoyment," not to mention fame and health. His elegies celebrate the very un-Roman virtues of peace and the pleasures of love, and express a longing for a return to primitivism. He enjoyed a great vogue with the contemporaries of Rousseau—four French translations of his works were published between 1776 and 1796. The content of his melodious elegies seems to us somewhat trivial, but his contemporaries may have seen them as a protest against the imperial regime, which favored values directly opposed to his.

The *Corpus Tibullianum* includes the elegies by two other poets: (1) Lygdamus, about whom nothing certain is known, but who was obviously a disciple of Tibullus, more given to tears and complaints than his master, and (2) Sulpicia, daughter of a prominent Roman and ward of Tibullus' patron Valerius Messalla. Her six short poems (a total of forty lines) are love notes addressed to a certain Cerinthus. Somewhat awkward in expression, they are remarkable for their candor.

Let others amass riches of yellow gold and own many acres of farmland; let others toil without respite in fear of the nearby enemy, their sleep chased by the blasts of trumpets summoning to battle. For myself, I will be content to lead an inactive life in poverty, provided that my hearth shine with a steady fire.

Quam iuvat immites ventos audire cubantem
  et dominam tenero continuisse sinu
aut, gelidas hibernus aquas cum fuderit Auster,
  securum somnos igne iuvante sequi!   *Ibid.*, *45*

Non ego laudari curo, mea Delia; tecum
  dum modo sim, quaeso segnis inersque vocer.
                                        Ibid., *57*

        Celari vult sua furta Venus.   *Id.*, *I*, *2*, *34*

Quid Tyrio recubare toro sine amore secundo
  prodest cum fletu nox vigilanda venit?   *Ibid.*, *75*

Quam bene Saturno vivebant rege, priusquam
  tellus in longas est patefacta vias!   *Ibid.*, *3*, *35*

Non domus ulla fores habuit, non fixus in agris,
  qui regeret certis finibus arva, lapis.   *Ibid.*, *43*

  Nec iurare time: veneris periuria venti
    inrita per terras et freta summa ferunt.
                                        Ibid., *4*, *21*

    Desine dissimulare; deus crudelius urit,
      quos videt invitos succubuisse sibi.   *Ibid.*, *8*, *7*

Munera ne poscas: det munera canus amator,
  ut foveat molli frigida membra sinu.
carior est auro iuvenis, cui levia fulgent
  ora nec amplexus aspera barba terit.   *Ibid.*, *29*

Quis furor est atram bellis accersere Mortem?
  imminet et tacito clam venit illa pede.
                                        Ibid., *10*, *33*

How pleasant to lie on my bed and hear the raging winds, with my mistress in my gentle embrace, or, when the winter storms bring their icy rains, to sleep safely by the comforting fire!

I have no care for glory, my Delia; provided I am with you, I am quite willing to be called sluggish and idle.

Venus likes her thefts to be concealed.

What good is it to lie on a Tyrian couch without luck in love, when night comes bringing not sleep but tears?

How good life was under the rule of Saturn, before the earth was opened for distant voyages!

No house had doors; no stone was set in the fields to mark the boundaries between farms.

Be not afraid to swear: the winds blow the vain perjuries of love away over land and sea.

Stop pretending: Cupid burns more cruelly those he sees succumbing to him against their will.

Never ask for gifts: let a white-haired lover offer them in order to warm his cold limbs against a soft bosom. More precious than gold is a young man: his face is shiny smooth with no beard to scratch in embrace.

What madness to bring down black death with wars! It is always close enough; it sneaks up on silent feet.

Iam Nox iungit equos, currumque sequuntur
matris lascivo sidera fulva choro,
postque venit tacitus furvis circumdatus alis
   Somnus et incerto Somnia nigra pede.   *Id., II, 1, 87*

Ferrea non venerem sed praedam saecula laudant.
                                        Ibid., 3, 35

Iam mala finissem leto, sed credula vitam
   spes fovet et fore cras semper ait melius.
                                        Ibid., 6, 19

LYGDAMUS

Carmine formosae, pretio capiuntur avarae:
   gaudeat, ut digna est, versibus illa novis.
                                  Elegiae, I, 7

A crudele genus nec fidum femina nomen!
   a pereat, didicit fallere si qua virum.
                                     Id., IV, 61

Nescis quid sit amor, iuvenis, si ferre recusas
   immitam dominam coniugiumque ferum.
                                     Ibid., 73

Ei mihi, difficile est imitari gaudia falsa,
   difficile est tristi fingere mente iocum.
                                     Id., VI, 33

Night is already yoking her horses, and the playful troupe of golden stars follows their mother's chariot. And then comes silent Sleep wrapped in somber wings, and dark Dreams on unsteady legs.

This iron age celebrates not love but booty.

I would by now have ended my sufferings by death, but gullible hope encourages me to live, keeps saying that tomorrow will be better.

LYGDAMUS*

Beautiful girls are won by poetry, greedy girls by money: may [Neaera] enjoy these verses as she deserves.

O cruel, faithless race of women! May they perish who have learned to betray a husband.

You don't know what love is, young man, if you will not bear with an ungentle mistress or a shrewish wife.

Ah me, it is hard to act joyful when you are unhappy, hard to pretend gaiety when the heart is sad.

* Cf. Note on Tibullus, p. 203.

SULPICIA

Tandem venit amor, qualem texisse pudori
 quam nudasse alicui sit mihi, Fama, magis.
                                    Elegidia, I, 1

 Exoluit promissa Venus: mea gaudia narret,
  dicetur si quis non habuisse sua.   *Ibid.,* 5

Sed peccasse iuvat, vultus componere famae
 taedet: cum digno digna fuisse ferar.   *Ibid.,* 9

 Ne tibi sim, mea lux, aeque iam fervida cura
  ac videor paucos ante fuisse dies,
 si quicquam tota commisi stulta iuventa
  cuius me fatear paenituisse magis,
 hesterna quam te solum quod nocte reliqui,
  ardorem cupiens dissimulare meum.   *Id., VI*

SULPICIA*

At last love has come, love such that, to conceal it, O Rumor, would shame me more than to proclaim it.

Venus has kept her word! Gossips: feel free to spread the news of my happiness—something that you yourselves have never known.

Yes, I glory in my fault, I won't put on a face for the sake of reputation. Let the world know that I am worthy of the man who is worthy of me.

My love, I confess that last night the only reason I left you alone was that I wanted to keep from you how ardently I desired you. If I don't regret this more than anything in my whole foolish youth, may you never again want me as passionately as I think you did a few days ago.

* Cf. Note on Tibullus, p. 203.

SEXTUS PROPERTIUS

c. 47 – c. 16 B.C.

Cynthia prima suis miserum me cepit ocellis,
    contactum nullis ante cupidinibus.
tum mihi constantis deiecit lumina fastus
    et caput impositis pressit Amor pedibus,
donec me docuit castas odisse puellas
    improbus et nullo vivere consilio.   *Elegiae, I, 1, 1*

Nudus Amor formae non amat artificem.
                        Ibid., 2, 8

Una si qua placet, culta puella sat est.
                        Ibid., 26

Nec tibi nobilitas poterit succurrere amanti:
    nescit Amor priscis cedere imaginibus.
                        Ibid., 5, 23

Hanc ego non auro, non Indis flectere conchis,
    sed potui blandi carminis obsequio.   *Ibid., 8, 39*

Me dolor et lacrimae merito fecere peritum;
    atque utinam posito dicar amore rudis!
                        Ibid., 9, 7

PROPERTIUS

Propertius was born in Umbria (probably at Assisi). Impoverished as a result of the proscriptions of Octavian and Antony, he came to Rome intending to study law, but turned to poetry instead. He left four books of elegies. The first, published in his lifetime, is the history of his passion for "Cynthia," whom he met at the age of eighteen; the three others contain pieces on a number of other subjects, including the famous "Queen of Elegies" (IV, 11) in which the ghost of a noble Roman matron comforts her widowed husband. As a poet of love, Propertius, who combines intense passion with ice-cold lucidity, has never been surpassed and rarely equaled.

Cynthia enslaved me with her lovely eyes. Alas! she was my first passion: before her, my heart had been untouched. Then wicked Cupid stripped me of my proud airs, ground me under his heel, until he had taught me to hate chaste girls and to live recklessly.

Cupid is naked and dislikes beauty contrived by art.

Admired by one man, a girl is sufficiently adorned.

Noble birth will be of no avail to you in love: Cupid is not impressed by family portraits.

Not with gold nor Indian pearls did I win her, but with the caress of my sweet song.

Experience is mine at the cost of tears and sufferings; if only I could renounce love and be a novice again!

Non sum ego qui fueram: mutat via longa puellas.
quantus in exiguo tempore fugit amor!

Id., I, 12, 11

Omnes humanos sanat medicina dolores:
solus amor morbi non amat artificem.

Id., II, 1, 57

Lilia non domina sint magis alba mea;
ut Maeotica nix minio si certet Hibero,
utque rosae puro lacte natant folia.

Ibid., 3, 10

Hostis si quis erit nobis, amet ille puellas:
gaudeat in puero, si quis amicus erit.

Ibid., 4, 17

Sed vobis facile est verba et componere fraudes:
hoc unum didicit femina semper opus.

Ibid., 9, 31

Quod si deficiant vires, audacia certe
laus erit: in magnis et voluisse sat est.

Ibid., 10, 4

Dum nos fata sinunt, oculos satiemus amore;
nox tibi longa venit, nec reditura dies.

Ibid., 15, 23

Errat, qui finem vesani quaerit amoris:
verus amor nullum novit habere modum.

Ibid., 29

Non semper placidus periuros ridet amantes
Iuppiter et surda neglegit aure preces.

Ibid., 16, 47

I am no longer what I used to be to her: a distant journey changes women. How much love has gone in so little time!

Medicine cures all human sufferings; the sickness of love alone refuses a physician.

Lilies are not whiter than my mistress: she is Maeotic snow vying with Iberian minium, or rose leaves floating on the purest milk.

May my enemies love women, may my friends delight in boys.

But it is easy for you to contrive lies and wiles: this art every woman has learned well.

Though strength be wanting, my daring is sure to win me praise: in great undertakings it is meritorious even to have the will.

So long as fate permits, let our eyes have their fill of love: the long night is on its way, with no day coming after it.

To seek an end to love's madness is a mistake: true love knows no bounds.

Not always does Jupiter smile serenely at lovers' perjuries and turn a deaf ear to their prayers.

Ut natura dedit, sic omnis recta figura est:
turpis Romano Belgicus ore color.

Ibid., 18, 25

Uni cuique dedit vitium natura creato.

Ibid., 22, 17

Qui videt, is peccat: qui te non viderit ergo,
non cupiet: facti lumina crimen habent.

Ibid., 32, 1

Expertus dico, nemo est in amore fidelis:
formosam raro non sibi quisque petit.

Ibid., 34, 3

Cedite Romani scriptores, cedite Grai!
nescio quid maius nascitur Iliade. *Ibid.*, 64

Non datur ad Musas currere lata via.

Id., III, 1, 14

Ergo sollicitae tu causa, pecunia, vitae;
per te immaturum mortis adimus iter;
tu vitiis hominum crudelis pabula praebes;
semina curarum de capita orte tuo.

Ibid., 7, 1

Frangitur ipsa suis Roma superba bonis.

Ibid., 13, 60

Frangit et attollit vires in milite causa;
quae nisi iusta subest, excutit arma pudor.

Id., IV, 6, 51

Sunt aliquid Manes: letum non omnis finit
luridaque evictos effugit umbra rogos.

Ibid., 7, 1

As nature made it, every face is right; Belgian rouge disgraces Roman cheeks.

Nature has conferred some vice on each created thing.

He sins who sees you; thus he who does not see you will not lust for you. It is the eyes that are guilty.

I speak from experience: no one is faithful in love. Rarely does a man fail to covet a beautiful woman for himself.

Give way, Roman writers, give way, Greeks! Something greater than the *Iliad* is being born. [*On Vergil's* Aeneid.]

There is no royal road to the arts.

So it is you, money, the cause of a restless life. Because of you we embark toward early death; on you men's vices cruelly feed, you, the seed and fountainhead of all our cares.

Proud Rome is now brought low by her wealth.

What breaks or exalts the soldier's strength is his cause. When it is not basically just, shame makes him drop his weapons.

The Shades really exist: death does not end all things, and the pale ghost, victorious, escapes the pyre.

Nunc tibi commendo communia pignora natos:
  haec cura et cineri spirat inusta meo.
Fungere maternis vicibus, pater: illa meorum
  omnis erit collo turba ferenda tuo.
Oscula cum dederis tua flentibus, adice matris:
  tota domus coepit nunc onus esse tuum.
Et si quid doliturus eris, sine testibus illis;
  cum venient, siccis oscula falle genis.

Ibid., 11, 73

PUBLIUS OVIDIUS NASO

43 B.C. – C. A.D. 17

Militat omnis amans, et habet sua castra Cupido. . . .
quae bello est habilis, Veneri quoque convenit aetas.
  turpe senex miles, turpe senilis amor.   *Amores, I, 9, 1*

  Cui peccare licet, peccat minus; ipsa potestas
    semina nequitiae languidiora facit.   *Id., III, 4, 9*

216

Now I commend to you our children, the pledges of our union; this care, unconsumed, lives on in my ashes. Father, perform a mother's duties: now you will have to bear the yoke of my little troop. When you kiss them to comfort their grief, kiss them for their mother too; the whole household now will be your burden. When you must cry yourself, make sure they are not there; should they surprise you, deceive their kisses with dry cheeks.

OVID

Born at Sulmona, in the Abruzzi, Ovid studied at Rome, intending to become a lawyer, but, like Propertius, he soon turned to poetry. A number of his works, including a tragedy, *Medea,* have not come down to us. Those extant include the *Amores,* which treats of the joys and sorrows of love; the *Heroides,* imaginary letters addressed by historical and mythological figures (e.g., Penelope, Phaedra, Sappho) to their lovers or husbands; the *Ars Amatoria* and *Remedia amoris,* which treat of the art of love, often in a humorous vein; the *Medicamina faciei,* on cosmetics; the *Metamorphoses,* his most famous poem, which in the Middle Ages was placed above the *Iliad;* the *Fasti,* on the festive days of the Roman calendar; the *Tristia* and the *Epistulae ex Ponto,* written after he was deported (in A.D. 9) to Tomi on the Black Sea, where he died. The reasons for his exile are not clear. He himself says that the emperor punished him for "a poem and a blunder" (*carmen et error*). The poem was probably the *Ars Amatoria*—Augustus, whose daughter Julia's indiscretions were notorious, frowned upon all light literature; as for the "error" or "blunder," there have been only conjectures, among them that Ovid was one of Julia's lovers.

(*Tr. G. Showerman*)

Every lover is a soldier, and Cupid has a camp of his own. . . . The age that is meet for the wars is also suited to Venus. 'Tis unseemly for the old man to soldier, unseemly for the old man to love.

She to whom erring is free errs less; very power makes less quick the seeds of sin.

Nitimur in vetitum semper cupimusque negata.

Ibid., 17

Ingenium quondam fuerat pretiosius auro;
at nunc barbaria est grandis, habere nihil.

Ibid., 8, 3

Cum rapiunt mala fata bonos—ignoscite fasso!—
sollicitor nullos esse putare deos.
vive pius—moriere; pius cole sacra—colentem
mors gravis a templis in cava busta trahet;
carminibus confide bonis—iacet, ecce, Tibullus:
vix manet e toto, parva quod urna capit!

Ibid., 9, 35

Luctantur pectusque leve in contraria tendunt
hac amor hac odium, sed, puto, vincit amor.
odero, si potero; si non, invitus amabo.

Ibid., 11, 33

Nil mihi rescribas, tu tamen ipse veni!

Heroides, 1, 2

Dicere quae puduit, scribere iussit amor.

Id., 4, 10

Non veniunt in idem pudor atque amor.

Id., 15, 121

Spectatum veniunt, veniunt spectentur ut ipsae.

Ars amatoria, I, 99

Utque viro furtiva Venus, sic grata puellae.
Vir male dissimulat; tectius illa cupit.

Ibid., 275

We ever strive for what is forbidden, and ever covet what is denied.

Time was when genius was more precious than gold, but now to have nothing is monstrous barbarism.

When evil fate sweeps away the good—forgive me who say it!—I am tempted to think there are no gods. Live the duteous life—you will die; be faithful in your worship—in the very act of worship heavy death will drag you from the temple to the hollow tomb; put your trust in beautiful song—behold, Tibullus lies dead: from his whole self there scarce remains what the slight urn receives!

Struggling over my fickle heart, love draws it now this way, and now hate that—but love, I think, is winning. I will hate, if I have strength; if not, I shall love unwilling.

Write nothing back to me—yourself come! [*Penelope to Ulysses*]

What modesty forbade me to say, love has commanded me to write. [*Phaedra to Hippolytus*]

Modesty and love are not at one. [*Sappho to Phaon*]

(*Tr. J. H. Mozley*)

They come to see, they come that they may be seen.

And as stolen love is pleasant to a man, so it is also to a woman; the man dissembles badly; she conceals desire better.

Promittas facito: quid enim promittere laedit?
  Pollicitis dives quilibet esse potest.　　*Ibid., 443*

Pessima sit, nulli non sua forma placet.
　　　　　　　　　　　　　　　Ibid., 614

Iuppiter ex alto periuria ridet amantum.
　　　　　　　　　　　　　Ibid., 633

Expedit esse deos, et, ut expedit esse putemus.
　　　　　　　　　　　　Ibid., 637

Ludite, si sapitis, solas impune puellas:
  hac minus est una fraude tuenda fides.
fallite fallentes: ex magna parte profanum
  sunt genus: in laqueos quos posuere, cadant.
　　　　　　　　　　　　Ibid., 643

Nomen amicitia est, nomen inane fides.
Ei mihi, non tutum est, quod ames, laudare sodali;
  cum tibi laudanti credidit, ipse subit.　　*Ibid., 740*

Heu facinus! non est hostis metuendus amanti;
  quos credis fidos, effuge, tutus eris.
Cognatum fratremque cave carumque sodalem:
  praebebit veros haec tibi turba metus.　　*Ibid., 751*

Ut dominam teneas, nec te mirere relictum,
  ingenii dotes corporis adde bonis.
forma bonum fragile est, quantumque accedit ad annos
  fit minor, et spatio carpitur ipsa suo.　　*Id., II, 111*

Non ego divitibus venio praeceptor amandi:
  nil opus est illi, qui dabit, arte mea;
secum habet ingenium qui cum libet, "accipe" dicit.
　　　　　　　　　　　　Ibid., 161

See that you promise: what harm is there in promises? In promises anyone can be rich.

Hideous though she be, there is none her own looks do not please.

Jupiter from on high smiles at the perjuries of lovers.

It is expedient there should be gods, and as it is expedient, let us deem that gods exist.

If you are wise, cheat women only, and avoid trouble; keep faith save for this one deceitfulness. Deceive the deceivers; they are mostly an unrighteous sort; let them fall into the snare which they have laid.

Friendship is but a name, faith is an empty name. Alas, it is not safe to praise to a friend the object of your love; as soon as he believes your praises, he slips into your place.

Ah, the reproach of it! no foe need a lover fear; fly those whom you deem faithful, and you will be safe. Kinsman, brother—beware of them and of thy boon companion; they will cause you real fears.

That you may keep your mistress, nor marvel to find yourself abandoned, add gifts of mind to bodily advantages. A frail advantage is beauty, that grows less as time draws on, and is devoured by its own years.

I come not to teach the rich to love; he who will give has no need of my art; he who when he pleases says, "Accept," has wit enough of his own.

Si nec blanda satis nec erit tibi comis amanti,
perfer et obdura; postmodo mitis erit.   *Ibid.*, *177*

Militiae species amor est; discedite segnes!
non sunt haec timidis signa tuenda viris.
Ibid., *233*

Nec dominam iubeo pretioso munere dones:
parva, sed e parvis callidus apta dato.   *Ibid.*, *261*

Quid tibi praecipiam teneros quoque mittere versus?
ei mihi! non multum carmen honoris habet!
carmina laudantur, sed munera magna petuntur:
dummodo sit dives, Barbarus ipse placet.
aurea nunc vere sunt saecula: plurimos auro
venit honos, auro conciliatur amor.   *Ibid.*, *273*

Littore quot conchae, tot sunt in amore dolores.
quae patimur, multo spicula felle madent.
Ibid., *519*

Nominibus mollire licet mala. fusca vocetur
nigrior Illyrica cui pice sanguis erit.
si paeta est, Veneri similis. Si flava, Minervae.
sit gracilis macie quae male viva sua est.
dic habilem quaecumque brevis; quae turgida, plenam;
et lateat vitium proximitate boni.   *Ibid.*, *657*

Nec quotus annus est, nec quo sit nata require
consule; quae rigidus munera censor habet.
Ibid., *663*

Prima sit in vobis morum tutela puellae.
ingenio facies conciliante placet.
certus amor morum est; formam populabitur aetas,
et placitus rugis vultus aratus erit.
De medicamine faciei feminae, *43*

Should she be neither kindly nor courteous to your wooing, persist and steel your resolve; one day she will be
kind.

Love is a kind of warfare; avaunt, ye laggards! These ban-
ners are not for timid men to guard.

Nor do I bid you give your mistress costly gifts; let them
be small, but choose your small gifts cunningly and well.

Shall I bid you send tender verses also? Alas, a poem is
not much honored. Poems are praised, but costly gifts are
sought; so he be wealthy, even a barbarian pleases. Now
truly is the age of gold: by gold comes many an honor,
by gold is affection gained.

As many as the shells that are on the shore, so many are
the pains of love; the darts that wound are steeped in
much poison.

With names you soften shortcomings; let her be called
swarthy whose blood is blacker than Illyrian pitch; if
cross-eyed, she is like Venus; yellow-haired, like Minerva;
call her slender whose thinness impairs her health; if short,
call her trim; if stout, of full body; let its nearness to a
virtue conceal a fault.

Ask not how old she is, nor under what consul she was
born; these are the duties of the stern Censor.

Think first ye women, to look to your behavior. The face
pleases when character commends. Love of character is
lasting: beauty will be ravaged by age, and the face that
charmed will be plowed by wrinkles.

Auferimur cultu; gemmis auroque teguntur
omnia; pars minima est ipsa puella sui.
Remedia amoris, 343

Successore novo vincitur omnis amor.
Ibid., 462

Qui nimium multis "non amo" dicit, amat.
Ibid., 648

In nova fert animus mutatas dicere formas
corpora. *Metamorphoses, I, 1*

Ante mare et terras et quod tegit omnia caelum
unus erat toto naturae vultus in orbe,
quen dixere Chaos; rudis indigestaque moles.
Ibid., 5

Os homini sublime dedit, caelumque tueri
iussit et erectos ad sidera tollere vultus. *Ibid., 85*

Aurea prima sata est aetas, quae vindice nullo,
sponte sua, sine lege fidem rectumque colebat.
Ibid., 89

Non bene conveniunt nec in una sede morantur
maiestas et amor. *Id., II, 846*

Ultima semper
expectanda dies homini, dicique beatus
ante obitum nemo supremaque funera debet.
Id., III, 135

Sum regina Iovisque
et soror et coniunx, certe soror. *Ibid., 265*

We are won by dress; all is concealed by gems and gold; a woman is the least part of herself.

All love is vanquished by a succeeding love.

He who says o'er much "I love not" is in love.

(Tr. F. J. Miller)

My mind is bent to tell of bodies changed into new forms.

Before the sea was, and the lands, and the sky that hangs over all, the face of Nature showed alike in her whole round, which state have men called chaos: a rough, un-ordered mass of things.

He gave to man an uplifted face and bade him stand erect and turn his eyes to heaven.

Golden was that first age, which, with no one to compel, without a law, of its own will, kept faith and did the right.

Majesty and love do not go well together, nor tarry long in the same dwelling place.

Man's last day must ever be awaited, and none to be counted happy till his death, till his last funeral rites are paid.

I am queen of heaven, the sister and the wife of Jove— at least his sister.

Spem sine corpore amat, corpus putat esse, quod umbra
est.   *Ibid.*, 417

Et placet et video; sed quod videoque placetque,
non tamen invenio; tantus tenet error amantem.
                                                        Ibid., 446

      Et felicissima matrum
dicta foret Niobe, si non sibi visa fuisset.
                                                        Id., VI, 155

      Aliudque cupido,
mens aliud suadet. Video meliora proboque,
deteriora sequor.   *Id.*, VII, 19

      Nulla est sincera voluptas
sollicitumque aliquid laetis intervenit.
                                                        Ibid., 453

      Labitur occulte fallitque volatilis aetas,
et nihil est annis velocius.   *Id.*, X, 518

      Utque rudis primoque cupidine tacta,
quid facit ignorans, amat et non sentit amorem.
                                                        Ibid., 636

Iamque opus exegi quod nec Iovis ira nec ignis
nec poterit ferrum nec edax abolere vetustas.
· · · · · · · ·
Quaque patet domitis Romana potentia terris,
ore legar populi, perque omnia saecula fama,
siquid habent veri vatum praesagia, vivam.
                                        Id., Epilogus, XV, 871, 877.

    In pretio pretium nunc est. dat census honores,
census amicitias; pauper ubique iacet.
                                                        Fasti, I, 217

He loves an unsubstantial hope and thinks that substance which is only shadow.

I am charmed and I see; but what I see and what charms me I cannot find—so great a delusion holds my love.

And Niobe would have been called most blessed of mothers, had she not seemed so to herself.

Desire persuades me one way, reason another. I see the better and approve it, but I follow the worse.

There is no pleasure unalloyed, and some care always comes to mar our joys.

Time glides by imperceptibly and cheats us in its flight, and nothing is swifter than the years.

All untutored, feeling for the first time the impulse of love, ignorant of what she does, she loves and knows it not.

And now my work is done, which neither the wrath of Jove, nor fire, nor sword, nor the gnawing tooth of time shall ever be able to undo . . . Wherever Rome's power extends over the conquered world, I shall have mention on men's lips, and, if the prophecies of bards have any truth, through all the ages shall I live in fame.

(Tr. Sir James G. Frazer)

Nowadays nothing but money counts: fortune brings honors, friendships, the poor man everywhere lies low.

Conscia mens recti famae mendacia risit,
sed nos in vitium credula turba sumus.

Id., IV, 311

Iam color unus inest rebus, tenebrisque teguntur
omnia: iam vigiles conticuere canes.   *Ibid.*, 489

Da modo lucra mihi, da facto gaudia lucro;
et fac ut emptori verba dedisse iuvet.

Id., V, 689

Carmina proveniunt animo deducta sereno;
nubila sunt subitis tempora nostra malis.
Carmina secessum scribentis et otia quaerunt;
me mare, me venti, me fera iactat hiems.
Carminibus metus omnis obest: ergo perditus ensem
haesurum iugulo iam puto iamque meo.

Tristia, I, 1, 39

Et veniam pro laude peto: laudatus abunde,
non fastiditus si tibi, lector, ero.   *Ibid.*, 7, 31

Non ego mordaci destrinxi carmine quemquam,
nec meus ullius crimina versus habet.
candidus a salibus suffusis felle refugi:
nulla venenato littera mixta ioco est.   *Ibid.*, 2, 563

Nil non mortale tenemus,
pectoris exceptis ingeniique bonis.

Id., III, 7, 43

En ego, cum patris caream, vobisque, domoque,
raptaeque sint, adimi quae potuere, mihi:
ingenio tamen ipse meo comitorque fruorque;
Caesar in hoc potuit iuris habere nihil.   *Ibid.*, 45

Conscious of innocence, she laughed at fame's untruths; but we of the multitude are prone to think the worst.

Now o'er the darkness stole a sober hue, and darkness hid the world; now the watchful dogs were hushed.

Only grant me profits, grant me the joy of profit made, and see to it that I enjoy cheating the buyer!

(Tr. A. L. Wheeler)

Poetry comes fine spun from a mind at peace; my days are clouded with unexpected woes. Poetry requires the writer to be in privacy and ease; I am harassed by the sea, by gales, by wintry storms. Poetry is injured by any fear; I in my ruin am ever and ever expecting a sword to pierce my throat.

Indulgence, then, instead of praise I ask; I shall have abundance of praise if you do not disdain me, reader.

I have never injured anybody with a mordant poem, my verse contains charges against nobody. Ingenuous, I have shunned wit steeped in gall—not a letter of mine is dipped in poisoned jest.

We possess nothing that is not mortal, except the blessings of heart and mind.

Behold me, deprived of native land, of you and my home, reft of all that could be taken from me; my mind is nevertheless my comrade and my joy; over this Caesar would have no right.

In causa facili cuivis licet esse diserto;
et minimae vires frangere quassa valent.

Ibid., 11, 21

Fleque meos casus: est quaedam flere voluptas:
expletur lacrimis egeriturque dolor.   *Id.*, IV, 3, 37

Sumque argumenti conditor ipse mei.

Id., V, 1, 10

Barbarus hic ego sum, quia non intelligor ulli:
et rident stolidi verba Latina Getae.

Ibid., 10, 37

Nescio qua natale solum dulcedine captos
ducit, et immemores non sinit esse sui.

Epistulae ex Ponto, I, 3, 35

Regia, crede mihi, res est succurrere lapsis.

Id., II, 9, 11

In an easy cause anybody may be eloquent; the slightest strength is enough to break what is already shattered.

Weep for my woe; in weeping there is a certain joy, for by tears grief is sated and relieved.

I myself provide the theme of which I write.

Here it is that I am a barbarian, understood by nobody; the Getae laugh stupidly at Latin words.

By what sweet charm I know not the native land draws all men nor allows them to forget it.

'Tis a royal deed, I assure thee, to help the fallen.

GAIUS VELLEIUS PATERCULUS

20 B.C. – after A.D. 31

Mummius tam rudis fuit, ut capta Corintho cum maximorum perfectas manibus tabulas ac statuas in Italiam portandas locaret, iuberet praedici conducentibus, si eas perdidissent, novas eos reddituros.

Historiae Romanae, I, 13, 4

Difficilis . . . in perfecto mora est, naturaliterque quod procedere non potest, recedit. *Ibid., 17, 6*

Non . . . ibi consistunt exempla, unde coeperunt. . . . et ubi semel recto deerratum est, in praeceps pervenitur, nec quisquam sibi putat turpe, quod alii fuit fructuosum.

Id., II, 3, 4

Naturaliter audita visis laudamus libentius et praesentia invidia, praeterita veneratione prosequimur et his nos obrui, illis instrui credimus. *Ibid., 92, 5*

PATERCULUS

Paterculus came of a prominent family. He served in the army as a tribune; under Tiberius he held the post of prefect of cavalry in Germany and Pannonia. Later he was questor and praetor. He wrote his *Historiae Romanae* after he had retired. Parts of Book I are lost, Book II covers the period from 146 B.C. to A.D. 30. The early sections are mostly a compilation; the sections on the reigns of Augustus and Tiberius contain valuable details. He was an enthusiastic partisan of Tiberius.

(Tr. Baker)

Mummius was so uninformed that after the taking of Corinth, when he was hiring people to carry to Italy the paintings and statues finished by the hands of the greatest artists, he ordered notice to be given to the contractors that if they should lose them, they must replace them with new ones.

To stand still on the summit of perfection is difficult, and in the natural course of things, what cannot go forward slips back.

Precedents do not stop where they began, and when people once deviate from the straight path, they are hurried down a precipice; nor does anyone think that scandalous in himself, which has proved profitable to another.

Such is our nature that we more readily bestow praise on actions that we hear of than on those which we see, and view the present with envy, the past with veneration— thinking ourselves obscured by the former but instructed by the latter.

MARCUS MANILIUS

C. 10 B.C. – A.D. 30

Carmine divinas artis et conscia fati
sidera diversos hominum variantia casus,
caelestis rationis opus, deducere mundo
aggredior.   *Astronomica, I, 1*

Omnia conando docilis sollertia vicit.
nec prius imposuit rebus finemque modumque
quam caelum ascendit ratio, cepitque profundam
naturam rerum.   *Ibid., 94*

Solvitque animis miracula rerum
eripuitque Iovi fulmen virisque Tonanti
et sonitum ventis concessit, nubibus ignem.
                                            Ibid., 103

Omnia mortali mutantur lege creata;
nec se cognoscunt terrae, vertentibus annis;
exutae variant faciem per saecula gentes.
at manet incolumis mundus, suaque omnia servat.
                                            Ibid., 504

Solvite, mortales, animos, curasque levate,
totque supervacuis vitam deplete querelis.
fata regunt orbem, certa stant omnia lege,
cunctaque per certos signantur tempora casus.
nascentes morimur, finisque ab origine pendet.
                                            Id., IV, 12

MANILIUS

Nothing is known of the life of Manilius, author of a poem in five books entitled *Astronomica*. Only the first book deals with astronomy, the rest with astrology.

[Translations of excerpts from Book I are by Edward Sherburne (1675); those from Book IV by Thomas Creech (1697)]

Divining arts, and stars foreknowing fate
Varying the diverse turns of human state
(The works of heaven's high reason) we bring down
In verse, from Heaven.

Ingenious industry made all things bend.
Nor put they to their curious search an end
Till Reason had scaled heaven, thence viewed this round
and nature latent in its causes found.

From error thus the wond'ring minds uncharm'd
Unsceptred Jove; the Thunderer disarm'd
Of name and power dispoyl'd him, and assign'd
Fire to the labouring clouds, Noise the Wind.

All things by human laws created change:
Lands to each other known, in time grow strange:
Nations in course of many years put on
A various face; but heaven wears always one.

Vain man forbear, of cares unload thy mind,
Forget thy hopes, and give thy fears to wind;
For Fate rules all, its stubborn laws must sway
The lower world, and man confin'd obey.
As we are born we die, our lots are cast,
And our first hour disposes of our last.

Quid mirum, noscere mundum
si possunt homines, quibus est et mundus in ipsis,
exemplumque dei quisque est in imagine parva?

Ibid., 893

Materiae ne quaere modum, sed perspice viris,
quas ratio, non pondus habet. ratio omnia vincit.

Ibid., 931

C. IULIUS PHAEDRUS

C. 15 B.C. – A.D. 45

Duplex libelli dos est: quod risum movet
et quod prudenti vitam consilio movet.

I, Prologus, 3

Numquam est fidelis cum potente societas.   *I, 5, 1*

Ego primum tollo, nominor quoniam leo.

Ibid., 7

Personam tragicam forte vulpes viderat.
"O quanta species," inquit, "cerebrum non habet!"

I, 7, 1

In principatu commutando saepius,
nil praeter domini nomen mutant pauperes.

I, 15, 1

Fortes indigne tuli
mihi insultare; te, naturae dedecus,
quod ferre cogor, certe bis videor mori!

I, 20, 10

Who can wonder that the world is known
So well by man, since himself is one?
The same composure in his form is shewed,
And man's the little image of the God.

Man know thy powers, and not observe thy size,
The noble power in piercing reason lies,
And reason conquers all, and rules the skies.

PHAEDRUS

Phaedrus was born in Thrace and lived as a freedman in Rome.
His fables, written in an unpretentious, sober style, are considered superior to Aesop's. Under Tiberius he was persecuted,
probably because he was suspected of political criticisms of the
powerful.

This little book has two qualities: it makes you laugh and
gives wise counsels for living.

Alliance with the powerful is never safe.

I'll help myself first, for my name is Lion.

A fox happened to see a tragedian's mask. "It's beautiful,"
he said, "but it has no brains!"

In changing rulers, the poor usually change nothing but
the name of their master.

I have been insulted by the brave, but to be subject to
your abuse, you disgrace to nature, is to die twice! [*The
dying lion to the donkey.*]

Humiles laborant ubi potentes dissident.

I, 30, 1

Est ardelionum quaedam Romae natio,
trepide concursans, occupata in otio,
gratis anhelans, multa agenda nil agens,
sibi molesta et aliis odiosissima.   *II, 5, 1*

Vulgare amici nomen, sed rara est fides.

III, 9, 1

Cito rumpes arcum, semper si tensum habueris,
at si laxaris, quum voles, erit utilis.   *III, 10, 1*

Hoc illis narro qui me non intelligunt.

III, 12, 8

Non semper ea sunt, quae videntur: decipit
frons prima multos; rara mens intelligit
quod interiore condidit cura angulo.   *IV, 1, 16*

Peras imposuit Iupiter nobis duas:
propriis repletam vitiis post tergum dedit,
alienis ante pectus suspendit gravem.   *IV, 10, 1*

Iniuriae qui addideris contumeliam.   *V, 3, 5*

Hoc qualecumque est Musa quod ludit mea,
nequitia pariter laudat et frugalitas;
sed haec simpliciter, illa tacite irascitur.

Fragmentum

The lowly suffer when the powerful disagree.

There is a nation of meddlers in Rome, who run about frantically, busy being idle, excited over nothing, doing much to no point, a nuisance to themselves, an object of hatred to others.

The name of friend is common, but true friendship is rare.

A bow kept taut will quickly break, kept loosely strung, it will serve you when you need it.

I am telling my tale to people who do not understand me.

Things are not always what they seem; outward form deceives many; rare is the mind that discerns what is carefully concealed within.

Jupiter makes us carry two sacks: the one in back is full of our own shortcomings, the one in front full of other people's.

You, who have added insult to injury.

Whatever diverts my Muse is equally praised by the wicked and the virtuous; the latter are sincere, the former silently resentful.

LUCIUS ANNAEUS SENECA

c. 4 b.c. — a.d. 65

Marcet sine adversario virtus; tunc apparet quanta sit
quantumque polleat, cum qui possit patientia ostendit.

De Providentia, II, 4

Ecce par deo dignum, vir fortis cum fortuna mala com-
positus, utique si et provocavit. *Ibid., 9*

Infelix est Mucius, quod dextra ignes hostium premit et
ipse a se exigit errores sui poenas? Quod regem, quem
armata manu non potuit, exusta fugat? Quid ergo? Felicior
esset, si in sinu amicae foveret manum? *Id., III, 5*

SENECA

The second son of Seneca the Elder, Seneca was taken to Rome as a boy and educated there. After a brilliant debut at the bar which almost cost him his life because it aroused the jealousy of Caligula, he devoted himself to the study of Stoic philosophy. In A.D. 41, under Claudius, he was banished to Corsica on a charge of immorality, but in A.D. 49 he was recalled to serve as tutor to Nero. In A.D. 65, charged with complicity in the Piso conspiracy, he committed suicide by Nero's order. He is best known for his moral essays, some in the form of consolations and others in the form of epistles to Lucilius—the latter perhaps the best written. Though occasionally singed by his own fiery sermonizing, Seneca displays remarkable psychological acumen and expresses lofty humanitarian ideas, much in advance of his time. As moralist, he has been one of the most frequently quoted Latin prose writers; many passages of Montaigne's *Essays* are derived almost verbatim from Seneca's work. Seneca also left nine tragedies, which influenced such European dramatists as Calderón, Camoëns, and Corneille. His other surviving works include a number of short poems; a satire on the death of Claudius; and *Questiones naturales,* whose purpose is also moral, but which offers interesting glimpses of the state of science in his time—Roger Bacon quoted from it extensively.

(*Tr. J. W. Basore*)

Without an adversary prowess shrivels. We see how great and efficient it really is only when it shows by endurance what it is capable of.

Lo! here a contest worthy of god—a brave man matched against ill fortune, and doubly so if his was also the challenge.

Is Mucius unfortunate because he grasps the flames of the enemy with his right hand and forces himself to pay the penalty of his mistake? because with his charred hand he routs the king whom with his armed hand he could not rout? Tell me, then, would he be happier if he were warming his hand in his mistress's bosom?

Prosperae res et in plebem ac vilia ingenia deveniunt; at calamitates terroresque mortalium sub iugum mittere proprium magni viri est. *Id., IV, 1*

Labor optimos citat. *Id., V, 4*

Ignis aurum probat, miseria fortes viros. *Ibid., 10*

Hunc affectum adversus omnis habet sapiens, quem adversus aegros suos medicus.
De Constantia Sapientis, XIII, 1

Nemo risum praebuit qui ex se cepit. *Id., XVII, 3*

Ad nocendum potentes sumus. *De Ira, I, iii, 2*

Facilius est excludere perniciosa quam regere et non admittere quam admissa moderari. *Ibid., vii, 2*

Ratio id iudicare vult quod aequum est; ira id aequum videri vult quod iudicavit. *Ibid., xviii, 1*

Si tantum irasci vis sapientem, quantum scelerum indignitas exigit, non irascendum illi sed insaniendum est.
Id., II, ix, 4

Turpissimam aiebat Fabius imperatori excusationem esse: "Non putavi," ego turpissimam homini puto.
Ibid., xxxi, 4

Hoc habent pessimum animi magna fortuna insolentes: quos laeserunt et oderunt. *Ibid., xxxiii, 1*

Dum inter homines sumus, colamus humanitatem.
Id., IV, xliii, 5

Non minus principi turpia sunt multa supplicia quam medico multa funera. *De Clementia, I, xxiv, 1*

Malivolum solacii genus est turba miserorum.
Ad Marciam de consolatione, XII, 5

Success comes to the common man, and even to commonplace ability; but to triumph over the calamities and terrors of mortal life is the part of a great man only.

Toil summons the best men.

Fire tests gold, misfortune brave men.

The wise man's feeling toward all men is that of the physician toward his patients.

No one becomes a laughingstock who laughs at himself.

We all have power to do harm.

It is easier to exclude harmful passions than to rule them, and to deny them admittance than to control them after they have been admitted.

Reason wishes the decision it gives to be just; anger wishes the decision it has given to seem the just decision.

If you expect the wise man to be angry as the shamefulness of crime compels, he must not be angry merely, but go mad.

Fabius used to say that the excuse, "I did not think," was the one most shameful for the commander; I think it most shameful for any man.

Men whose spirit has grown arrogant from the great favor of fortune have this most serious fault: those whom they injured they also hate.

So long as we live among men, let us cherish humanity.

Numerous executions are not less discreditable to a prince than are numerous funerals to a physician.

The solace that comes from having company in misery smacks of ill-will.

Si mortuorum aliquis miseretur, et non natorum misereatur.

Id., XIX, 5

Nihil est tam fallax quam vita humana, nihil tam insidiosum; non me hercules quisquam illam accepisset, nisi daretur inscientibus.

Id., XXII, 3

Ad hoc sacramentum adacti sumus, ferre mortalia nec perturbari iis, quae vitare non est nostrae potestatis. In regno nati sumus; deo parere libertas est.

De vita beata, XV, 7

Saepe grandis natu senex nullum aliud habet argumentum, quo se probet diu vixisse, praeter aetatem.

De tranquillitate animi, III, 8

Humanius est deridere vitam quam deplorare.   *Id., XV, 2*

Nullum magnum ingenium sine mixtura dementiae fuit.

Id., XVII, 10

Vivere tota vita discendum est et, quod magis fortasse miraberis, tota vita discendum est mori.

De brevitate vitae, VII, 3

Magna servitus est magna fortuna.

Ad Polybium de consolatione, VI, 5

Multos experimus ingratos, plures facimus.

De beneficiis, I, i, 4

Ingratus est, qui remotis arbitris agit gratias.

Id., II, xxiii, 2

Tutius est quosdam offendere quam demeruisse; argumentum enim nihil debentium odio quaerunt.

Ibid., xxiv, 1

If anyone pities the dead, he must also pity those who have not been born.

Nothing is so deceptive as human life, nothing is so treacherous. Heaven knows! not one of us would have accepted it as a gift, were it not given to us without our knowledge.

This is the sacred obligation by which we are bound—to submit to the human lot and not to be disquieted by those things which we have the power to avoid. We have been born under a monarchy; to obey God is freedom.

Often a man who is very old in years has no evidence to prove that he has lived a long life other than his age.

It better befits a man to laugh at life than to lament over it.

No great genius has ever existed without a touch of madness. [*Aristotle*]

It takes the whole of life to learn how to live, and—what will perhaps make you wonder more—it takes the whole of life to learn how to die.

A great fortune is a great slavery.

Many men we find ungrateful, but more we make so.

The man who returns his thanks only when witnesses have been removed shows himself ungrateful.

It is safer to offend some men than to have done them a service; for in order to prove that they owe nothing they have recourse to hatred.

Ingratus est qui beneficium accepisse se negat, quod accepit; ingratus est qui dissimulat; ingratus qui non reddit, ingratissimus omnium, qui oblitus est. *Id., III, i, 3*

Illustres quaedam ac nobiles feminae non consulum numero sed maritorum annos suos computant. *Ibid., xvi, 2*

Opinionem quidem et famam eo loco habeamus, tamquam non ducere sed sequi debeat. *Id., VI, xliii, 3*

Non qui parum habet, sed qui plus cupit, pauper est.
Epistulae morales, II, 6

Si cum hac exceptione detur sapientia, ut illam inclusam teneam nec enuntiem, reiciam. Nullius boni sine socio iucunda possessio est. *Id., VI, 4*

Necesse est aut imiteris aut oderis. *Id., VII, 7*

Sic vive cum hominibus, tamquam deus videat; sic loquere cum deo, tamquam homines audiant. *Id., X, 5*

Philosophia . . . animum format et fabricat, vitam disponit, actiones regit, agenda et omittenda demonstrat, sedet ad gubernaculum et per ancipitia fluctuandum derigit cursum. Sine hac nemo intrepide potest vivere, nemo secure. *Id., XVI, 3*

Quicquid bene dictum est ab ullo, meum est. *Ibid., 7*

The man is ungrateful who denies that he has received a benefit which he has in fact received; he is ungrateful who pretends that he has not received one; he, too, is ungrateful who fails to return one; but the most ungrateful of all is the man who has forgotten a benefit.

Certain illustrious and noble ladies reckon their years not by the number of consuls, but by the number of their husbands.

As for rumor and reputation, let us consider them as matters that must not guide, but follow our actions.

(*Tr. R. M. Gummere*)

It is not the man who has little, but the man who craves more, that is poor.

If wisdom were given me under the express condition that it must be kept hidden and not uttered, I should refuse it. No good thing is pleasant to possess, without friends to share it.

You must either imitate or loathe [the world].

Live among men as if God beheld you; speak with God as if men were listening.

Philosophy . . . molds and constructs the soul, guides our conduct, shows us what we should do and what we should leave undone; it sits at the helm and directs our course as we waver amid uncertainties. Without it, no one can live fearlessly or in peace of mind.

Whatever is well said by anyone is mine.

Profunda super nos altitudo temporis veniet, pauca ingenia caput exerent et in idem quandoque silentium abitura oblivioni resistent ac se diu vindicabunt. *Id., XXI, 5*

Paucos servitus, plures servitutem tenent. *Id., XXII, 11*

Nemo quam bene vivat, sed quam diu, curat, cum omnibus possit contingere, ut bene vivant, ut diu, nulli. *Ibid., 17*

Unum bonum est, quod beatae vitae causa et firmamentum est, sibi fidere. *Id., XXXI, 3*

Qui amicus est, amat; qui amat, non utique amicus est. Itaque amicitia semper prodest, amor aliquando etiam nocet. *Id., XXXV, 1*

Effugere non potes necessitates, potes vincere.
Id., XXXVII, 3

Vis tu cogitare istum, quem servum tuum vocas, ex isdem seminibus ortum eodem frui caelo, aeque spirare, aeque vivere, aeque mori! *Id., XLVII, 10*

Non est extrinsecus malum nostrum; intra nos est, in visceribus ipsis sedet, et ideo difficulter ad sanitatem pervenimus, quia nos aegrotare nescimus. *Id., L, 4*

Somnium narrare vigilantis est, et vitia sua confiteri sanitatis indicium est. *Id., LIII, 8*

Otium sine litteris mors est et hominis vivi sepultura.
Id., LXXXII, 3

The deep flood of time will roll over us; some few great men will raise their heads above it, and, though destined at the last to depart into the same realms of silence, will battle against oblivion and maintain their ground for long.

There are a few men whom slavery holds fast, but there are many more who hold fast to slavery.

Men do not care how nobly they live, but only how long, although it is within the reach of every man to live nobly, but within no man's power to live long.

There is only one good, the cause and support of a happy life—trust in oneself.

A friend loves you, of course; but one who loves you is not in every case your friend. Friendship, accordingly, always profits you, but love sometimes even wounds you.

You cannot escape necessities, but you can overcome them.

Kindly remember that he whom you call your slave sprang from the same stock, is smiled upon by the same skies, and on equal terms with yourself breathes, lives, and dies.

The evil that afflicts us is not external, it is within us, situated in our very vitals; for that reason we attain soundness with all the more difficulty, because we do not know that we are diseased.

Only he who is awake can recount his dream, and similarly a confession of sin is a proof of sound mind.

Leisure without study is death; it is a tomb for the living man.

De liberalibus studiis quid sentiam, scire desideras: nullum suspicio, nullum in bonis numero, quod ad aes exit.

Id., LXXXVIII, 1

Felix illud saeculum ante architectos fuit, ante tectores.

Id., XC, 8

Non sumus in ullius potestate, cum mors in nostra potestate sit. *Id., XCI, 21*

Plus dolet quam necesse est, qui ante dolet quam necesse sit. *Id., XCVIII, 8*

Postquam docti prodierunt, boni desunt. *Id., XCV, 13*

A natura discedimus, populo nos damus nullius rei bono auctori. *Id., XCIX, 17*

Excutienda vitae cupido est discendumque nihil interesse, quando patiaris, quod quandoque patiendum est. Quam bene vivas refert, non quam diu; saepe autem in hoc est bene, ne diu. *Id., CI, 15*

Non potest gratis constare libertas. Hanc si magno aestimas, omnia parvo aestimanda sunt. *Id., CIV, 34*

Quemadmodum omnium rerum, sic litterarum quoque intemperantia laboramus; non vitae sed scholae discimus.

Id., CVI, 12

Ducunt volentem fata, nolentem trahunt. *Id., CVII, 11*

You have been wishing to know my views with regard to liberal studies. My answer is this: I respect no study, and deem no study good, which results in money-making.

Believe me, that was a happy age, before the days of architects, before the days of builders!

We are in the power of nothing when once we have death in our own power.

He suffers more than is necessary, who suffers before it is necessary.

When savants have appeared, sages have become rare.

We abandon nature and surrender to the mob who are never good advisers in anything.

We must get rid of this craving for life, and learn that it makes no difference when your suffering comes, because at some time you are bound to suffer. The point is not how long you live, but how nobly you live. And often this living nobly means that you cannot live long.

Liberty cannot be gained for nothing. If you set a high value on liberty, you must set a low value on everything else.

Just as we suffer from excess in all things, so we suffer from excess in literature; thus we learn our lessons not for life, but for the lecture room.

The willing soul fate leads, but the unwilling drags along.

Dum fata sinunt
vivite laeti; properat cursu
vita citato volucrique die
rota praecipitis vertitur anni.

Hercules Furens, 177

Quod nimis miseri volunt
hoc facile credunt.

Id., 313

Ars prima regni est posse invidiam pati.

Id., 353

Cogi qui potest nescit mori.

Id., 426

Non est ad astra mollis e terris via.

Id., 437

Lycus: Quemcumque miserum videris, hominem scias.
Amphitryon: Quemcumque fortem videris, miserum neges.

Id., 463

Tibi crescit omne
et quod occasus videt et quod ortus
—parce venturis—tibi, mors, paramur.
sis licet segnis, properamus ipsi;
prima quae vitam dedit hora, carpit.

Id., 870

Violenta nemo imperia continuit diu,
moderata durant.

Troades, 258

Ego esse quicquam sceptra nisi vano putem
fulgore tectum nomen et falso comam
vinclo decentem?

Id., 271

Qui non vetat peccare, cum possit, iubet.

Id., 291

Quod non vetat lex, hoc vetat fieri pudor.

Id., 334

While the fates permit, live happily; life speeds on with hurried step, and with winged days the wheel of the headlong year is turned.

What the wretched overmuch desire, they easily believe.

'Tis the first art of kings, the power to suffer hate.

Who can be forced has not learned how to die.

There is no easy way to the stars from earth.

Lycus: Whome'er thou shalt see wretched, know him man.
Amphitryon: Whome'er thou shalt see brave, call him not wretched.

For thee, O Death, all things are growing; all that the setting sun, all that the rising, sees—oh, spare thou those who are sure to come—for thee we are all preparing. Though thou be slow, we hasten of ourselves; the hour which first gave life is plucking it away.

Ungoverned power no one can long retain; controlled, it lasts.

Should I count sovereignty anything but a name bedecked with empty glamor, a brow adorned with a lying coronet?

He who, when he may, forbids not sin, commands it.

What law forbids not, shame forbids be done.

Post mortem nihil est ipsaque mors nihil,
velocis spatii meta novissima.
spem ponant avidi, solliciti metum;
tempus nos avidum devorat et chaos.   *Id., 397*

Fortuna fortes metuit, ignavos premit.
                                    Medea, 159

Qui nil potest sperare, desperet nihil.   *Id., 163*

Nutrix: Abieri Colchis, coniugis nulla est fides
nihilque superest opibus tantis tibi.
Medea: Medea superest.   *Id., 165*

Iniqua numquam regna perpetuo manent.
                                       Id., 196

Qui statuit aliquid parte inaudita altera,
aequum licet statuerit, haud aequus fuit.
                                       Id., 199

Venient annis saecula seris,
quibus Oceanus vincula rerum
laxet et ingens pateat tellus
Tethysque novos detegat orbes
nec sit terris ultima Thule.   *Id., 375*

Per alta vade spatia sublimi aethere;
testare nullos esse, qua veheris, deos.
                                       Id., 1026

Deum esse amorem turpis et vitio furens
finxit libido, quoque liberior foret
titulum furori numinis falsi addidit.
                                Hippolytus, 195

There is nothing after death, and death itself is nothing, the final goal of a course full swiftly run. Let the eager give up their hopes; their fears, the anxious; greedy time and chaos engulf us altogether.

Fortune fears the brave, the cowardly overwhelms.

Whoso has naught to hope, let him despair of naught.

Nurse: The Colchians are no longer on thy side, thy husband's vows have failed, and there is nothing left of all thy wealth.
Medea: Medea is left.

Unjust rule never abides continually.

He who has judged aught, with the other side unheard, may have judged righteously, but was himself unrighteous.

There will come an age in the far-off years when Ocean shall unloose the bonds of things, when the whole broad earth shall be revealed, when Tethys shall disclose new worlds and Thule not be the limit of the lands.

Go on through the lofty spaces of high heaven and bear witness, where thou ridest, that there are no gods.

'Tis base and sin-mad lust that has made love into a god and, to enjoy more liberty, has given to passion the title of an unreal divinity.

Pars sanitatis velle sanari fuit. *Id., 249*

Curae leves loquuntur, ingentes stupent.
Id., 607

Res humanas ordine nullo
Fortuna regit sparsitque manu
munera caeca, peiora fovens;
vincit sanctos dira libido,
fraus sublimi regnat in aula. *Id., 978*

Quidquid in altum Fortuna tulit,
ruitura levat. modicis rebus
longius aevum est; felix mediae
quisquis turbae sorte quietus
aura stringit litora tuta
timidusque mari credere cumbam
remo terras propiore legit. *Agamemnon, 101*

Res est profecto stulta nequitiae modus.
Id., 150

Agamemnon: Victor timere quid potest?
Cassandra: Quod non timet. *Id., 799*

Electra: Mortem aliquid ultra est?
Aegisthus: Vita, si cupias mori. *Id., 996*

Regem non faciunt opes,
non vestis Tyriae color,
non frontis nota regiae,
non auro nitidae fores;
rex est qui posuit metus
et diri mala pectoris. *Thyestes, 345*

Illi mors gravis incubat
qui, notus nimis omnibus,
ignotus moritur sibi. *Id., 401*

The wish for healing has ever been the half of health.

Light troubles speak; the weighty are struck dumb.

Fate without order rules the affairs of men, scatters her gifts with unseeing hand, fostering the worst; dire lust prevails against pure men, and crime sits regnant in the lofty palace.

Whatever Fortune has raised on high, she lifts but to bring low. Modest estate has longer life; then happy he whoe'er content with the common lot with soft breeze hugs the shore and fearing to trust his skiff to the wider sea, with unambitious oar keeps close to land.

Surely 'tis folly to stop midway in crime.

Agamemnon: What can a victor fear?
Cassandra: What he doth not fear.

Electra: Is aught worse than death?
Aegisthus: Yes, life if thou longest to die.

A king neither riches make, nor robe of Tyrian hue, nor crown upon the royal brow, nor doors with gold bright-gleaming; a king is he who has laid fear aside and the base longing of an evil heart.

On him does death lie heavily, who, but too well known to all, dies to himself unknown.

Peior est bello timor ipse belli. *Id., 572*

Vitae est avidus quisquis non vult
mundo secum pereunte mori. *Id., 882*

O quam contempta res est homo, nisi supra humana
surrexerit! *Naturales quaestiones, I, praef. 5*

Tum consummatum habet plenumque bonum sortis humanae cum calcato omni malo petit altum et in interiorem
naturae sinum venit. *Ibid., 7*

Antiquus ordo revocabitur. Omne ex integro animal gen-
erabitur dabiturque terris homo inscius scelerum et meli-
oribus auspiciis natus. Sed illis quoque innocentia non
durabit, nisi dum novi sunt. Cito nequitia subrepit. Virtus
difficile inventu est, rectorem ducemque desiderat; etiam
sine magistro vitia discuntur. *Id., III, xxx, 7*

Haec ex quibus causis accidant, digna res excuti. Quod,
inquis, erit pretium operae? Quo nullum maius est, nosse
naturam. . . . Utrum mundus terra stante circumeat an
mundo stante terra vertatur. Fuerunt enim qui dicerent nos
esse quos rerum natura nescientes ferat, nec caeli motu
fieri ortus et occasus, nos ipsos oriri et occidere.
Id., VII, ii, 2

Worse than war is the very fear of war.

Greedy indeed for life is he who would not die when the world is perishing in his company.

(Tr. John Clarke)

What a despicable thing is man, unless he rises above the human condition!

The full consummation of human felicity is attained when, all vice trampled under foot, the soul seeks the heights and reaches the inner recesses of nature.

The ancient order of things will be recalled. Every living creature will be created afresh. The earth will receive a new man ignorant of sin, born under happier stars. But they, too, will retain their innocence only while they are new. Vice quickly creeps in; virtue is difficult to find, she requires ruler and guide. But vice can be acquired even without a tutor.

What the causes are that bring these things [earthquakes] to pass is certainly worth discussing. What, you say, will be the reward of our labor? That reward, I say, which surpasses all others, the knowledge of nature. . . . [We endeavor to ascertain] whether the earth stands still while the universe revolves around it, or whether the converse is the truth, the universe standing still while the earth revolves. There have been persons who made bold to say that it is we that all unwitting are borne round by the frame of things, that the sun rises and sets not because of a movement of the heavens, and that we ourselves rise and set.

Veniet tempus quo ista quae nunc latent in lucem dies
extrahat et longioris aevi diligentia. Ad inquisitionem
tantorum aetas una non sufficit. . . . Itaque per succes-
siones ista longas explicabuntur. Veniet tempus quo pos-
teri nostri tam aperta nos nescisse mirentur.

Ibid., xxv, 4, 5

Quam multa animalia hoc primum cognovimus saeculo,
quam multa negotia ne hoc quidem! Multa venientis aevi
populus ignota nobis sciet; multa saeculis tunc futuris cum
memoria nostri exoleverit reservantur. Pusilla res mundus
est, nisi in illo quod quaerat omnis mundus habeat.

Ibid., xxx, 5

GAIUS PLINIUS SECUNDUS

A.D. 23 – 79

Deus est mortali iuvare mortalem.

Historia naturalis, II, 5, 18

Solum ut inter ista vel certum sit nihil esse certi nec quicquam miserius homine aut superbius.   *Ibid., 25*

The day will yet come when the progress of research through long ages will bring to light the mysteries of nature that are now concealed. A single lifetime does not suffice for the investigations of problems of such complexity. . . . It must therefore require long successive ages to unfold all. The day will yet come when posterity will be amazed that we remained ignorant of things that will to them seem so plain.

How many animals we have come to know for the first time in our own days! Many, too, that are unknown to us, the people of a coming day will know. Many discoveries are reserved for the ages still to be, when our memory shall have perished. The world would be a puny thing if future ages found in it nothing to investigate.

PLINY THE ELDER

Pliny was born at Comum (on Lake of Como) and educated in Rome. He held several important administrative posts. While admiral at Misenum, scientific curiosity led him in A.D. 79 to make an on-the-spot investigation of the eruption which had just destroyed Herculaneum and Pompeii. He died from the effects of the volcanic fumes. He was a tireless reader and writer. The variety of his interests, as well as his Stoic beliefs, critical attitude to contemporary life, and pessimistic outlook is reflected in his only surviving work, The encyclopaedic *Historia naturalis*. It is based on notes taken from Latin and Greek writers on astronomy, physics, geography, zoology, botany, agriculture, trade, medicine, and the arts and crafts. There are interesting digressions, including a survey of the history of painting and sculpture.

(Tr. H. Rackham and W. S. Jones)

For mortal to aid mortal—this is God.

Among these things but one thing seems certain—that nothing certain exists, and that nothing is more pitiable or more presumptuous than man.

Miraque humani ingeni peste sanguinem et caedes condere annalibus iuvat, ut scelera hominum noscantur mundi ipsius ignaris. *Ibid., 6, 43*

Leonum feritas inter se non dimicat, serpentium morsus non petit serpentis, ne maris quidem beluae ac pisces nisi in diversa genera saeviunt: at Hercule homini plurima ex homine sunt mala. *Id., VII, Praef., 5*

Quid non miraculo est cum primum in notitiam venit? quam multa fieri non posse priusquam sunt facta iudicantur! *Ibid., 1, 6*

Ritus naturae capite hominem gigni, mos est pedibus efferri. *Ibid., 8, 46*

Natura vero nihil hominibus brevitate vitae praestitit melius. *Ibid., 50, 168*

Vulgare Graeciae dictum, Semper Africam aliquid novi afferre. *Id., VIII, 16, 17*

Mihi contuenti semper suasit rerum natura nihil incredibile existimare de ea. *Id., XI, 2, 6*

Volgoque veritas iam attributa vino est. *Id., XIV, 28, 141*

Nisi carenti doloribus morbisque, vita ipsa poena fiat. *Id., XXVIII, 1*

Apelli fuit alioqui perpetua consuetudo numquam tam occupatum diem agendi, ut non lineam ducendo exerceret artem. *Id., XXXV, 36, 84*

Owing to a curious disease of the human mind we are pleased to enshrine in history records of bloodshed and slaughter, so that persons ignorant of the facts of the world may be acquainted with the crimes of mankind.

Fierce lions do not fight among themselves, the serpent's bite attacks not serpents, even the monsters of the sea and the fishes are only cruel against different species; whereas to man, I vow, most of his evils come from his fellow men.

What is not deemed miraculous when first it comes into knowledge? how many things are judged impossible before they actually occur!

It is nature's method for a human being to be born head first, and it is the custom for him to be carried to burial feet first.

Nature has granted man no better gift than the shortness of life.

The common Greek saying that Africa is always bringing us something new.

When I have observed Nature, she has always induced me to deem no statement about her incredible.

Truth has come to be proverbially credited to wine. [*The proverb is* In vino veritas—"*Wine tells the truth.*"]

Life itself becomes a punishment for those who are not free from pains and diseases.

It was a regular custom with Apelles never to let a day of business be so fully occupied that he did not practice his art by drawing at least a line. [*Origin of the proverb* Nulla dies sine linea—"*No day without a line.*"]

Ne supra crepidam sutor iudicaret, quod et ipsum in proverbium abiit. *Ibid., 36, 85*

C. PETRONIUS ARBITER

c. A.D. 26? – 66

Grandis et ut ita dicam pudica oratio non est maculosa nec
turgida, sed naturali pulchritudine exsurgit. *Satyricon, 2*

Medicus enim nihil aliud est quam animi consolatio.
Id., 42

Numquam autem recte faciet, qui cito credit, utique homo
negotians. *Id., 43*

Corcillum est quod homines facit, certa quisquilia omnia.
Id., 75

[*Apelles asked a shoemaker to appraise the shoes in one of his paintings. When the man went on to discuss the rest of the work, Apelles rebuked him, saying that*] a shoemaker must not go beyond the sandal [*a remark that has also passed into a proverb:* Ne sutor ultra crepidam— *"A cobbler should stick to his last."*]

PETRONIUS

Author of a novelistic masterpiece, the *Satyricon* (only parts of it have come down to us) and a distinguished poet, Petronius is generally assumed to be identical with the Arbiter elegantiae referred to by Tacitus (*Annals*, XX, 18). Victim of a court intrigue, he was ordered by Nero to remain at Cumae, and committed suicide. He died, says Tacitus, surrounded by his friends and exchanging with them "not thoughts on the immortality of the soul or on the theories of the philosophers, but light poetry and playful verses."

(Tr. M. Heseltine)

Great style, which, if I may say so, is also modest style, is never blotchy and bloated. It rises supreme by virtue of its natural beauty.

A doctor is nothing but a sop to conscience.

A man who is always ready to believe what is told him will never do well, especially a businessman.

A bit of sound sense is what makes men; the rest is all rubbish.

Nomen amicitiae sic, quatenus expedit, haeret;
   calculus in tabula mobile ducit opus.
Cum fortuna manet, vultum servatis, amici;
   cum cecidit, turpi vertitis ora fuga.   *Id.*, *80*

Raram fecit mixturam cum sapientia forma.   *Id.*, *94*

Nihil est hominum inepta persuasione falsius nec ficta sev-
eritate ineptius.   *Id.*, *132*

Sicut muta animalia cibo inescantur, sic homines non
caparentur nisi spei aliquid morderent.   *Id.*, *140*

> Qui voltur iecur intimum pererrat
> et pectus trahit intimasque fibras,
> non est quem lepidi vocant poetae,
> sed cordis mala, livor atque luxus.
>
> *Fragmenta, xxv*

Inveniet quod quisque velit: non omnibus unum est
   quod placet: his spinas colligit, ille rosas.
Cf. *Baehrens, Poetae Latini Minores, Vol. 4, 74* (Attr.)

Iam nunc algentes autumnus fecerat umbras
atque hiemem tepidis spectabat Phoebus habenis,
iam platanus iactare comas, iam coeperat uvas
adnumerare suas defecto palmite vitis:
ante oculos stabat quidquid promiserat annus.   *Id.*, *75*

> Primus in orbe deos fecit timor.   *Id.*, *76*

Uxor, legis onus, debet quasi census amari.
   nec censum vellem semper amare meum.
                                                    Id., *78*

Linque tuas sedes alienaque litora quaere,
   o iuvenis: maior rerum tibi nascitur ordo.   *Id.*, *79*

The name of friendship endures so long as there is profit in it; the counter on the board plays a changeable game. While my luck holds you give me your smiles, my friends; when it is out, you turn your faces away in shameful flight.

Beauty and wisdom make a rare conjunction.

There is nothing more insincere than people's silly convictions, or more silly than their sham morality.

Just as dumb creatures are snared by food, human beings would not be caught unless they had a nibble of hope.

The vulture who explores our inmost liver, and drags out our heart and inmost nerves, is not the bird of whom our dainty poets talk, but those diseases of the soul, envy and wantonness.

Every man shall find his own desire; there is no one thing which pleases all: one man gathers thorns and another roses.

Now autumn had brought its chill shades, and Phoebus was looking winterwards with cooler reins. Now the plane tree had begun to shed her leaves, now the young shoots had withered on the vine, and she had begun to number her grapes: the whole promise of the year was standing before our eyes.

It was fear first created gods in the world.

A wife is a burden imposed by law, and should be loved like one's fortune. But I do not wish to love even my fortune for ever.

Leave thine home, O youth, and seek out alien shores: a larger range of life is ordained for thee.

Pervixi: neque enim fortuna malignior unquam
   eripiet nobis quod prior hora dedit.   *Id., 84*

Non est forma satis nec quae vult bella videri
   debet vulgari more placere sibi.
Dicta, sales, lusus, sermonis gratia, risus
   vincunt naturae candidioris opus.
Condit enim formam quicquid consumitur artis,
   et nisi velle subest, gratia nuda perit.   *Id., 89*

   Foeda est in coitu et brevis voluptas
   et taedet Veneris statim peractae.
   Non ergo ut pecudes libidinosae
   caeci protinus irruamus illuc
   (nam languescit amor peritque flamma);
   sed sic sic sine fine feriati
   et tecum iaceamus osculantes.
   Hic nullus labor est ruborque nullus:
   hoc iuvit, iuvat et diu iuvabit;
   hoc non deficit incipitque semper.   *Id., 101*

Somnia quae mentes ludunt volitantibus umbris
non delubra deum nec ab aethere numina mittunt,
sed sibi quisque facit. Nam cum prostrata sopore
urget membra quies et mens sine pondere ludit,
quidquid luce fuit tenebris agit.   *Id., 121*

I have had life in full; for never can harder fortune take away what was given us in time overpast.

Outward beauty is not enough, and the woman who would appear fair must not be content with any common manner. Words, wit, play, sweet talk and laughter, surpass the work of too simple nature. For all expense of art seasons beauty, and naked loveliness is wasted all in vain, if it have not the will to please.

(Tr. Ben Jonson)

Doing, a filthy pleasure is, and short;
And done, we straight repent us of the sport:
Let us not then rush blindly on unto it,
Like lustfull beasts, that onely know to doe it:
For lust will languish, and that heat decay,
But thus, thus, keeping endlesse Holy-day,
Let us together closely lie, and kisse,
There is no labour, nor no shame in this;
This hath pleas'd, doth please, & long will please; never
Can this decay, but is beginning ever.

(Tr. M. Heseltine)

It is not the shrines of the gods, nor the powers of the air, that send the dreams which mock the mind with flitting shadows; each man makes dreams for himself. For when rest lies about the limbs subdued by sleep, and the mind plays with no weight upon it, it pursues in the darkness whatever was its task by daylight.

SILIUS ITALICUS

A.D. 26 – 101

Ingenio motus avidus fideique sinister
is fuit, exsuperans astu, sed devius aequi.
armatus nullus divum pudor; improba virtus
et pacis despectus honos; penitusque medullis
sanguinis humani flagrat sitis.   *Punica, I, 56*

    Asper amore
sanguinis, et metui demens credebat honorem.
                               Ibid., 149

    Explorant adversa viros, perque aspera duro
nititur ad laudem virtus interrita clivo.
                               Id., IV, 603

Pelle moras: brevis est magni Fortuna favoris.
                               Ibid., 732

    Deforme sub armis
vana superstitio est; dea sola in pectore virtus
bellantum viget.   *Id., V, 125*

    (Crede experto, non fallimus) aegris
nil movisse salus rebus.   *Id., VII, 395*

SILIUS ITALICUS

Tiberius Catius Ascomius Silius Italicus was probably born at Padua. He came of a prominent family, was a brilliant orator, held the office of consul in 68 (last year of Nero's reign), and was governor of Asia Minor in 69. He was a passionate collector and, being a very wealthy man, could afford to purchase the houses in which Cicero and Vergil had lived. He practiced a veritable religious cult to the memory of Vergil. His poem on the Second Punic War—the longest Latin poem—was much praised in his lifetime but was forgotten soon after his death; it was not rediscovered until 1414. It is a work overladen with mythology, written "with more care than talent," as Pliny the Younger put it (*"maiore cura quam ingenio"*). At the age of seventy-five, suffering from an incurable disease, he starved himself to death.

(Tr. J. D. Duff)

By nature he was eager for action and faithless to his plighted word, a past master in cunning, but a strayer from justice. Once armed he had no respect for Heaven; he was brave for evil and despised the glory of peace, and a thirst for human blood burned in his inmost heart. [*Characterization of Hannibal*]

Thirst for blood hardened his heart, and he had the folly to believe that to be feared is glory. [*Hasdrubal*]

Manhood is tested by trial, and valor climbs unterrified the rocky path and difficult ascent that leads to glory.

Make haste! The flood tide of Fortune soon ebbs.

Groundless superstition ill becomes an army; valor is the only deity that rules in the warrior's breast.

Take the word of experience, I speak the truth: inaction is safest in peril.

Velle ac nolle ambobus idem societaque toto
mens aevo ac parvis dives concordia rebus.
occubuere simul; votisque ex omnibus unum
id Fortuna dedit, iunctam inter proelia mortem.

Id., IX, 406

Stat nulla diu mortalibus usquam,
Fortuna titubante, fides.   *Id., XI, 3*

Pax optima rerum,
quas homini novisse datum est; pax una triumphis
innumeris potior; pax, custodire salutem
et cives aequare potens.   *Ibid., 592*

Nec ira deum tantum nec telum nec hostes,
quantum sola noces animis illapsa, Voluptas.

Id., XV, 94

VALERIUS MAXIMUS

fl. c. a.d. 30

Deos enim reliquos accepimus, Caesares dedimus.
Facta et dicta memorabilia, Praefatio

Lento enim gradu ad vindictam sui divina procedit ira
tarditatemque supplicii gravitate pensat.   *Id., I, 1 ext. 3*

In liking and disliking they never differed; it was a lifelong marriage of two minds; and brotherly love made them rich in poverty. In death they were not divided, and of all their prayers Fortune granted them one only—to die in battle side by side.

Nowhere do men remain loyal for long when Fortune proves unstable.

Peace is the best thing that men may know; peace is better than a thousand triumphs; peace has power to guard our lives and secure equality among fellow citizens.

Neither the wrath of Heaven nor the attacks of foemen are as fatal as Pleasure alone when she infects the mind.

VALERIUS MAXIMUS

Valerius Maximus lived in the period of Emperor Tiberius. He defines his book as "the description of human life in its various aspects." It is actually a compilation of historical anecdotes with moralizing commentaries, made for the use of orators. It enjoyed great popularity in the Middle Ages. The phrase from the preface, quoted below, is not meant as a criticism but as a compliment to Tiberius, to whom his book is dedicated.

The other gods were handed down to us, the Caesars we made gods ourselves.

Divine anger is slow to mete out justice, but in its severity makes up for the delay in punishment.

Aspero enim et abscisso castigationis genere militaris disciplina indiget, quia vires armis constant; quae, ubi a recto tenore desciverunt, oppressura sunt, nisi opprimantur.

Id., II, 7, 14

Multo enim multoque seipsum quam hostem superare operosius est. *Id., IV, 1, 2*

Speciosius aliquanto iniuriae beneficiis vincuntur quam mutui odii pertinacia pensantur. *Ibid., 2, 4*

Ubi idem et maximus et honestissimus amor est, aliquanto praestat morte iungi quam vita distrahi. *Ibid., 6, 3*

Verum nulla tam modesta felicitas est, quae malignitatis dentes vitare possit. *Ibid., 7 ext. 2*

Military discipline requires that punishment be harsh and speedy. For the strength of the state depends on the army; once the latter leaves the path of duty, it is bound to become oppressive unless checked in time.

It is harder, much harder, to vanquish oneself than one's enemy.

It is nobler to wipe out wrongs with kindness than to go on stubbornly paying back hatred with hatred.

When reciprocal love is very strong and very true, it is far preferable to be joined in death than parted in life.

No happiness, however virtuous, is safe from malicious backbiting.

AULUS PERSIUS FLACCUS

A.D. 34–62

Magister artis ingenique largitor
venter, negatas artifex sequi voces.

Saturae, Prologus, 10

O mores, usque adeone
scire tuum nihil est, nisi te scire hoc sciat alter?

Id., I, 26

At pulchrum est digito monstrari et dicier "hic est."

Ibid., 27

O curvae in terris animae et caelestium inanis!

Id., II, 61

Magne pater divum, saevos punire tyrannos
haut alia ratione velis, cum dira libido
moverit ingenium ferventi tincta veneno:
virtutem videant intabescantque relicta.

Id., III, 35

Ut nemo in sese temptat descendere, nemo
sed praecedenti spectatur mantica tergo!

Id., IV, 23

PERSIUS

Born at Volaterrae in Etruria, Persius studied grammar and rhetoric at Rome, and philosophy under the Stoic Cornutus. He left six satires (a total of 650 hexameters) in which he treats the subjects of the frivolity of contemporary poets, false religion, the need for self-knowledge, true freedom, and the deleterious effects of sloth and avarice. They are inspired by Lucilius (the first satire begins with *"O curas hominum! O quantum est in rebus inane!"* a direct quotation from the old satirist; cf. p. 40), but his style is overcharged with literary allusions, and his tone is severely moralizing. A French critic likened him to a "young Puritan preacher."

(Tr. G. G. Ramsay)

That master of the arts, that dispenser of genius, the belly, who has a rare skill in getting at words which are not his own.

Good heavens! Is all your knowledge to go utterly for nothing unless other people know that you possess it?

O but it's a fine thing to have a finger pointed at one and to hear people say, That's the man!

O souls bowed to earth and void of all heavenly thoughts!

O mighty father of the gods! Be it thy will to punish tyrants whose souls have been stirred by the deadly poison of evil lust in no other way but this—that they may look on virtue and pine away because they have lost her!

Not a soul is there, no, not one, who seeks to get down into his own self; all watch the wallet on the back that walks before!

Caedimus inque vicem praebemus crura sagittis.
vivitur hoc pacto, sic novimus.   *Ibid., 42*

Tecum habita: noris quam sit tibi curta supellex.
                                                   Ibid., 52

Mille hominum species et rerum discolor usus;
velle suum cuique est, nec voto vivitur uno.
                                                   Id., V, 52

Stat contra ratio et secretam garrit in aurem,
ne liceat facere id quod quis vitiabit agendo.
                                                   Ibid., 96

Indulge genio, carpamus dulcia, nostrum est
quod vivis, cinis et manes et fabula fies.
vive memor leti, fugit hora, hoc quod loquor inde est.
                                                   Ibid., 151

We keep smiting by turns and by turns presenting our own legs to the arrow. That is the rule of life; that is the lesson of experience.

Live in your own house, and recognize how poorly it is furnished.

Men are of a thousand kinds, and diverse are the colors of their lives. Each has his own desires; no two men offer the same prayers.

Reason forbids, and whispers privately into the ear that no man be allowed to do what he will spoil in the doing of it.

Give your genius a chance. Let us gather our sweets! Our life is our own today, tomorrow you will be a dust, a shade, a tale that is told. Live mindful of death, the hour flies, the word that I speak is so much taken from it.

MARCUS FABIUS QUINTILIANUS

C. A.D. 35 – C. 95

Natura tenacissimi sumus eorum, quae rudibus animis percepimus. . . . Et haec ipsa magis pertinaciter haerent, quo deteriora sunt. Nam bona facile mutantur in peius; num quando in bonum verteris vitia?

Institutio oratoria, I, i, 5

Nihil est peius iis, qui paulum aliquid ultra primas litteras progressi falsa sibi scientiae persuasionem induerunt.

Ibid., 8

Id in primis cavere oportebit, ne studia, qui amare nondum potest, oderit et amaritudinem semel perceptam etiam ultra rudes annos reformidet. Lusus hic sit.   *Ibid., 20*

Licet ipsa vitium sit ambitio, frequenter tamen causa virtutum est.   *Ibid., ii, 22*

Studium discendi voluntate, quae cogi non potest, constat.

Ibid., iii, 8

QUINTILIAN

Quintilian was born at Calagurris, Spain, and was brought as a child to Rome, where he studied under the most reputed rhetoricians. Emperor Vespasian appointed him public teacher of oratory in Rome; among his pupils were Pliny the Younger and the future emperor Hadrian. Domitian made him tutor to his grand nephews. At the age of forty-six he retired from teaching and, urged by his friends, composed the celebrated *Institutio oratoria*, in twelve books, which contains a complete plan for the training of an orator. His ideas on the education of children have lost none of their validity. Book 10 offers a valuable review of Latin literature.

(Tr. H. E. Butler)

We are by nature most tenacious of childish impressions. . . . Further, it is the worst impressions that are most durable. For, while what is good readily deteriorates, you will never turn vice into virtue.

There are none worse than those who, as soon as they have progressed beyond a knowledge of the alphabet, delude themselves into the belief that they are the possessors of real knowledge.

Above all things we must take care that the child, who is not yet old enough to love his studies, does not come to hate them and dread the bitterness which he has once tasted, even when the years of infancy are left behind. His studies must be made an amusement.

Though ambition may be a fault in itself, it is often the mother of virtues.

Study depends on the good will of the student, a quality that cannot be secured by compulsion.

Caedi vero discentes, quamlibet et receptum sit et Chrysippus non improbet, minime velim. Primum, quia deforme atque servile est et certe (quod convenit, si aetatem mutes) iniuria est. *Ibid.*, 13

Quare hoc dixisse satis est; in aetatem infirmam et iniuriae obnoxiam nemini debet nimium licere. *Ibid.*, 17

Consuetudiem sermonis vocabo consensum eruditorum, sicut vivendi consensum bonorum. *Ibid.*, vi, 45

Facilius est multa facere quam diu. *Ibid.*, xii, 7

Facile remedium est ubertati; sterilia nullo labore vincuntur. *Id.*, II, iv, 6

Dum satis putant vitio carere, in id ipsum incidant vitium, quod virtutibus carent. *Ibid.*, 9

Sermo rectus et secundum naturam enuntiatus nihil habere ex ingenio videtur; illa vero, quae utcunque deflexa sunt, tanquam exquisitiora miramur. *Ibid.*, v, 11

In omnibus fere minus valent praecepta quam experimenta. *Ibid.*, 15

Natura materiae doctrinae est; haec fingit, illa fingitur. Nihil ars sine materia, materiae etiam sine arte pretium est, ars summa materia optima melior. *Ibid.*, xix, 3

Mendacem memorem esse oportere. *Id.*, IV, ii, 91

I disapprove of flogging, although it is the regular custom and meets with the acquiescence of Chrysippus [the Stoic philosopher], because in the first place it is a disgraceful form of punishment, and in any case it is an insult, as you will realize if you imagine its infliction at a later age.

I will content myself with saying that children are helpless and easily victimized, and that therefore no one should be given unlimited power over them.

I will define usage in speech as the agreed practice of educated men, just as where our way of life is concerned I should define it as the agreed practice of all good men.

It is easier to do many things than to do one thing for a long time continuously.

Exuberance is easily remedied, but barrenness is incurable, be your efforts what they may.

While they [dry teachers] are content that their work should be devoid of faults they fall into the fault of being devoid of merit.

We have come to regard direct and natural speech as incompatible with genius, while all that is in any way abnormal is admired as exquisite.

There are no subjects in which, as a rule, practice is not more valuable than precept.

Nature is the raw material for education: the one forms, the other is formed. Without material art can do nothing; material without art does possess a certain value, while the perfection of art is better than the best material.

A liar should have a good memory.

Quae non possunt valere, quia magna sint, valebunt, quia multa sunt. . . . Singula levia sunt et communia, universa vero nocent etiamsi non ut fulmine, tamen ut gradine.

Id., V, xii, 5

Tanto est accusare quam defendere, quanto facere quam sanare vulnera, facilius. *Ibid., xiii, 3*

Adversus miseros . . . inhumanus est iocus.

Id., VI, iii, 33

Ubi vinci necesse est, expedit cedere. *Ibid., iv, 16*

Id ipsum optime fiat, quod nos aliquid non optime fecisse simulamus. *Id., VIII, ii, 24*

Verbum omne, quod neque intellectum adiuvat neque ornatum, vitiosum dici potest. *Ibid., iii, 55*

Non ut edam vivo, sed ut vivam edo. *Id., IX, iii, 85*

Ubicunque ars ostentatur, veritas abesse videatur.

Ibid., 102

Modesto tamen et circumspecto iudicio de tantis viris pronuntiandum est, ne, quod plerisque accidit, damnent quae non intelligunt. *Id., X, i, 26*

Multa magis quam multorum lectione formanda mens.

Ibid., 59

Ennium sicut sacros vetustate lucos adoremus, in quibus grandia et antiqua robora iam non tantam habent speciem quantam religionem. *Ibid., 88*

Arguments which have no individual force on the ground of strength will acquire force in virtue of their number. . . . These arguments are trivial and commonplace in detail, but their cumulative force is damaging. They may not have the overwhelming force of a thunderbolt, but they will have all the destructive force of hail.

It is just so much easier to accuse than to defend as it is easier to inflict than to heal a wound.

Jests directed against the unfortunate are inhuman.

Where defeat is inevitable, it is wisest to yield.

The pretended admission of a fault on our part creates an excellent impression.

Every word which neither helps the sense nor the style may be regarded as faulty.

I do not live to eat, but eat to live.

Wherever the orator displays his art unveiled, the hearer says, "The truth is not in him."

Modesty and circumspection are required in pronouncing judgment on such great men [famous authors], since there is always the risk of falling into the common fault of condemning what one does not understand.

We must form our minds by reading deep rather than wide.

Ennius deserves our reverence, but only as those groves whose age has made them sacred, but whose huge and sacred trunks inspire us with religious awe rather than with admiration for their beauty.

Cito scribendo non fit, ut bene scribatur; bene scribendo fit, ut cito. *Id., X, iii, 10*

Pectus est . . . quod disertos facit, et vis mentis.
Ibid., vii, 15

Qui stultis videri eruditi volunt, stulti eruditis videntur.
Ibid., 21

Rarum est . . . ut satis se quisque vereatur. *Ibid., 24*

Et aperte tamen gloriari nescio an sit magis tolerabile vel ipsa vitii huius simplicitate, quam illa iactatio perversa, si abundans opibus pauperem se neget, nobilis obscurum et potens infirmum et disertus imperitum plane et infantem vocet. *Id., XI, i, 21*

Maledicus a malefico non distat nisi occasione.
Id., XII, ix, 9

MARCUS VALERIUS MARTIALIS

c. a.d. 40 – c. 104

Innocuos censura potest permittere lusus:
lasciva est nobis pagina, vita proba.
Epigrammata, I, 4, 7

Non est, crede mihi, sapientis dicere "Vivam";
sera nimis vita est crastina: vive hodie.
Ibid., 15, 11

Write quickly and you will never write well, write well
and you will soon write quickly.

It is feeling and force of imagination that make us eloquent.

Speakers who wish to seem learned to fools are merely
regarded as fools by the learned.

It is rare for anyone to be sufficiently critical of himself.

And yet I am not sure that open boasting is not more
tolerable, owing to its sheer straightforwardness, than that
perverted form of self-praise, which makes the millionaire
say that he can barely support himself, the man of mark
describe himself as obscure, the powerful pose as weak,
and the eloquent as unskilled and even inarticulate.

The evil speaker differs from the evil doer only in respect
of opportunity.

MARTIAL

Born at Bilbilis, Spain, Martial came to Rome at the age of
twenty-two, under Nero, and lived on the sale of his books and
the gifts of his patrons, among them Emperors Titus and Domitian. He expressed his gratitude in the form of flattery. His epigrams have become the model of the genre.

Censorship need not frown upon innocuous entertainment:
though my writing be wanton, my life is decent.

Believe me, a wise man never says, "I shall live"; to live
tomorrow is too late: live today.

Sunt bona, sunt quaedam mediocria, sunt mala plura,
quae legis hic: aliter non fit, Avite, liber.   *Ibid., 16*

Cineri gloria sera venit.   *Ibid., 25, 8*

Non amo te, Sabidi, nec possum dicere quare:
hoc tantum possum dicere, non amo te.   *Ibid., 32*

Quem recitas meus est, o Fidentine, libellus:
sed male cum recitas, incipit esse tuus.

Ibid., 38

Non bene olet, qui bene semper olet.

Id., II, 12, 4

Non sunt longa quibus nihil est quod demere possis,
sed tu, Cosconi, disticha longa facis.   *Ibid., 77, 7*

Sum, fateor, semperque fui, Callistrate, pauper
sed non obscurus nec male notus eques,
sed toto legor orbe frequens et dicitur "Hic est,"
quodque cinis paucis hoc mihi vita dedit.

Id., V, 13, 1

Odi dolosas munerum et malas artes:
imitantur hamos dona: namque quis nescit
avidum vorata decipi scarum musca?
quotiens amico diviti nihil donat,
o Quintiane, liberalis est pauper.   *Ibid., 18, 6*

Extra fortunam est quidquid donatur amicis:
quas dederis solas semper habebis opes.

Ibid., 42, 7

This book you are reading has some good things, some indifferent, and many bad. There's no other way, Avitus, to make a book.

To the dead fame comes too late.

I don't like you, Sabidius, and I can't say why: all I can say is, I don't like you.

The book you're reading out loud, Fidentinus, is mine. But the way you're mangling it, you're making it yours.

The man who is always well scented doesn't smell good.

What cannot be shortened is never long, but your two-line poems, Cosconius, are rather long.

I confess, Callistratus, I am and always have been poor, though as a member of the equestrian order, never obscure nor ill-reputed. Many people read me all over the world and say, "That's him": life has given me what death gives to few.

I detest the fraud and trickery of gift-giving. Presents are like fishhooks. Who doesn't know that the fly, once swallowed, lands the greedy fish? Whenever a poor man gives nothing to a rich friend, O Quintianus, he is being generous.

Whatever you give to friends is secure against fortune: property given away is the only kind that will forever be yours.

Cui tradas, Lupe, filium magistro
quaeris sollicitus diu rogasque.
omnes grammaticosque rhetorasque
devites moneo: nihil est illi
cum libris Ciceronis aut Maronis. . . .
si versus facit, abdices poetam. . . .
si duri puer ingeni videtur,
praeconem facias vel architectum.   *Ibid.*, 56

Cras the victurum, cras dicis, Postume, semper.
  dic mihi, cras istud, Postume, quando venit?
                                        Ibid., 58, 1

Semper pauper eris, si pauper es, Aemiliane.
  dantur opes nullis nunc nisi divitibus.   *Ibid.*, 81

Iurat capillos esse, quos emit, suos
Fabulla: numquid ergo, Paule, peierat?
                                        Id., VI, 12

Laudat, amat, cantat nostros mea Roma libellos,
  meque sinus omnes, me manus omnis habet.
ecce rubet quidam, pallet, stupet, oscitat, odit.
  hoc volo: nunc nobis carmina nostra placent.
                                        Ibid., 60

Non est vivere, sed valere vita est.
                                        Ibid., 70, 15

Cur non mitte meos tibi, Pontiliane, libellos?
  ne mihi tu mittas, Pontiliane, tuos.   *Id.*, VII, 3

Aera domi non sunt, superest hoc, Regule, solum
  ut tua vendamus munera: numquam emis?
                                        Ibid., 16

You ask, Lupus, to what master you should entrust your son: this has been worrying you a long time. My advice: steer shy of grammarians and rhetoricians: your son has no business with Cicero and Vergil. . . . If you catch him writing poetry, disinherit him. . . . If you think the boy isn't very bright, make him an auctioneer or an architect.

You'll start to live tomorrow, Postumus, tomorrow, you're always saying. Tell me now, Postumus, when does your tomorrow come?

If you are poor, Aemilianus, you'll always be so. Nowadays only the rich get rich.

Fabulla swears that the hair she buys is hers: could it be, Paulus, that she swears falsely?

Rome, my city, loves and recites my verses; you'll find them in every pocket, every hand. Look! there is a man blushing, turning pale, he's aghast, his jaw drops, how he hates them. That's how I want it: that's when I enjoy my own verses.

Life's not just living, it's living in health.

Why don't I send you my books, Pontianus? So that you, Pontianus, won't send me yours.

I haven't a penny, Regulus, all I can do now is sell the things you've given me: want to buy them back?

Qui fingit sacros auro vel marmore vultus,
non facit ille deos: qui rogat, ille facit.
Id., VIII, 24, 5

Munera qui tibi dat locupleti, Gaure, senique,
si sapis et sentis, hoc tibi ait "Morere."
Ibid., 27

Sint Maecenates, non derunt, Flacce, Marones.
Ibid., 56, 5

Omnis aut vetulas habes amicas
aut turpis vetulisque foediores.
has ducis comites trahisque tecum
per convivia porticus theatra.
sic formosa, Fabulla, sic puella es.
Ibid., 79

Nubere vis Prisco: non miror, Paula; sapisti.
ducere te non vult Priscus: et ille sapit.
Id., IX, 5

Hoc lege, quod possit dicere vita "Meum est."
non hic Centauros, non Gorgonas Harpyiasque
invenies: hominem pagina nostra sapit.
Id., X, 4, 8

Nubere Paula cupit nobis, ego ducere Paulam
nolo: anus est. vellem, si magis esset anus.
Ibid., 8

Hunc servare modum nostri novere libelli,
parcere personis, dicere de vitiis. *Ibid., 33, 9*

Rebus in angustis facile est contemnere vitam.
Id., XI, 56, 15

Non potes in nugas dicere plura meas
ipse ego quam dixi. *Id., XIII, 2, 4*

A man who sculptures holy images in gold or marble is not making gods: it's the man who prays that makes them.

Gaurus, you rich old man, anyone who sends you a present—don't you see—is telling you, "It's time to die."

Were there more Maecenases, there would be more Vergils, Flaccus.

All your women friends are old or ugly, which is worse than old. They are always with you, you drag them along with you in the streets, to dinners, to theaters. That's how you keep young and pretty, Fabulla.

Paula, you want to marry Priscus: I am not surprised, you have good taste. Priscus doesn't want to marry you: he has good taste too.

Read of what life can recognize as her own. You won't find Centaurs, Gorgons, or Harpies in my books; my pages have the flavor of mankind.

Paula is dying to marry me, I don't want to marry Paula: she's old. I might be willing if she were older.

My books have stayed within these bounds: to spare the person, to denounce vice.

Contempt for life is easy in distress.

You cannot be harder on my trifling verses than I have been myself.

MARCUS ANNAEUS LUCANUS

A.D. 39 – 65

In se magna ruunt: laetis hunc numina rebus
crescendi posuere modum.   *Pharsalia, I, 81*

Victrix causa deis placuit, sed victa Catoni.
                                          Ibid., 128

          Stat magni nominis umbra.   *Ibid., 135*

     Non in Caesare tantum
nomen erat nec fama ducis, sed nescia virtus
stare loco, solusque pudor non vincere bello.
                                          Ibid., 143

       Quisque pavendo
dat vires famae, nulloque auctore malorum,
quae finxere, timent.   *Ibid., 484*

O faciles dare summa deos eademque tueri
difficiles!   *Ibid., 510*

     Caesar in omnia praeceps,
nil actum credens, cum quid superesset agendum.
                                     Id., II, 656

LUCAN

Born at Córdoba, Spain, Lucan was brought to Rome as a child. He was introduced to the court of Nero by his uncle, Seneca. According to Tacitus (*Annals,* XV, 47), Nero "tried to disparage the fame of his poems and, with the foolish vanity of a rival, forbade him to publish them." Out of resentment, Lucan became involved in the conspiracy of Piso and was compelled by Nero to commit suicide at the age of twenty-six. He left a number of works, including a tragedy, but only his (unfinished) *Pharsalia* has survived, an epic poem on the war between Caesar and Pompey, which has been criticized for its flamboyant rhetoric and admired for many brilliant characterizations and incisive epigrams. The young Shelley preferred him to Vergil.

Greatness collapses of itself: such limit the gods have set to the growth of prosperous states.

The victorious party found favor with the gods, the vanquished with Cato.

He [Pompey] stands, the shadow of a great name.

Not only had Caesar a great name and a general's glory, but his valor knew no rest, and the only thing he looked upon as a disgrace was not winning a battle.

Each by his terror gives new strength to rumor, and fears unfounded evils of his own imagining.

How willing are the gods to grant supreme power, how unwilling to uphold it!

Caesar, always prompt to act, believed nothing had been done while anything was left to be done.

Aut nihil est sensus animis a morte relictum
aut mors ipsa nihil.   *Id., III,* 39

    Servat multos fortuna nocentes,
et tantum miseris irasci numina possunt.
                                                Ibid., 448

    Victurosque dei celant, ut vivere durent,
felix esse mori.   *Id., IV,* 517

Mors, utinam pavidos vitae subducere nolles,
sed virtus te sola daret!   *Ibid.,* 580

    Audendo magnus tegitur timor.   *Ibid.,* 702

    Quicquid multis peccatur, inultum est.
                                                Id., V, 260

    Fortissimus ille est,
qui promptus metuenda pati, si comminus instent,
et differre potest.   *Id., VII,* 105

Ex populis qui regna ferunt, sors ultima nostra est,
quos servire pudet.   *Ibid.,* 444

Libera fortunae mors est; capit omnia tellus,
quae genuit; caelo tegitur, qui non habet urnam.
                                                Ibid., 818

    Sidera terra
ut distant et flamma mari, sic utile recto.
Sceptrorum vis tota perit, si pendere iusta
incipit, evertitque arces respectus honesti.
                                                Id., VIII, 487

    Exeat aula,
qui vult esse pius. virtus et summa potestas
non coeunt.   *Ibid.,* 493

Either the soul feels nothing after death, or death itself is nothing.

Fortune often saves the guilty, while the gods vent their anger on poor wretches.

From those destined to live the gods conceal that death is a blessing, so that they may go on living.

O death, would that you did not rob cowards of life, but were given to the brave alone!

Boldness can mask great fear.

Crimes perpetrated by a multitude remain unavenged.

The bravest man is he who is prepared both to cope with present dangers and to await a better time.

Of all the nations who tolerate kings, our fate is the worst, because to be slaves makes us ashamed.

Death is free from fortune's sway; the earth takes back all she gave birth to; the sky covers the man who has no burial urn.

The useful is as distant from the right as the stars from the earth and fire from water. The whole strength of rulers goes when justice begins to be weighed, and respect for truth undermines their citadels.

Let him who would be just quit the imperial courts. Virtue and supreme power are incompatible.

Nulla fides umquam miseros elegit amicos.

Ibid., 535

Scire mori sors prima viris, sed proxima cogi.

Id., IX, 211

Sortilegis egeant dubii semperque futuris
casibus ancipites: me non oracula certum,
sed mors certa facit.   *Ibid.*, 581

Tota teguntur
Pergama dumetis: etiam periere ruinae.

Ibid., 969

C. VALERIUS FLACCUS

c. A.D. 40 – c. 90

At regina virum (neque deus amovet ignem)
persequitur lustrans oculisque ardentibus haeret;
et iam laeta minus praesentis imagine pugnae
castigatque metus et quas alit inscia curas.

Argonautica, VI, 657

Ac velut ante comas ac summa cacumina silvae
lenibus adludit flabris levis auster, at illum
protinus immanem miserae sensere carinae:
talis ad extremos agitur Medea furores.   *Ibid.*, 664

Loyalty never chose the unfortunate for friends.

Man's first happiness is to know how to die, his second to be forced to die.

Let those who are irresolute, who are always uncertain of the future, run to soothsayers. What gives me confidence is not oracles, but the certainty of death.

All Pergamum is covered with thorn bushes: even its ruins have perished.

VALERIUS FLACCUS

Valerius Flaccus, born at Padua (or Setia), held the office of *quindecemvir sacris faciundis* (one of the custodians of the Sybilline books). He was a friend of Pliny the Younger, Juvenal, and Quintilian. The last-named makes brief reference to his death: *Multum in Valerio Flacco nuper amisimus,* "We have recently suffered a grievous loss in Valerius Flaccus." His unfinished *Argonautica,* a poem on the quest for the Golden Fleece, is remarkable chiefly for its romantic treatment of the heroine, Medea.

(Tr. J. H. Mozley)

But the princess with roving gaze follows the hero (for the god quenches not the fire), upon him her burning eyes are ever fixed; and now she has less delight in the battle scene before her, and chides her fears and the trouble cherished she knows not why.

And just as at first the South wind makes gentle sport as it softly stirs the leaves and topmost branches of the woodland, but soon the unlucky ships are feeling all its terrible strength: even so is Medea led on to the height of madness.

Obvius ut sera cum se sub nocte magistris
impingit pecorique pavor, qualesve profundum
per chaos occurrunt caecae sine vocibus umbrae;
haut secus in mediis noctis nemorisque tenebris
inciderant ambo attoniti iuxtaque subibant,
abietibus tacitis aut immotis cyparissis
adsimiles, rabidus nondum quas miscuit auster.

Id., VII, 400

PUBLIUS PAPINIUS STATIUS

C. A.D. 40 – 96

Pax secura locis et desidis otia vitae
et numquam turbata quies somnique peracti.
nulla foro rabies aut strictae in iurgia leges:
morum iura viris solum et sine fascibus aequum.

Silvae, III, v, 85

As when in the deep of night panic fear comes with full
shock on herd and herdsman, or as when sightless, voiceless ghosts meet in the abyss of hell: so in the midnight
shadows of the grove did they two meet and draw nigh
each other, awe-struck, like silent firs and motionless cypresses, when the mad South wind hath not yet inter-
twined their boughs.

P. P. STATIUS

Statius was born at Naples. His father was a teacher of rhetoric
and a poet. Vespasian summoned him to Rome as tutor to Domitian. The young Statius was victorious at the Augustalia contest in Naples, and later won a prize at Alba for a poem cele-
brating Domitian's exploits in the war against the Dacians. He
spent his last years in Naples. His surviving works are the *Silvae*, a collection of occasional verse, the *Thebais*, an epic poem
in twelve books on the civil war between the sons of Oedipus
and Jocasta, and the unfinished *Achilleis*, on the education of
Achilles by the centaur Chiron. He was much read in the Middle Ages. Among his admirers are Dante, Chaucer, Boccaccio,
Tasso, Malherbe, and Corneille. The most famous of his poems is
the invocation to Sleep, which inspired Sidney, Wordsworth,
and Keats, among others.

(Tr. J. H. Mozley)

Peace untroubled reigns there, and life is leisurely and
calm, with quiet undisturbed and sleep unbroken. No
madness of the forum, no laws unsheathed in quarrel; our
citizens admit but duty's ordinance, and Right holds sway
without rod or axe. [*Refers to poet's life in Naples*]

Crimine quo merui, iuvenis placidissimus divum,
quove errore miser, donis ut solus egerem,
Somne, tuis? tacet omne pecus volucresque feraeque
et simulant fessos curvata cacumina somnos,
nec trucibus fluviis idem sonus; occidit horror
aequoris, et terris maria adclinata quiescunt.

Id., V, iv, 1

Nec te totas infundere pennas
luminibus compello meis—hoc turba precetur
laetior—: extremo me tange cacumine virgae,
sufficit, aut leviter suspenso poplite transi.

Ibid., 16

Cui verba sonosque
monstravi questusque et vulnera caeca resolvi,
reptantemque solo demissus ad oscula nostra
erexi, blandoque sinu iam iamque cadentes
exsopire genas dulcesque accersere somnos.

Ibid., v, 81

Iamque per emeriti surgent confinia Phoebi
Titanis late, mundo subvecta silenti,
rorifera gelidum tenuaverat aera biga:
iam pecudes volucresque tacent, iam Somnus avaris
inrepsit curis pronusque ex aethere nutat,
grata laboratae referens oblivia vitae.   Thebais, I, 336

Exedere animum dolor iraque demens
et, qua non gravior mortalibus addita curis,
spes, ubi longa venit.   Id., II, 319

O youthful Sleep, gentlest of the gods, by what crime or error of mine have I deserved that I alone should lack thy bounty? Silent are all the cattle, and the wild beasts and the birds, and the weary tree tops have the semblance of weary slumber, nor do the raging torrents roar as they were wont; the ruffled waves have sunk to rest, and the sea leans against the earth's bosom and is still.

Nor do I bid thee shower all the influence of thy wings upon my eyes—that be the prayer of the happier folk!— touch me but with thy wand's extremest tip, 'tis enough, or pass over me with lightly hovering step.

I taught thee sounds and words and soothed thy complainings and thy hidden hurts, and as thou didst crawl on the ground, I stooped and lifted thee to my kisses, and lovingly on my bosom lulled to sleep thy drooping eyes, and bade sweet slumber take thee. [*Lament for his son*]

(*Tr. Alexander Pope*)

'Twas now the Time when Phoebus yields to Night,
And rising *Cynthia* sheds her silver Light
Wide o'er the World in solemn Pomp she drew
Her airy Chariot, hung with Pearly Dew;
All Birds and Beasts lye hush'd; Sleep steals away
The wild desires of Men, and Toils of Day,
And brings, descending thro' the silent Air,
A sweet forgetfulness of Human Care.

(*Tr. J. H. Mozley*)

Anguish devours the mind, and furious wrath, and hope than which the heart can bear no heavier burden, when 'tis long deferred.

O caeca nocentum
consilia! o semper timidum scelus!

Ibid., 489

Flammeus aeratis lunae tremor errat in armis.

Ibid., 532

Madidos ubi lucidus agros
ortus et algentes laxavit sole pruinas.

Id., III, 468

Cernis, ut ingentes murorum porrigat umbras
campus, et e speculis moriens intermicet ignis?
Moenia sunt iuxta; modo nox magis ipsa tacebat,
solaque nigrantes laxabant astra tenebras.

Id., XII, 250

O blind and guilty counsels! O ever timorous crime!

The flickering moonlight plays upon the brazen armor.

When the sun rising bright has melted the cold hoarfrost on the humid field.

Seest thou how the plain outstretched the vast shadow of the wall, and how the dying fires flicker from the watch towers? The city is hard by; night herself was more silent, and only the stars broke through the pitchy gloom.

P. CORNELIUS TACITUS

c. a.d. 55 – 117

In ingenio quoque, sicut in agro, quamquam grata quae diu serantur atque elaborentur, gratiora tamen quae sua sponte nascuntur. *Dialogus de Oratoribus, 6*

Is est orator qui de omni quaestione pulchre et ornate et ad persuadendum apte dicere pro dignitate rerum, ad utilitatem temporum, cum voluptate audientium possit.

Id., 30

Quo modo nobiles equos cursus et spatia probant, sic est aliquis oratorum campus, per quem nisi liberi et soluti ferantur debilitatur ac frangitur eloquentia. *Id., 39*

Memoriam quoque ipsam cum voce perdidissemus, si tam in nostra potestate esset oblivisci quam tacere.

De Vita et Moribus Iulii Agricolae, 2

Nerva Caesar res olim dissociabiles miscuerit, principatum ac libertatem. *Id., 3*

TACITUS

The most illustrious of all Roman historians, Tacitus was quaestor under Vespasian, edile under Titus, and praetor under Domitian. In A.D. 78 he married the daughter of Agricola, governor of Britain; he was proconsul of Asia from 112 to 116. Tacitus enjoyed a great reputation as an orator, but his speeches, as well as a book of verse, are lost. His extant works are *Dialogus de Oratoribus*, an inquiry into the causes of the decline of oratory; a *Life of Agricola; De Germania*, a description of the German tribes; the first four books and part of the fifth of the *Historiae;* and Books I to IV, XI to XV of the *Annals*, plus fragments of Books V, VI, and XVI. His unique qualities as an artist and student of human nature were not, apparently, appreciated in the centuries immediately after his death. He emerged momentarily from oblivion under the third-century Roman emperor Tacitus (275–76) who claimed proudly that he was a descendant of the historian and gave orders that his statue and works be placed in all libraries. His present fame began with the discovery of manuscripts of his works in the fifteenth century.

(Tr. Church and Brodribb)

As with earth, so with genius. Though time must be spent in the sowing and cultivation of some plants, yet those which grow spontaneously are the more pleasing.

The orator is he who can speak on every question with grace, elegance and persuasiveness, suitably to the dignity of his subject, the requirements of the occasion, and the taste of his audience.

Just as a spacious course tests a fine horse, so the orator has his field, and unless he can move in it freely and at ease, his eloquence grows feeble and breaks down.

We should have lost memory as well as voice, had it been in our power to forget as it was to keep silent.

Nerva Caesar blended things once irreconcilable: sovereignty and freedom.

Ut corpora nostra lente augescunt, cito extinguuntur, sic ingenia studiaque oppresseris facilius quam revocaveris.

Ibid.

Ego facilius crediderim naturam margaritis deesse quam nobis avaritiam. *Id.*, 12

Omne ignotum pro magnifico est. *Id.*, 30

Auferre trucidare rapere falsis nominis imperium, atque ubi solitudinem faciunt pacem appellant. *Ibid.*

Pessimum inimicorum genus, laudantes. *Id.*, 41

Proprium humani ingenii est odisse quem laeseris. *Id.*, 42

Tu vero felix, Agricola, non vitae tantum claritate, sed etiam opportunitate mortis. *Id.*, 45

Quotiens bella non ineunt, multum venatibus, plus per otium transigunt, dediti somno ciboque . . . ipsi hebent, mira diversitate naturae, cum idem homines sic ament inertiam et oderint quietem. *De Germania*, 15

Nemo enim illic vitia ridet, nec corrumpere et corrumpi saeculum vocatur. *Id.*, 19

Sanctius . . . ac reverentius visum de actis deorum credere quam scire. *Id.*, 34

Rara temporum felicitate, ubi sentire quae velis, et quae sentias dicere licet. *Historiae, I*, 1

Non esse curae deis securitatem nostram, esse ultionem.

Ibid., 3

Just as our bodies grow slowly but perish in a moment, so it is easier to crush talent and the arts than to revive them.

I could myself more readily believe that the natural properties of the pearls are in fault than our keenness for gain.

The unknown always passes for the marvellous.

To robbery, slaughter, plunder, they give the lying name of empire; they make a solitude and call it peace.

That worst class of enemies—the men who praise.

It is human nature to hate the man whom you have injured.

You were indeed fortunate, Agricola, not only in the splendor of your life, but also in the opportune moment of your death.

Whenever they are not fighting, they pass much of their time in the chase, and still more in idleness, giving themselves up to sleep and to feasting. . . . They themselves lie buried in sloth, a strange combination in their nature that the same men should be so fond of idleness, so averse to peace.

No one in Germany laughs at vice, nor do they call it the fashion to corrupt and to be corrupted.

It has been thought more pious and reverential to believe in the actions of the gods than to inquire about them.

The rare happiness of times when we may think what we please, and express what we think.

The gods have no concern for our happiness, but only for our punishment.

309

Cupidine ingenii humani libentius obscura credendi.

Ibid., 22

Mox, ut in magnis mendaciis, interfuisse se quidam et vidisse adfirmabant. *Ibid., 34*

Maior privatu visus dum privatus fuit, et omnium consensu
capax imperii nisi imperasset. *Ibid., 49*

Amicitias dum magnitudine munerum, non constantia
morum contineri putat, meruit magis quam habuit.

Id., III, 86

Etiam sapientibus cupido gloriae novissima exuitur.

Id., IV, 6

Dux Claudius Sanctus effosso oculo dirus ore, ingenio
debilior. *Ibid., 62*

Nondum victoria, iam discordia erat. *Ibid., 69*

Acerrima proximorum odia . . . *Ibid., 70*

Sine ira et studio. *Annales, I, 1*

Eam condicionem esse imperandi, ut non aliter ratio con-
stet quam si uni reddatur. *Ibid., 6*

At Romae ruere in servitium consules, patres, eques:
quanto quis illustrior, tanto magis falsi ac festinantes, vul-
tuque composito, ne laeti excessus principis, neu tristiores
primordio, lacrimas, guadium, questus adulationem mis-
cebant. *Ibid., 7*

. . . with that inclination so natural to the human mind readily to believe in the mysterious.

Soon, as happens with these great fictions, men asserted that they had been present and seen the deed.

He seemed greater than a subject while he was yet in a subject's rank, and by common consent would have been pronounced equal to empire, had he never been emperor.

Believing that friendship may be retained by munificent gifts rather than by consistency of character, he should have had more friends than he did.

The desire for glory is the last infirmity cast off even by the wise.

Their leader was Claudius Sanctus; one of his eyes had been destroyed; he was repulsive in countenance and even more feeble in intellect.

The victory was yet to be gained; dissension had already begun.

The extreme bitterness of family feuds . . .

Without either bitterness or partiality.

The condition of holding empire is that an account cannot be balanced unless it be rendered to one person.

Meanwhile at Rome people plunged into slavery—consuls, senators, knights. The higher a man's rank, the more eager his hypocrisy, and his looks the more carefully studied, so as neither to betray joy at the decease of one emperor nor sorrow at the rise of another, while he mingled delight and lamentations with his flattery.

Maiestate salva, cui maior e longinquo reverentia.

Ibid., 47

Deorum iniurias dis curae. *Ibid., 73*

Nulli iactantius maerent quam qui maxime laetantur.

Id., II, 77

Quanto plura recentium seu veterum revolvo, tanto magis
ludibria rerum mortalium cunctis in negotiis obversantur.

Id., III, 18

Adeo maxima quaeque ambigua sunt, dum alii quoquo
modo audita pro compertis habent, alii vera in contrarium
vertunt et gliscit utrumque posteritate. *Ibid., 19*

Corruptissima re publica plurimae leges. *Ibid., 27*

Nisi forte rebus cunctis inest quidam velut orbis, ut quem
ad modum temporum vices, ita morum vertantur; nec omnia apud priores meliora, sed nostra quoque aetas multa
laudis et artium imitanda posteris tulit. *Ibid., 55*

Praecipuum munus annalium reor ne virtutes sileantur
utque pravis dictis factisque ex posteritate et infamia
metus sit. *Ibid., 65*

Memoriae proditur Tiberium, quotiens curia egrederetur,
Graecis verbis in hunc modum eloqui solitum: "O homines
ad servitutem paratos!" *Ibid.*

Sed praefulgebant Cassius atque Brutus, eo ipso quod ef-
figies eorum non videbantur. *Ibid., 76*

Neque femina amissa pudicitia alia abnuerit. *Id., IV, 3*

Without compromising the imperial dignity, which inspired greater awe at a distance.

Wrongs done to the gods are the gods' concern.

None mourn more ostentatiously [over the death of Germanicus] than those who most rejoice in it.

The wider the scope of my reflection on the present and the past, the more I am impressed by their mockery of human plans in every transaction.

So obscure are the greatest events, that as some take for granted any hearsay, whatever its source, and others turn truth into falsehood, both errors find encouragement with posterity.

Laws were most numerous when the commonwealth was most corrupt.

Possibly there is in all things a kind of cycle, and there may be moral revolutions just as there are changes of seasons. Nor was everything better in the past, but our own age too has produced many specimens of excellence and culture for posterity to imitate.

This I regard as history's highest function, to let no worthy action be uncommemorated, and to hold out the reprobation of posterity as a terror to evil words and deeds.

Tradition says that Tiberius as often as he left the Senate-House used to exclaim in Greek, "How ready these men are to be slaves!"

But Cassius and Brutus outshone them all, from the very fact that their likenesses were not to be seen.

A woman after having parted with her virtue will hesitate at nothing.

Beneficia eo usque laeta sunt, dum videntur exsolvi posse:
ubi multum antevenere, pro gratia odium redditur.

Ibid., 18

Cunctas nationes et urbes populus aut primores aut singuli
regunt: delecta ex iis et consociata rei publicae forma
laudari facilius quam evenire, vel si evenit, haud diuturna
esse potest. *Ibid., 33*

Pauci prudentia honesta ab deterioribus, utilia ab noxiis
discernunt, plures aliorum eventis docentur. *Ibid.*

Etiam gloria ac virtus infensos habet, ut nimis ex propin-
quo diversa arguens. *Ibid.*

Libros per aediles cremandos censuere patres: sed man-
serunt, occultati et editi. Quo magis socordiam eorum in-
ridere libet, qui praesenti potentia credunt extingui posse
etiam sequentis aevi memoriam. Nam contra punitis ingeniis gliscit auctoritas, neque aliud externi reges aut qui
eadem saevitia usi sunt, nisi dedecus sibi atque illis
gloriam peperere. *Ibid., 35*

Insigne visum est earum Caesaris litterarum initium. . . .
"Quid scribam vobis, patres conscripti, aut quo modo
scribam aut quid omnino non scribam hoc tempore, quam
perir me cotidie sentio, si scio." Adeo facinora atque flagitia
sua ipsi quoque in supplicium verterant. *Id., VI, 6*

Populi imperium iuxta libertatem, paucorum dominatio
regiae libidini propior est. *Ibid., 42*

Benefits received are a delight to us as long as we think we can requite them; when that possibility is far exceeded, they are repaid with hatred instead of gratitude.

All nations and cities are ruled by the people, the nobility, or by one man. A constitution, formed by selection out of these elements, is easier to commend than to produce; or, if it is produced, it cannot be lasting.

It is but few who have the foresight to distinguish right from wrong or what is sound from what is hurtful, while most men learn wisdom from the fortunes of others.

Even honor and virtue make enemies, condemning, as they do, their opposites by too close a contrast.

His books, so the Senators decreed, were to be burnt by the aediles; but some copies were left which were concealed and afterwards published. And so one is all the more inclined to laugh at the stupidity of men who suppose that the despotism of the present can actually efface the memories of the next generation. On the contrary, the persecution of genius fosters its influence; foreign tyrants, and all who have imitated their oppression, have merely procured infamy for themselves and glory for their victims.

The beginning of the emperor's [Tiberius'] letters seemed very striking. . . . "May all the gods and goddesses destroy me more miserably than I feel myself to be daily perishing, if I know at this moment what to write to you, Senators, how to write it, or what, in short, not to write." So completely had his crimes and infamies recoiled, as a penalty, on himself.

Popular government almost amounts to freedom, while the rule of the few approaches closely to a monarch's caprice.

Haud ignarus summa scelera incipi cum periculo, peragi cum praemio. *Id., XII, 67*

Nihil rerum mortalium tam instabile ac fluxum est quam fama potentiae non sua vi nixae. *Id., XIII, 19*

Additurum principem defunctae templum et aras et cetera ostentandae pietati. *Id., XIV, 3*

Habet aliquid ex iniquo omne magnum exemplum, quod contra singulos utilitate publica rependitur. *Ibid., 44*

Plura saepe peccantur, dum demeremur quam dum offendimus. *Id., XV, 21*

Initia magistratuum nostrorum meliora ferme et finis inclinat, dum in modum candidatorum suffrage conquirimus. *Ibid.*

Auctor nominis eius Christus Tiberio imperitante per procuratorem Pontium Pilatum supplicio adfectus erat; repressaque in praesens exitiabilis superstitio rursum erumpebat, non modo per Iudaeam, originem eius mali, sed per urbem etiam, quo cuncta undique atrocia aut pudenda confluunt celebranturque. *Ibid., 44*

Impunitatis cupido. . . . magnis semper conatibus adversa. *Ibid., 50*

Cupido dominandi cunctis adfectibus flagrantior est. *Ibid., 53*

He knew that the greatest crimes are perilous in their inception, but well rewarded after their consummation.

Of all things human the most precarious and transitory is a reputation for power which has no strong support of its own.

"The emperor would add the honor of a temple and of shrines to the deceased lady, with every other display of filial affection." [*Nero's admiral, after telling him how to destroy Agrippina*]

There is some injustice in every great precedent, which, though injurious to individuals, has its compensation in the public advantage.

More faults are often committed while we are trying to oblige than while we are giving offense.

Our magistrates' early career is generally better than its close, which deteriorates when we are anxiously seeking votes, like candidates.

Christus, from whom the name [of Christians] had its origin, suffered the extreme penalty during the reign of Tiberius at the hands of one of our procurators, Pontius Pilatus, and most mischievous superstition, thus checked for the moment, again broke out not only in Judaea, the first source of the evil, but even in Rome where all things hideous and shameful from every part of the world find their center and become popular.

The desire of escape, that foe to all great enterprises.

The lust of dominion inflames the heart more than any other passion.

Interrogatusque a Nerone, quibus causis ad oblivionem sacramenti processisset, "Oderam te," inquit, "nec quisquam tibi fidelior militum fuit, dum amari meruisti. Odisse coepi, postquam parricida matris et uxoris, auriga et histrio et incendiarius extitisti."

Ibid., 67

AETNA

(c. a.d. 60)

Plurima pars scaenae rerum est fallacia: vates
sub terris nigros viderunt carmine manes
atque inter cineres Ditis pallentia regna:
mentiti vates Stygias undasque canesque.

Aetna, 75

Debita carminibus libertas ista; sed omnis
in vero mihi cura: canam quo fervida motu
aestuet Aetna novosque rapax sibi congerat ignes.

Ibid., 91

Nosse fidem rerum dubiasque exquirer causas,
ingenium sacrare caputque attollere caelo,
scire quot et quae sint magno natalia mundo
principia . . .
   divina est animi ac iucunda voluptas. *Ibid.*, 224

   Artificis naturae ingens opus aspice.

Ibid., 601

Questioned by Nero as to the motives which had led him on to forget his oath of allegiance, "I hated you," he replied, "yet not a soldier was more loyal to you while you deserved to be loved. I began to hate you when you became the murderer of your mother and your wife, a charioteer, an actor, and an incendiary."

AETNA

This didactic poem is an investigation into the causes of earthquakes. It was ascribed to Vergil and others, but all we know of its author is that he was a contemporary of Seneca. He displays enthusiasm for science and rejects mythological explanations of natural phenomena.

Most of the things we see on the stage are lies. In their verses poets evoke the shades of the underworld and the ashes of the dead in the lurid kingdom of Dis: their stories of Stygian waters and hounds are fictions.

Such liberties are the prerogative of poetry; for myself I am concerned solely with truth. I shall sing the movements that agitate fiery Aetna.

To know the truth, to inquire into uncertain causes, to immortalize genius, to lift one's head to the sky, to grasp the number and nature of the great universe's first principles . . .
    this is the mind's divine and gratifying joy.

Look upon the immense work of the artist Nature.

DECIMUS IUNIUS IUVENALIS

c. a.d. 60–117

Difficile est saturam non scribere. nam quis iniquae
tam patiens urbis, tam ferreus, ut teneat se . . .

Saturae, I, 30

Probitas laudatur et alget.
criminibus debent hortos praetoria mensas,
argentum vetus et stantem extra pocula caprum.

Ibid., 74

Si natura negat, facit indignatio versum.

Ibid., 79

Nil erit ulterius quod nostris moribus addat
posteritas, eadem facient cupientque minores,
omne in praecipiti vitium stetit. *Ibid., 147*

Ultra Sauromatas fugere hinc libet et glacialem
Oceanum, quotiens aliquid de moribus audent
qui Curios simulant et Bacchanalia vivunt. *Id., II, 1*

Quis tulerit Gracchos de seditione querentes?

Ibid., 24

Dat veniam corvis, vexat censura columbas.

Ibid., 63

JUVENAL

Juvenal, who is admired as the greatest Latin satirist, was born at Aquinum in Apulia and studied under Quintilian. He practiced for some time at the bar, and was banished for having written a poem ridiculing the actor Paris, one of Domitian's favorites. His satires, published under Trajan and Hadrian, castigate Domitian (he admits that it would be unwise to denounce the living). He attacks the vices of the plutocrats, the wickedness and immorality of women and foreigners (particularly Greeks), and laments the decline of the ancient aristocratic virtues.

It is hard not to write satire. For who is so tolerant of this unjust city, so unfeeling, as to hold himself back?

Honesty is praised and left out in the cold. Gardens, palaces, rich tables, old silver, and those embossed goats on the cups—men owe these to their crimes.

When talent fails, indignation writes the verse.

Posterity can add nothing more to our ways; those who come after will do likewise and lust after the same things. Every vice is at its pinnacle.

Whenever those who pose as Curii and live one long bacchanal venture a comment on morals, I long to flee to the Sarmatians and the Frozen Sea.

Who'd put up with complaints of sedition from the Gracchi?

Our censors are indulgent to the crows, but harass the doves.

Quid Romae faciam? mentiri nescio.

Id., *III*, *41*

Nil habet infelix paupertas durius in se,
quam quod ridiculos homines facit. *Ibid.*, *152*

Ventre nihil novi frugalius. *Id.*, *V*, *6*

Multa Pudicitiae veteris vestigia forsan
aut aliqua exstiterint et sub Iove, sed Iove nondum
barbato. *Id.*, *VI*, *14*

Rara avis in terris nigroque simillima cycno.

Ibid., *165*

Omnia Graece . . .
hoc sermone pavent, hoc iram gaudia curas,
hoc cuncta effundunt animi secreta: qui ultra?
concumbunt Graece. *Ibid.*, *187*

Hoc volo, sic iubeo; sit pro ratione voluntas.

Ibid., *223*

Praestabat castas humilis fortuna Latinas
quondam, nec vitiis contingi parva sinebant
tecta labor somnique breves et vellere Tusco
vexatae duraeque manus ac proximus urbi
Hannibal et stantes Collina turre mariti.
nunc patimur longae pacis mala: saevior armis
luxuria incubuit victumque ulciscitur orbem.

Ibid., *287*

"Pone seram, cohibe." sed quis custodiet ipsos
custodes, qui nunc lascivae furta puellae
hac mercede silent? crimen commune tacetur:
prospicit hoc prudens et ab illis incipit uxor.

Ibid., *347*

What am I to do in Rome? I don't know how to lie.

What is hardest to bear in dire poverty is that it makes a man a laughingstock.

I know nothing more easily satisfied than the belly.

Many vestiges of ancient modesty—well, at least some— may have survived even under Jove, but not after Jove had grown a beard.

[A chaste woman is] a rare bird on this earth, something like a black swan.

Nowadays everything's in Greek . . . in that language they express their fears, their anger, joy, worries, in it they pour out their heart's secrets: why, they even make Greek love!

This is what I want, such are my orders: my desire is reason enough!

Humble circumstances formerly kept the Latin women chaste; they were spared contact with vice because their houses were small, they worked hard, slept little, and their hands were roughed and calloused from working Tuscan wool, because Hannibal was just outside the gates and their men were on duty at the Collina tower. Now we are suffering the evils of a long peace: more destructive than war, luxury has come to stay with us and we are punished for our conquest of the world.

"Lock her up, confine her." But who will guard the guards themselves, who are rewarded for keeping quiet about the secret loves of their lascivious mistresses? You don't talk when you are an accomplice. The prudent wife foresees this and begins with them.

Summmum crede nefas animam praeferre pudori,
et propter vitam vivendi perdere causas.

Id., VIII, 83

Cantabit vacuus coram latrone viator.

Id., X, 22

Qui dabat olim
imperium fasces legiones omnia, nunc se
continet atque duas tantum res anxius optat,
panem et circenses. *Ibid., 78*

Mulier saevissima tunc est,
cum stimulos odio pudor admovet. *Ibid., 328*

Orandum est ut sit mens sana in corpore sano;
fortem posce animum mortis terrore carentem,
qui spatium vitae extremum inter munera ponat
naturae, qui ferre queat quoscumque labores,
nesciat irasci, cupiat nihil et potiores
Herculis aerumnas credat saevosque labores
et venere et cenis et pluma Sardanapali. *Ibid., 356*

Nullum numen habes, si sit prudentia: nos te,
nos facimus, Fortuna, deam caeloque locamus.

Ibid., 365

Ut sit magna, tamen certe lenta ira deorum est.

Id., XII, 100

Ploratur lacrimis amissa pecunia veris.

Id., XIII, 134

Humani generis mores tibi nosse volenti
sufficit una domus. *Ibid., 159*

Think it the greatest impiety to prefer life to disgrace, and for the sake of life to lose the reason for living.

The traveler with empty purse can whistle when a thief stops him.

Those who formerly made consuls and generals, had legions in their gift, and all the rest are content with much less now: they clamor for only two things—bread and games.

A woman is never more ruthless than when shame gives a spur to her hatred.

We should pray for a sound mind in a sound body; for a heart that fears not death, deems mortality one of nature's gifts, can endure any kind of hard work, knows no anger and covets naught, and thinks Hercules' labors and hardships better than love-making, banquets, or the soft couches of Sardanapalus.

You would not be a divine being were mankind more intelligent: it is we who make you a goddess, Fortune, we who place you in heaven.

However great it may be, the anger of the gods is certainly slow.

One sheds real tears when one loses one's own money.

If you would study the ways of the human race, one household is enough.

Quippe minuti
semper et infirmi est animi exiguique voluptas
ultio. Continuo sic collige, quod vindicta
nemo magis gaudet quam femina.   *Ibid., 189*

Scelus intra se tacitum qui cogitat ullum
facti crimen habet.   *Ibid., 209*

Maxima debetur puero reverentia.
          Id., XIV, 47

Crescitur amor nummi quantum ipsa pecunia crevit.
          Ibid., 139

Mollissima corda
humano generi dare se natura fatetur,
quae lacrimas dedit; haec nostri pars optima sensus.
          Ibid., 131

Sed iam serpentum maior concordia.
          Ibid., 159

Yes, revenge is always the pleasure of a petty, insignificant, weak mind. Infer this directly from the fact that no one enjoys revenge more than women.

Who silently meditates a crime within himself is already guilty.

We owe the greatest respect to a child.

The richer you get, the more you love money.

Nature, who gave us tears, acknowledges that she endowed the human race with a tender heart: this is the noblest part of our moral nature.

But nowadays there is more concord among snakes [than among men].

GAIUS PLINIUS
CAECILIUS SECUNDUS

A.D. 61 or 62 – c. 114

Meminimus, quanto maiore animo honestatis fructus in conscientia quam in fama reponatur. Sequi enim gloria, non adpeti debet.   *Epistulae, I, 8*

Hoc pluribus visum est. Numerantur enim sententiae, non ponderantur; nec aliud in publico consilio potest fieri, in quo nihil est tam inaequale quam aequalitas ipsa. Nam, cum sit impar prudentia, par omnium ius est.   *Id., II, 12*

Dicere enim solebat nullum esse librum tam malum, ut non aliqua parte prodesset.   *Id., III, 5*

Quatenus nobis denegatur diu vivere, relinquamus aliquid, quo nos vixisse testemur.   *Ibid., 7*

Nescio quo pacto vel magis homines iuvat gloria lata quam magna.   *Id., IV, 12, 7*

Mihi autem videtur acerba semper et immatura mors eorum, qui immortale aliquid parant.   *Id., V, 5*

PLINY THE YOUNGER

Born at Comum (on Lake Como), nephew and adoptive son of
Pliny the Elder, Pliny studied under Quintilian. After a brilliant
career as a lawyer, he was praetor, prefect of the treasury, consul, and governor of Bithynia under Trajan. He was a close
friend of Tacitus and a patron of Suetonius and Martial, and
used his great wealth to found schools, libraries, temples, etc.
He left the *Panegyricus,* a speech addressed to Trajan when accepting the consulship (in A.D. 100), and ten books of *Letters,*
which he himself arranged for publication.

(Tr. Melmoth, revised by W. M. L. Hutchison)

I am sensible how much nobler it is to place the reward of
virtue in the silent approbation of one's own breast than in
the applause of the world. Glory ought to be the conse-
quence, not the motive of our actions.

That was what seemed good to the majority. Votes go by
number not weight, nor can it be otherwise in assemblies
of this kind where nothing is more unequal than that
equality which prevails in them; for though every member
has the same right of suffrage, every member has not the
same strength of judgment to direct it.

It was a maxim of his [Pliny the Elder's] that no book was
so bad but some profit might be gleaned from it.

Since it is not granted us to live long, let us transmit to
posterity some memorial that we *have* at least *lived.*

I know not how it is, mankind are generally more pleased
with an extensive than even a great reputation.

For my part I regard every death as cruel and premature
that removes one who is preparing some immortal work.

Hominis est enim adfici dolore, sentire, resistere tamen et solacia admittere, non solaciis non egere.   *Id., VIII, 16*

Est dolendi modus, non est timendi. Doleas enim, quantum scias accidisse, timeas quantum possit accidere.

Ibid., 17

Quis vitia odit, homines odit.   *Ibid., 22*

Alius alium, ego beatissimum exisitimo, qui bonae mansuraeque famae praesumptione perfruitur certusque posteritatis cum futura gloria vivit.   *Id., IX, 3*

Impensa monumenti supervacua est; memoria nostra durabit si vita meruimus.   *Ibid., 19*

Nihil peccat nisi quod nihil peccat.   *Ibid., 26*

Ut satius est unum aliquid insigniter facere quam plurima mediocriter, ita plurima mediocriter, si non possis unum aliquid insigniter.   *Ibid., 29*

Neque enim soli iudicant, qui maligne legunt.   *Ibid., 38*

Sine auctore vero propositi libelli nullo crimine locum habent debere. Nam et pessimi exempli, nec nostri saeculi est.   *Id., X, 97 (Traianus Plinio)*

Melius omnibus quam singulis creditur. Singuli enim decipere et decipi possunt: nemo omnes, neminem omnes fefellerunt.   *Panegyricus, 62*

Cum essent civium domini, libertorum erant servi.

Ibid., 88

For it is the very essence of human nature to feel those impressions of sorrow, which it yet endeavors to resist, and to admit, not to be above, consolation.

Grief has limits, whereas apprehension has none. For we grieve only for what we know *has* happened, but we fear all that possibly *may* happen.

He who hates vice, hates mankind.

Men differ in their notions of supreme happiness, but in my opinion it consists in the foretaste of an honest and abiding fame, the assurance of being admired by posterity, the realization, while yet living, of future glory.

A monument is a useless expense; our memory will endure if we have earned it by our life.

His only fault is that he has no faults.

As it is far better to excel in any single art than to arrive only at a mediocrity in several, so on the other hand a moderate skill in several is to be preferred where one cannot attain to excellency in any.

For the malicious is not, I trust, the only judicious reader.

Information without the accuser's name subscribed must not be admitted in evidence against anyone, as it is introducing a very dangerous precedent, and by no means agreeable to the spirit of the age. [*Trajan to Pliny, on Christians*]

It is better to believe the world than individuals. For individuals can deceive and be deceived, whereas no one ever fooled the world, nor did the world fool one individual.

Though they were the masters of the citizens, they were slaves of freedmen. [*Refers to the predecessors of Trajan*]

GAIUS SUETONIUS TRANQUILLUS

A.D. 70 – C. 140

Tu enim, Caesar, civitatem dare potes hominibus, verbo non potes. *De Grammaticis, XXII*

Cur non illi quoque eadem furta temptarent? Verum intellecturos facilius esse Herculi clavam quam Homero versum subripere. *Vita Vergilii, XLVI*

Adeo . . . consternatum ferunt, ut per continuos menses barba capilloque summisso caput interdum foribus illideret vociferans: "Quintili Vare, legiones redde!"
De Vita Caesarum, Divus Augustus, XXIII, 2

Urbem . . . excoluit adeo, ut iure sit gloriatus marmoream se relinquere, quam latericiam accepisset.
Id., XXVIII, 3

Cum aliquos numquam soluturos significare vult, "ad Kalendas Graecas soluturos" ait. *Id., LXXXVII, 1*

Supremo die . . . amicos admissos percontatus, ecquid iis videretur mimum vitae commode transegisse.
Id., XCIX, 1

SUETONIUS

Suetonius was probably born in Rome. He practiced at the bar, declined an appointment as military tribune for which he was recommended by Pliny the Younger, and later held an important secretarial post under Hadrian. Dismissed, possibly for disrespect to Hadrian's shrewish wife, he devoted himself to writing the *Lives of the Caesars*. He also composed a number of scholarly works, now lost except for fragments from the lives of grammarians and Roman poets. As a historian, he is remarkable for biographical detail and documentation: in his post under Hadrian he had access to the imperial archives.

You, Caesar, can grant citizenship to people, but not to words. [*Marcus Pomponius Marcellus, a grammarian criticizing an improper usage in a speech by Tiberius*]

I wish they'd try stealing from him! They'd learn it is easier to take Hercules' club away from him than one line from Homer. [*Vergil on critics who accused him of plagiarizing Homer*]

So great was his [the emperor Augustus'] dismay, it is said, that for months on end he did not shave or have his hair cut, and from time to time beat his head against the door, shouting, "Quintilius Varus, give me back my legions!"

He made so many improvements in Rome, he could rightly boast that he had found it brick and left it marble.

When he wanted to suggest that a debt would never be made good, he used the expression, "He'll pay on the Greek calends."

On the day of his death, he had his friends in and asked what they thought of his performance in life's comedy.

Praesidibus onerandas tributo provincias suadentibus rescripsit boni pastores esse tondere pecus, non deglubere.

Id., Tiberius, XXXII, 2

Infensus turbae faventi adversus studium suum exclamavit, "Utinam p.R. unam cervicem haberet!"

Id., Caligula, XXX, 2

Cum de supplicio cuiusdam capite damnati ut ex more subscriberet admoneretur: "Quam vellem," inquit, "nescire litteras."

Id., Nero, X, 2

Qualis artifex pereo!

Ibid., XLIX, 1

Reprehendenti filio Tito, quod etiam urinae vectigal commentus esset, pecuniam ex prima pensione admovit ad nares, scistitans num odore offenderetur.

Id., Divus Vespasianus, XXIII, 3

Puto deus fio.

Ibid., 4

Recordatus quondam super cenam, quod nihil cuiquam toto die praestitisset, memorabilem illam meritoque laudatam vocem edidit: "Amici, diem perdidi."

Id., Divus Titus, VIII, 1

Condicionem principum miserrimam aiebat, quibus de coniuratione comperta non crederetur nisi occisis.

Id., Domitianus, XX

To provincial governors who wanted to raise taxes, he [Tiberius] wrote that good shepherds shear their sheep but do not skin them.

Enraged at the mob for favoring a proposal against his wishes, he [Caligula] exclaimed, "Would that the Roman people had but a single neck!"

When he [Nero] was asked to sign the usual warrant for a man's execution, he said, "How I wish I had never learned to write!"

What an artist is lost with me!
[*Nero, shortly before his death*]

When his son Titus criticized him [Vespasian] for making people pay to use the public urinals, he held up to his nose one of the first coins so collected, asking him whether its smell was offensive.

I believe I'm turning into a god. [*Vespasian, before dying*]

On one occasion, recalling at dinner that he [Titus] had not granted a single favor all day, he uttered this memorable and justly praised remark: "Friends, I have lost a day."

[Domitian] used to say that the lot of rulers was the worst, because nobody would believe that their lives were threatened by a conspiracy until after they had been killed.

PUBLIUS ANNIUS FLORUS

fl. c. A.D. 74

Mulier intra pectus omnis celat virus pestilens;
dulce de labris loquuntur, corde vivunt noxio.
De Qualitate Vitae, III

Quando ponebam novellas arbores mali et piri,
cortici summae notavi nomen ardoris mei.
nulla fit exinde finis vel quies cupidinis:
crescit arbor, gliscit ardor: animus implet litteras.
Id., V

Cive Romano per orbem nemo vivit rectius:
quippe malim unum Catonem quam trecentos Socratas.
Id., VII, 2

Consulent fiunt quotannis et novi proconsules:
solus aut rex aut poeta non quotannis nascitur.
Id., IX

Ne pereant lege mane rosas: cito virgo senescit.
Id., XI, 9

Difficilius est provincias obtinere quam facere; viribus pa-
rantur, iure retinentur.
*Epitomae de Tito Livio Bellorum Omnium Annorum DCC
Libri II, II, xxx, 29*

FLORUS

Florus, a native of Africa (or Spain) lived in Rome under Trajan and Hadrian. He wrote light verse, some of which has survived, and an abridged history of Rome (based on Livy), which was much read in the Middle Ages.

Every woman conceals a destructive poison in her breast. While women's lips speak sweetly, they are plotting mischief.

When I was planting young apple trees and pear trees, I cut the name of my dearest on the bark. Since, there has been no end or peace to my passion: as the tree grows, my love glows; the heart gives body to the letters.

No one in the world lives more uprightly than the citizen of Rome; indeed, I prefer a single Cato to three hundred Socrateses.

New consuls and proconsuls are made every year, only patrons or poets are not born every year.

Pick roses in the morning, lest they fade: a maiden soon grows old.

It is harder to keep provinces than to conquer them; acquired by force, they are held by justice.

PUBLIUS AELIUS HADRIANUS

A.D. 76 – 138

Animula vagula blandula,
hospes comesque corporis,
quae nunc abibis in loca,
pallidula, rigida, nudula,
nec ut soles dabis iocos?

AULUS GELLIUS

C. A.D. 123 – C. 165

Nihil cum fidibus graculo, nihil cum amaracino sui.

Noctes Atticae, Praefatio, 19

Si sine uxore pati possemus, Quirites, omnes ea molestia
careremus; sed quoniam ita natura tradidit, ut nec cum
illis satis commode, nec sine illis ullo modo vivi possit,
saluti perpetuae potius quam brevi voluptati consulendum
est.

Id., I, 6, 1

HADRIAN

Proclaimed emperor in 117, Hadrian was a cousin of Trajan. He was a student of philosophy and literature, proficient in all the arts, and a writer of undistinguished verse. One poem, composed on his deathbed, has become famous.

(Tr. Lord Byron)

Ah! gentle, fleeting, wav'ring sprite,
Friend and associate of this clay!
To what unknown region borne
Wilt thou now wing thy distant flight?
No more with wonted humour gay,
But pallid, cheerless, and forlorn.

AULUS GELLIUS

Aulus Gellius studied literature at Rome and philosophy at Athens. On his return to Rome he practiced law. His *Attic Nights* is a collection of scattered notes dealing with philosophy, criticism, jurisprudence, biography, and other matters—"a kind of literary storehouse" (*quasi quoddam litterarum penus*), as he describes it. He wrote it to amuse and instruct his children. It has preserved for us excerpts from many Greek and Latin writings otherwise lost.

The jackdaw has no use for a lyre, nor the hog for sweet-smelling ointment. [*Proverb*]

Could we dispense with wives, Romans, we would have one nuisance less. However, since nature has decreed that we cannot live very comfortably with them and without them not at all, we should look rather to our long-term welfare than to our short-term pleasure. [*Quotation from a speech by Quintus Metellus Numidicus, consul 109* B.C.]

Di immortales virtutem approbare, non adhibere debent.

Id., I, 6, 8

Religentem esse oportet; religiosum nefas. *Id., IV, 9*

Video barbam et pallium: philosophum nondum video.

Id., IX, 2, 1

Alius quidam veterum poetarum cuius nomen mihi nunc
memoriae non est, veritatem temporis filiam esse dixit.

Id., XII, 11, 7

Consuetudo vicit: quae cum omnium domina rerum, tum
maxime verborum est. *Ibid., 13, 4*

Turpius esse dicebat Favorinus philosophus exigue atque
frigide laudari, quam insectanter et graviter vituperari.

Id., XIX, 3, 1

QUINTUS SEPTIMIUS
FLORENS TERTULLIANUS

c. a.d. 160 – c. 223

Cum odio sui coepit veritas. Simul atque apparuit, inimica
est. *Apologeticus, VII, 3*

Caecitatis duae species facile concurrunt, ut qui non vident
quae sunt, videre videantur quae non sunt. *Id., IX, 20*

We may expect the immortal gods to approve virtue, not to endow us with it. [*Same as above*]

It is reasonable to be religious, abominable to be superstitious. [*Anonymous poet*]

I see the beard and the cloak: I have yet to see the philosopher. [*Herodes Atticus*]

Another old poet whose name I cannot recall just now, said that truth is the daughter of time.

Usage won out—the supreme authority in all things, and especially in language.

The philosopher Favorinus used to say that it is worse to get lukewarm or faint praise than unrelieved vicious abuse.

TERTULLIAN

Born in Carthage of pagan parents, Tertullian studied law, rhetoric, and philosophy. Impressed by the courage of the martyrs, he became a Christian. He wrote about fifty books; thirty-two have survived. The best known are the *Apologeticus*, a spirited defense of Christianity in which he uses irony and sarcasm with great effectiveness. During a stay in Rome (c. 204), he composed *De Spectaculis* (on public spectacles), which displeased the Roman clergy because of its harshness. Back in Africa, he fell in with Montanist heretics and broke with the Church; later he left Montanism to found a new sect.

The first reaction to truth is hatred. The moment it appears, it is treated as an enemy.

Two kinds of blindness are readily combined: people who cannot see what really is are the very ones who see what is not.

341

Invisibilis est, etsi videatur; incomprehensibilis, etsi per gratiam repraesentetur; inaestimabilis, etsi humanis sensibus aestimetur. *Id., XVII, 2*

O testimonium animae naturaliter Christianae! *Ibid., 6*

Haec et nos risimus aliquando. De vestris sumus. Fiunt, non nascuntur Christiani. *Id., XVIII, 4*

Et nunc adventum eius expectant, nec alia magis inter nos et illos conpulsatio est quam quod iam venisse non credunt. *Id., XXI, 15*

[Existimant] Omnis publicae cladis, omnis popularis incommodi Christianos esse in causam. . . . Si caelum stetit, si terra movit, si fames, si lues, statim Christianos ad leonem! adclamatur. Tantos ad unum? *Id., XL, 2*

Plures efficimur quotiens metimur a vobis; semen est sanguis Christianorum. *Id., L, 13*

Ut est aemulatio divinae rei et humanae, cum damnamur a vobis, a deo absolvimur. *Ibid., 16*

Omne enim spectaculum sine concussione spiritus non est. Ubi enim voluptas, ibi est studium, per quod scilicet voluptas sapit; ubi studium, ibi et aemulatio, per quam studium sapit. Porro et ubi aemulatio, ibi et furor et bilis et ira et dolor et cetera ex his, quae cum his non conpetunt disciplinae. *De spectaculis, XV*

Certum est quia impossibile. *De Carne Christi, V*

[God] is invisible, although seen, incomprehensible although revealed by grace, unfathomable although fathomed by the human senses.

O evidence of a soul naturally Christian! [*The belief in a supreme being*]

There was a time when we, too, laughed at these things [*Christian dogmas*]. We are of your number. Christians are made, not born.

Even now they [the Jews] await His coming, nor is there any greater contention between us and them, than that they do not believe He has already come.

They hold the Christians responsible for every public calamity, for every common misfortune. . . . If the sky stops moving, if the earth moves, if there is a famine, if there is a plague, at once the cry goes up: The Christians to the lion! So many Christians to one lion?

Every time you mow us down we spring up more numerous: the blood of Christians is seed.

God's ways are at odds with human ways: condemned by you, we are acquitted by God.

There is no public entertainment that does not inflict spiritual damage. For where there is pleasure, there is eagerness, which adds spice to pleasure; where there is eagerness there is taking of sides, which adds spice to eagerness. And where there is taking of sides, there is rage, and bile and anger and pain and all the other things that follow from them, which like them are incompatible with spiritual discipline.

It is certain because it is impossible.

Iam illa obiici solita vox: non habeo aliquid quo vivam. Districtius repercuti potest: vivere ergo habes?

De idololatria, V

MINUCIUS FELIX

fl. c. a.d. 180

Quod est in liberis amabilius—adhuc annis innocentibus et adhuc dimidiata verba temptantibus, loquellam ipso offensantis linguae fragmine dulciorem.   *Octavius, II, 1*

Hic non videri potest: visu clarior est; nec comprehendi: tactu purior est; nec aestimari: sensibus maior est, infinitus, immensus et soli sibi tantus, quantus est, notus.

Id., XVIII, 8

Ita corpus in sepulcro, ut arbores in hiberno: occultant virorem ariditate mentita. . . . Expectandum nobis etiam corporis ver est.   *Id., XXXIV, 11*

Vos scelera admissa punitis, apud nos et cogitare peccare est; vos conscios timetis, nos etiam conscientiam solam.

Id., XXXV, 6

Nobilitate generosus es? Parentes tuos laudas? Omnes tamen pari sorte nascimur, sola virtute distinguimur.

Id., XXXVII, 10

Non eloquimur magna sed vivimus.   *Id., XXXVIII, 6*

The [Christian idol-maker's] usual objection is: "I have no other way of making a living." To which the somewhat harsh reply can be made: "Do you have to live?"

MINUCIUS FELIX

Minucius Felix was born in Africa and distinguished himself as a lawyer in Rome. A convert to Christianity, he defended his new faith in *Octavius*, a dialogue. His arguments stress the moral values of the Christian religion.

(Tr. G. H. Rendall)

Children still at the lovable stage of the years of innocence, trying to form broken words, in the pretty prattle which the broken efforts of a stumbling tongue render still sweeter . . .

God cannot be seen: he is too bright for sight; nor grasped: he is too pure for touch; nor measured: for he is beyond all sense, infinite, measureless, his dimension known to himself alone.

The body in the grave is like trees in winter; they conceal their greenness under a show of dryness. . . . We too must wait for the springtime of the body.

You punish crimes committed, with us the thought of crime is sin; you fear the voice of witnesses, we the sole voice of conscience.

Are you of noble lineage? proud of your ancestry? Yet we are all born equal, virtue alone gives mark.

We do not preach great things but we live them.

Contra verbosos noli contendere verbis:
sermo datur cunctis, animi sapientia paucis.   *I, 10*

Officium alterius multis narrare memento;
at quaecumque aliis benefeceris ipse, sileto.   *I, 15*

Qui simulat verbis nec corde est fidus amicus,
to quoque fac simules: sic ars deluditur arte.   *I, 26*

Linque metum leti; nam stultum est tempore in omni,
dum mortem metuas, amittere gaudia vitae.   *II, 3*

Rebus in adversis animum submittere noli:
spem retine; spes una hominem nec morte relinquit.

II, 25

Instrue praeceptis animum, ne discere cessa;
nam sine doctrina vita est quasi mortis imago.

III, 1

Uxorem fuge ne ducas sub nomine dotis,
nec retinere velis, si coeperit esse molesta.

III, 12

Cum sis incautus nec rem ratione gubernes,
noli Fortunam, quae non est, dicere caecam.   *IV, 3*

Cum tibi praeponas animalia bruta timore,
unum hominem scito tibi praecipue esse timendum.

IV, 11

This collection of moral aphorisms, sometimes ascribed to a certain Cato of Córdoba, comprises 145 couplets. It was very popular in the Carolingian epoch, and used in schools.

Do not fight verbosity with words: speech is given to all, intelligence to few.

Remember to speak often of another's kindness, but keep silent about your own good deeds.

With him who dissembles in words and is not a loyal friend at heart, be sure to dissemble too. So cunning outwits cunning.

Give up fearing death; it is at all times foolish to miss life's pleasures for fear of death.

In adversity do not lose heart; hold on to hope: hope alone does not desert a man even at death.

Furnish your mind with precepts, never stop learning; for life without learning is but an image of death.

Avoid taking a wife for the sake of her dowry, nor should you keep one when she grows troublesome.

When you are imprudent and fail to steer your course by reason, do not call Fortune blind, for she is not.

When your mind is obsessed with fear of brute beasts, know that it is man you should fear above all.

Tempora longa tibi noli promittere vitae:
quocumque incedis, sequitur Mors corporis umbra.

IV, 37

THASCIUS CAECILIUS CYPRIANUS

C. A.D. 200 – 258

Habere non potest Deum patrem qui ecclesiam non habet
matrem.   *De catholicae ecclesiae unitate, VI*

Inexpiabilis et gravis culpa discordiae nec passione purga-
tur. Esse martyr non posset qui in ecclesia non est.

Id., XIV

Mundus ecce nutat et labitur et ruinam sui non iam senectute rerum sed fine testatur.   *De mortalitate, XXV*

Madet orbis mutuo sanguine . . . homicidium quum ad-
mittunt singuli, crimen est, virtus vocatur quum publice
geritur.   *Epistulae, I, 6*

TERENTIANUS MAURUS

fl. A.D. 200

Habent sua fata libelli.   *De syllabis, 1, 1286*

Do not promise yourself a long life: wherever you go, Death goes too, like your body's shadow.

ST. CYPRIAN

A father of the Church, St. Cyprian was born at Carthage. He taught rhetoric, became a Christian in 246, and bishop of Carthage in 248. He was beheaded for refusal to sacrifice to the gods.

He who does not have the Church for mother cannot have God for father.

The grave, inexpiable sin of schism is not to be atoned for by suffering. A man not in the Church cannot be a martyr.

The world is tottering to its ruin, evidence not merely of decrepitude but of final collapse.

The world is drenched in mutual slaughter. . . . Held to be a crime when committed by individuals, homicide is called a virtue when committed by the state.

TERENTIANUS MAURUS

A grammarian, author of *De litteris syllabis et metris Horatii* (in verse).

Books have their own destiny.

M. AURELIUS OLYMPIUS
NEMESIANUS

C. A.D. 260

Cantet, amat quod quisque: levant et carmina curas.

Ecloga, IV

Omnia tempus alit, tempus rapit: usus in arto est.

Ibid., 32

PENTADIUS

C. A.D. 290

Hic est ille, suis nimium qui credidit undis
Narcissus vero dignus amore puer.
cernis ab irriguo repetentem gramine ripas
ut per quas periit crescere possit aquas.

Narcissus

Crede ratem ventis, animum ne crede puellis;
namque est feminea tutior unda fide.　*De femina*

PERVIGILIUM VENERIS

C. A.D. 350

Cras amet qui nunquam amavit quique amavit cras amet:
ver novum, ver iam canorum, ver renatus orbis est;
vere concordant amores, vere nubunt alites,
et nemus comam resolvit de maritis imbribus.　　*1*

NEMESIANUS

A native of Africa, Nemesianus won a poetic contest against Emperor Numerianus without losing the latter's favor. He is the author of four eclogues and a didactic poem on hunting.

Let everyone sing of what he loves: songs, too, relieve love's anxieties.

Time feeds all things, time takes them away; enjoyment lasts but a brief space.

PENTADIUS

Pentadius was an African-born author of epigrams and elegies.

This is Narcissus, the youth worthy of genuine love, who trusted his native waters too far. You see him turning from the moist meadow to the river's edge, seeking to become a flower in the very waters which spelled his doom.

Entrust your boat to the winds, but not your heart to girls; the waves are safer than a woman's promise.

PERVIGILIUM VENERIS

The author of this famous hymn to Venus is unknown, and its date is purely conjectural.

(Tr. J. W. Mackail)

Tomorrow shall be love for the loveless, and for the lover tomorrow shall be love. Spring is young, spring now is singing, spring is the world reborn. In spring the loves make accord, in spring the birds mate, and the woodland loosens her tresses under nuptial showers.

Illa cantat, nos tacemus: quando ver venit meum?
quando fiam uti chelidon ut tacere desinam?   *XXII*

DECIMUS MAGNUS AUSONIUS

c. a.d. 310 – 395

Cum glaucus opaco
respondet colli fluvius, frondere videntur
fluminei latices et palmite consitus amnis.
quis color ille vadis, seras cum propulit umbras
Hesperus et viridi perfundit monte Mosellam!

Mosella, 189

Uxor, vivamus quod viximus, et teneamus
nomina, quae primo sumpsimus in thalamo:
nec ferat ulla dies, ut commutemur in aevo;
quin tibi sim iuvenis tuque puella mihi.

Epigrammata, XL, Ad Uxorem, 1

Nos ignoremus, quid sit matura senectus.
scire aevi meritum, non numerare decet.

Ibid., 7

She sings, we are mute: when is my spring coming? When shall I be as the swallow, that I may cease to be voiceless?

AUSONIUS

Ausonius was born at Bordeaux. After practicing at the bar, he became a teacher of rhetoric, and in 367 was appointed tutor to Emperor Valentinian's son, Gratian. Later he was governor of Gaul. His works include idylls, eclogues, epistles, epigrams, and a poem on the Moselle, etc., all of which reflect intimate knowledge of the classics. A number of his pieces are merely complicated word games, more or less humorous, in which he displays his technical skill. One of these, the *Cento nuptialis*, is made up entirely of half verses from the *Aeneid*, with a risqué twist. He sometimes expresses religious feelings, but his Christianity is skin-deep. *Satis precum datum Deo* ("Now I have prayed enough!") he exclaims at the end of a poem describing his daily devotions. He excels in evocations of everyday life and descriptions of nature.

When the sky-blue river reflects the darkened hill, the flowing stream seems to put forth leaves, and the river to be planted with the shoots of vines. How colorful the waters when Hesperus casts late shadows and the green mountain is spread over the Moselle!

Wife, let us live as we have lived, and keep calling each other by the names we first used when we married. May the day never come that we should change, may I always be your young man, and you my girl.

Let us never know what old age is. Let us know the happiness time brings, not count the years.

Lais anus Veneri speculum dico: dignum habeat se
aeterna aeternum forma ministerium.
at mihi nullus in hoc usus, quia cernere talem,
qualis sum, nolo, qualis eram, nequeo.
De Laide dicante Veneri speculum suum,
Epigrammata, LXV

Nil homine terra peius ingrato creat.
Epigrammata, CXL, 1

Prima urbes inter, divum domus, aurea Roma.
Ordo nobilium Urbium, I

Omne aevum curae: cunctis sua displicet aetas.
Idyllia, XV, 10

Optima Graiorum sententia, quippe homini aiunt,
non nasci esse bonum, natum aut cito morte potiri.
Ibid., 49

Nemo silens placuit; multi brevitate loquendi.
Epistolae, XIV, 44

I, the aged Lais, dedicate my mirror to Venus; let eternal beauty receive the eternal tribute it deserves. The mirror is no longer of any use to me, for I do not want to see myself as I am, and I cannot see myself as I was.

The earth produces nothing worse than an ungrateful man.

First among cities, home of the gods, golden Rome.

Every age has its troubles: everyone dislikes his own time of life.

The Greeks have an excellent maxim: they say that the best thing for a man is not to be born, or, once born, to die quickly.

No one pleases by silence; many please by brevity of speech.

AMMIANUS MARCELLINUS

A.D. 330 – after 391

Paucae domus studiorum seriis cultibus antea celebratae, nunc ludibriis ignavae torpentis exundant. . . . Pro philosopho cantor, et in locum oratoris doctor artium ludicrarum accitur, et bibliothecis sepulcrorum ritu in perpetuum clausis, organa fabricantur hydraulica, et lyrae ad speciem carpentorum ingentes. *Res gestae, XIV, vi, 18*

Cum nos cauti vel (ut verius dixerim) timidi, nihil exaggeremus, praeter ea quae fidei testimonia neque incerta monstrarunt. *Id., XVIII, vi, 23*

Christianam religionem absolutam et simplicem anili superstitione confundens, in qua scrutanda perplexius quam componenda gravius excitavit discidia plurima, quae progressa fusius aluit concertatione verborum, ut catervis antistitum iumentis publicis ultro citroque discurrentibus per synodos (quas appellant), dum ritum omnem ad suum trahere conatur arbitrium, rei vehiculariae succederet nervos. *Id., XXI, xvi, 18*

AMMIANUS MARCELLINUS

Born at Antioch, author of a history that was intended to be a continuation of Tacitus, Ammianus Marcellinus is remarkable for his objectivity and impartiality. He offers interesting glimpses of the cultural decay of his age, the dissensions among the various Christian sects, and the attempts of the emperors to exploit them for their own purposes. The historian himself served under Julian the Apostate in the Persian campaign, and a great deal of his history is based on firsthand observation. The work originally had thirty-one books, but the first thirteen are lost; the surviving portion covers the period from 352 to 378.

(Tr. John C. Rolfe)

The few houses that were formerly famed for devotion to serious pursuits now teem with the sports of sluggish indolence. . . . In place of the philosopher the singer is called in, and in place of the orator the teacher of stagecraft, and while the libraries are shut up forever like tombs, water-organs are manufactured and lyres as large as carriages.

For I am too cautious or (to speak more truly) too timid, to exaggerate anything beyond what is proven by trustworthy and sure evidence.

The plain and simple religion of the Christians he [Constantius] obscured by a dotard's superstition, and by subtle and involved discussions about dogma. Rather than by seriously trying to make them agree, he aroused many controversies; and as these spread more and more, he fed them with contentious words. And since throngs of bishops hastened hither and thither on the public post horses to the various synods, as they call them, while he sought to make the whole ritual conform to his own will, he cut the sinews of the courier service.

Dissidentes Christianorum antistites cum plebe discissa in palatium intromissos, monebat civilius, ut discordiis consopitis, quisque nullo vetante, religioni suae serviret intrepidus. Quod agebat ideo obstinate ut dissensiones augente licentia, non timeret unanimantem postea plebem, nullas infestas hominibus bestias, ut sunt sibi ferales plerique Christianorum expertus. *Id., XXII, v, 3, 4*

Illud autem erat inclemens, obruendum perenni silentio, quod arcebat docere magistros rhetoricos et grammaticos, ritus Christiani cultores. *Ibid., x, 7*

Superstitiosus magis quam sacrorum legitimus observator, innumeras sine parsimonia pecudes mactans, ut aestimaretur (si revertisset de Parthis), boves iam defuturos.
Id., XXV, iv, 17

Damasus et Ursinus, supra humanum modum ad rapiendam episcopi sedem ardentes, scissis studiis asperrime conflictabantur, ad usque mortis vulnerumque discrimina adiumentis utriusque progressis. . . . In basilica Sicinini, ubi ritus Christiani est conventiculum, uno die centum triginta septem reperta cadavera peremptorum. . . . Qui esse poterant beati re vera, si magnitudine urbis despecta, quam vitiis opponunt, ad imitationem antistitum quorundam provincialium viverent, quos tenuitas edendi potandique parcissime, vilitas etiam indumentorum, et supercilia humum spectantia, perpetuo numini, verisque eius cultoribus, ut puros commendant, et verecundos.
Id., XXVII, iii, 12, 13, 15

He [Julian] summoned to the palace the bishops of the Christians, who were of conflicting opinions, and the people, who are also at variance, and politely advised them to lay aside their differences, and each fearlessly and without opposition to observe his own beliefs. On this he took a firm stand, to the end that, as this freedom increased their dissension, he might afterwards have no fear of a united populace, knowing as he did from experience that no wild beasts are such enemies to mankind as are most of the Christians in their deadly hatred of one another.

But this one thing was inhumane, and ought to be buried in eternal silence, namely, that he forbade teachers of rhetoric to practise their profession, if they were followers of the Christian religion.

Superstitious rather than truly religious, he sacrificed innumerable victims without regard to cost, so that one might believe that if he had returned from the Parthians, there would soon be a scarcity of cattle.

Damasus and Ursinus, burning with a superhuman desire of seizing the bishopric, engaged in bitter strife because of their opposing interests; and the supporters of both parties went even so far as conflicts ending in bloodshed and death. . . . In the basilica of Sicininus, where the assembly of the Christian sect is held, in a single day one hundred and thirty-seven corpses of the slain were found. . . . These men might be truly happy, if they would disregard the greatness of the city behind which they hide their faults, and live after the manner of some provincial bishops, whose moderation in food and drink, plain apparel also, and gaze fixed upon the earth, commend them to the Eternal Deity and to his true servants as pure and reverent men.

AURELIUS AMBROSIUS

c. A.D. 333 – 397

Non in dialectica complacuit Deo salvum facere populum
suum.   *De fide, I, 5, 42*

Imperator . . . intra ecclesiam, non supra ecclesiam est.
                              Sermo contra Auxentium, 35

Quando hic sum, non ieiuno Sabbato; quando Romae sum,
ieiuno Sabbato.   (*Augustinus Epistulae, 36, 14*)

S. HIERONYMUS

c. A.D. 340 – 420

Praeproperus sermo; confusa turbatur oratio; amor or-
dinem nescit.   *Epistulae, VII, 6*

Romanus orbis ruit et tamen cervix nostra erecta non
flectitur.   *Id., LX, 16*

AMBROSE

St. Ambrose was the son of a high dignitary. At an early age he held the post of governor of Milan. Elected bishop, he vigorously fought the Arians, defended the Church against encroachments of imperial authority, and wrote dogmatic treatises and hymns.

It is not the will of God to save his people through dialectics.

The emperor . . . is in the Church, not above the Church.

When I am here [at Milan], I do not fast on the Sabbath; when I am at Rome, I do fast on the Sabbath.

ST. JEROME

Born at Stridon, Dalmatia, St. Jerome studied in Rome and was converted there. For a time he lived in a Syrian desert as a hermit. In 382 he returned to Rome, where he became the spiritual counselor of a group of noble ladies. In 386 he retired to a monastery in Bethlehem and devoted himself to writing. Aside from his epistles, the best known of which are addressed to his spiritual wards, he wrote biographies and commentaries on the Scriptures, and made the Latin translation of the Bible that came to be known as the Vulgate.

My thoughts rush headlong; my words are confused and incoherent; but love knows not order.

The Roman world is collapsing and yet we do not bow our heads.

Aliae sunt leges Caesarum, aliae Christi; aliud Papinianus, aliud Paulus noster praecipit. Apud illos in viris pudicitiae frena laxantur et solo stupro atque adulterio condemnato passim per lupanaria et ancillulas libido permittitur, quasi culpam dignitas faciat, non voluptas. Apud nos, quod non licet feminis, aeque non licet viris.   *Id., LXXVII, 3*

Facito aliquid operis, ut semper te diabolus inveniat occupatum.   *Id., CXXV, 11*

Nec putemus in verbis Scripturarum esse Evangelium, sed in sensu: non in superficie, sed in medulla; non in sermonum foliis, sed in radice rationis.
                    In epististulam ad Galatas commentarii, I, 1, 11

Pereant qui ante nos nostra dixerunt.
                            In Ecclesiasten commentarius, I

FLAVIUS VEGETIUS RENATUS

fl. A.D. 380

Qui desiderat pacem praeparet bellum.
                            Epitoma rei militaris, Prologium, 3

Caesar's laws are one thing, Christ's another; Papinian makes one ruling, our Paul another. Among them, restraints on modesty are loosened for men, only rape and adultery are condemned; casual lust is permitted in brothels and with slave girls, as if sin were a matter of the woman's status, not of sensuality. Among us, what is forbidden women is equally forbidden men.

Be sure to keep busy, so that the devil may always find you occupied.

We must not suppose that the Gospel is in the words of the Scriptures, but in their meaning, not on the surface but within, not in the leaves of discourse but in the root of reason.

Perish those who said what we are saying before we did!

VEGETIUS

Vegetius Renatus was the author of a treatise on warfare, *Epitoma rei militaris*.

If you want peace prepare for war.

AURELIUS CLEMENS PRUDENTIUS

A.D. 348 – C. 405

Dicendum mihi: "quisquis es,
  mundum quem coluit, mens tua perdidit.
  non sunt illa Dei, quae studuit, cuius habeberis."
atqui fine sub ultimo
  peccatrix anima stultitiam exuat:
  saltem voce Deum concelebret, si meritis nequit.

Liber Cathemerinon, Praefatio, 31

Non fero Romanum nomen sudataque bella
et titulos tanto quaesitos sanguine carpi.
detrahit invictis legionibus et sua Romae
praemia deminuit, qui, quidquid fortiter actum est,
adscribit Veneri, palmam victoribus aufert.

Contra orationem Symmachi, II, 551

Vivere commune est, sed non commune mereri.

Ibid., 807

Peccante nil est taetrius,
  nil tam leprosum aut putidum;
  cruda est cicatrix criminum,
  oletque ut antrum Tartari.

Peristephanon Liber, II, 285

PRUDENTIUS

Sometimes referred to as the foremost Christian Latin poet, Prudentius was a native of Spain, successively lawyer, judge, governor, and high dignitary at the court of Emperor Honorius. At the age of fifty-seven (see first of the excerpts below) he decided to devote himself to furthering Christianity with the written word. His works, much read in the Middle Ages, include didactic poems, epigrams, and lyrics. The *Cathemerinon* and the *Peristephanon* are collections of hymns. *Contra orationem Symmachi* is a polemical work against the prefect of Rome, Symmachus, one of the last and most eloquent defenders of the dying ancient religion. The *Hamartigenia* is a didactic poem on the origin of evil.

It is time I said to myself: "Whoever you may be, your soul has lost the world it loved; the things it pursued do not belong to God, who is to judge you." And so, as my last day approaches, let my sinful soul divest itself of its folly; let it at least celebrate God in words, if it cannot in deeds.

I will not permit the name of Rome, whose wars cost so much toil, and whose glory was purchased at such cost of blood, to be disparaged. He who credits Venus with Rome's great exploits belittles the unconquered legions, destroys Rome's honor, takes away the palm from the victors.

To live is common to all, but to be worthy of living is not.

Nothing is more hideous than a sinner, nothing so leprous or stinking. His crimes are a running sore and smell like the cave of Tartarus.

En omne sub regnum Remi
mortale concessit genus,
idem loquuntur dissoni
ritus, it ipsum sentiunt.
hoc destinatum quo magis
ius Christiani nominis
quodcumque terrarum iacet
uno inligaret vinculo.   *Ibid., 425*

Nil est amore veritatis celsius.   *Id., X, 388*

"Removete lumen," dicet insanabilis,
"iniurosa est nil videnti claritas."   *Ibid., 593*

Auri namque fames parto fit maior ab auro.
                                    Hamartigenia, 257

S. AURELIUS AUGUSTINUS

A.D. 354 – 430

Ab exordio generis humani, quicumque in eum credi-
derunt, eumque utcumque intellexerunt, et secundum eius
praecepta pie iusteque vixerunt, quandolibet et ubilibet
fuerint, pro eo procul dubio salvi facti sunt.
                              Epistulae, 102, 12

Lo, the whole human race has come under the rule of Remus: men of different ways of life now speak and think alike. This was preordained so that the rightful authority of the Christian name might unite in one bond all lands.

Nothing is more sublime than love of truth.

"Take away the light [of the faith]," he who is beyond saving will say. "Its radiance hurts the eyes of those who cannot see."

The hunger for gold grows greater as gold is acquired.

ST. AUGUSTINE

St. Augustine was born at Tagaste, Numidia, of a pagan father and a Christian mother, Monica. In his autobiographical *Confessions* he tells us that it was Cicero's treatise *Hortensius* (now lost) that awakened him to philosophy. For a long time he was a Manichaean. In 384 he became a professor of rhetoric in Milan, where he was converted under the influence of Ambrose. Back in Africa he received priest's orders and eventually became bishop at Hippo. St. Augustine's influence on subsequent thought is not confined to theology. The link between the pagan and the Christian world, he reinterpreted the ideals of antiquity, and in a sense created the modern soul with its conflicts and its unfathomable depths. He was a tireless writer, producing, in addition to a number of important theological and philosophical treatises, more than five hundred sermons and nearly three hundred long epistles.

From the beginning of mankind, those who believed in Him [Christ] and knew Him in any way, and lived a pious and just life according to His precepts, wherever and whenever they may have been, were beyond doubt saved by Him.

Absit namque ut hoc in nobis Deus oderit, in quo nos reliquis animantibus excellentiores creavit. Absit, inquam, ut ideo credamus, ne rationem accipiamus sive quaeramus; cum etiam credere non possemus, nisi rationales animas haberemus. *Id., 120, 1, 3*

Inexcusabilis est omnis peccator vel reatu originis vel additamento etiam propriae voluntatis, sive qui novit sive qui ignorat, sive qui iudicat sive qui non iudicat; quia et ipsa ignorantia in iis, qui intelligere noluerunt, sine dubitatione peccatum est, in iis autem qui non potuerunt, poena peccati. *Id., 194, 6, 27*

Martyres non facit poena sed causa.
Enarrationes in Psalmos, XXXIV, 2

Est autem fides credere quod nondum vides; cuius fidei merces est videre quod credis. *Sermones, 43, 1, 1*

Ne te sanum putes. Sanitas immortalitas erit. Nam haec longa aegritudo erit. *Id., 77, 4*

De Deo loquimur, quid mirum si non comprehendis? Si enim comprehendis, non est Deus. Sit pia confessio ignorantiae magis quam temeraria professio scientiae. Attingere aliquantum mente Deum magna beatitudo est, comprehendere autem impossibile. *Id., 117, 3*

Vult homo non esse concupiscentias. . . . Velimus, nolimus, habemus illas: velimus, nolimus, titillant, blandiuntur, stimulant. . . . Premuntur nondum exstinguuntur.
Id., 128, 9

Appetitio igitur beatae vitae philosophis Christianisque communis est. . . . Dic, Epicurice, quae res faciat beatum? Respondit: voluptas corporis. Dic, Stoice? Virtus animi. Dic, Christiane? Donum Dei. *Id., 150, 3, 7*

No, God does not hate that part of us by which He has made us superior to other living creatures. No, we must not believe in such a way that we should reject or ask for a reason: for we could not even believe unless we had rational souls.

Every sinner is inexcusable, whether because of the original sin or because of an additional offense due to his own will, whether he knows or does not know it, whether he condemns or does not condemn it; because in those unwilling to understand ignorance itself is beyond doubt a sin, and in those unable to understand, this inability is the penalty of sin.

Not the punishment but the cause makes the martyr.

Faith is to believe what you do not see; the reward of this faith is to see what you believe.

Don't think yourself healthy. Health will be immortality. This life will be a long sickness.

We are speaking of God—is it surprising if you don't understand? A pious admission of ignorance must be preferred to a rash profession of knowledge. To touch God to some extent with the mind is a great bliss, but to grasp Him is altogether impossible.

Man does not want to have desires . . . Whether we like it or not, we have them; whether we like it or not they tickle us, caress us, excite us. . . . They press upon us until they are extinguished.

The quest for a happy life is thus common to the philosophers and the Christians. . . . Tell us, Epicurean, what things make us happy? His answer is: Bodily pleasure. And you, Stoic? Intellectual virtue. And you, Christian? The gift of God.

Semper tibi displiceat quod es, si vis pervenire ad id quod nondum es. Nam ubi tibi placuisti, ibi remansisti. Si autem dixeris Sufficit; et peristi. Semper adde. Semper ambula, semper profice: noli in via remanere noli retro redire, noli deviare.   *Id., 169, 18*

De vitiis nostris scalam nobis facimus si vitia ipsa calcamus.
Id., 176, 4

Summum bonum appetere est bene vivere, ut nihil sit aliud bene vivere, quam toto corde, tota anima, tota mente Deum diligere: a quo exsistit, ut incorruptus in eo amor atque integer custodiatur, quod est temperantiae; et nullis frangatur incommodis, quod est fortitudinis; nulli alii serviat, quod est iustitiae; vigilet in discernendis rebus, ne fallacia paulatim dolusve subrepat, quod est prudentiae.
De moribus ecclesiae catholicae, 1, 3, 6

Credibilium tria sunt genera. Alia sunt quae semper creduntur et numquam intelleguntur: sicut est omnis historia, temporalia et humana gesta percurrens. Alia quae mox, ut creduntur, intelleguntur: sicut sunt omnes rationes humanae, vel de numeris, vel de quibuslibet disciplinis. Tertium, quae primo creduntur, et postea intelleguntur: qualia sunt ea, quae de divinis rebus non possunt intelligi, nisi ab his qui mundo sunt corde.
De diversis quaestionibus, LXXXIII, 48

Laudare te vult homo, aliqua portio creaturae tuae. tu excitas, ut laudare te delectet, quia fecisti nos ad te et inquietum est cor nostrum, donec requiescat in te.
Confessiones, I, 1

Et illa erant fercla, in quibus mihi esurienti te inferebatur sol et luna, pulchra opera tua.   *Id., III, 6*

370

If you would attain to what you are not yet, you must always be displeased by what you are. For where you were pleased with yourself there you have remained. But once you have said, "It is enough," you are lost. Keep adding, keep walking, keep advancing: do not stop, do not turn back, do not turn from the straight road.

We can fashion a ladder for our vices by trampling them underfoot.

To seek the highest good is to live well; to live well is nothing else but to love God with all our heart, all our soul, all our mind; hence it is obvious that this love must be preserved whole and uncorrupt, which is the part of temperance; it must not be distracted by difficulties, which is the part of courage; it must serve nothing else, which is the part of justice; it must be vigilant in discriminating among things lest falseness or fraud steal in, which is the part of prudence.

There are three kinds of credible things: (1) Those which are always believed and never understood: such is all history, all temporal things and human actions. (2) Those which are understood as soon as they are believed: such are all human reasonings, concerning numbers or any other discipline. (3) Those which are believed first and understood afterward: such are those concerning divine things which can be understood only by those clean of heart.

(*Tr. John K. Ryan*)

Man, this part of your creation, wishes to praise you. You arouse him to take joy in praising you, for you have made us for yourself, and our heart is restless until it rests in you.

Such were the platters on which the sun and the moon, your beauteous works, were brought to me while I hungered for you.

371

Fieri non potest ut filius istarum lacrimarum pereat.

Ibid., 12

Grande profundum est ipse homo, cuius etiam capillos tu, domine, numeratos habes et non minuuntur in te: et tamen capilli eius magis numerabiles quam affectus eius et motus cordis eius.

Id., IV, 14

At ego adulescens miser valde . . . etiam petieram a te castitatem et dixeram: "da mihi castitatem et continentiam, sed noli modo."

Id., VIII, 7

Unde hoc monstrum? et quare iste? Imperat animus corpori, et paretur statim: imperat animus sibi, et resistitur.

Ibid., 9

Tolle lege, tolle lege.

Ibid., 12

Nec ego ipse capio totum, quod sum. Ergo animus ad habendum se ipsum angustus est.

Id., X, 8

Et eunt homines mirari alta montium, et ingentes fluctus maris, et latissimos lapsus fluminum, et Oceani ambitum, et gyros siderum, et relinquunt se ipsos.

Ibid.

Quid ergo sum, deus meus? quae natura sum? varia, multimoda vita et immensa vehementer.

Ibid., 17

Cum . . . te, deum meum, quaero, vitam beatam quaero. quaeram te, ut vivat anima mea.

Ibid., 20

Quid est ergo tempus? si nemo ex me quaerat, scio; si quaerenti explicare velim, nescio.

Id., XI, 14

Domine deus, pacem da nobis—omnia enim praestitisti nobis—pacem quietis, pacem sabbati, pacem sine vespera. Omnis quippe iste ordo pulcherrimus rerum valde bonarum modis suis peractis transiturus est: et mane quippe in eis factum est et vespera.

Id., XIII, 35

It is impossible that the son of such tears should perish.

Man is a mighty deep, whose very hairs you have numbered, O Lord, and they are not lessened before you. But man's hairs are easier to count than his affections and the movements of his heart.

But I, a most wretched youth . . . had ever sought chastity from you, and had said, "Give me chastity and continence, but not yet!"

Whence comes this monstrous state? Why should it be? Mind commands body, and it obeys forthwith. Mind gives orders to itself and is resisted.

Take up and read. Take up and read.

I do not comprehend all that I am. Is the mind, therefore, too limited to possess itself?

Men go forth to marvel at the mountain heights, at huge waves in the sea, at the broad expanse of flowing rivers, at the wide reaches of the ocean, and at the circuits of the stars, but themselves they pass by.

What then am I, O my God? What is my nature? A life varied and manifold and mightily surpassing measurement.

When I seek you, my God, I seek the happy life. Let me seek you "so that my soul may live."

What, then, is time? If no one asks me, I know; if I want to explain it to someone who does ask me, I do not know.

O Lord God, give us peace, for you have given all things to us, the peace of rest, the peace of the Sabbath, the peace without an evening. The entire most beautiful order of things that are very good, when their measures have been accomplished, is to pass away. For truly in them a morning has been made, and an evening also.

Securus iudicat orbis terrarum.

Contra epistulam Parmeniani, III, 24

Ad sapientiam pertinet aeternarum rerum cognitio intellectualis, as scientiam vero temporalium rerum cognitio rationalis. *De Trinitate, XII, 15, 25*

Quae autem scientia Dei est, ipsa et sapientia; et quae sapientia, ipsa essentia sive substantia; quia in illius naturae simplicitate mirabili non est aliud sapere, aliud esse; sed quod est sapere, hoc est et esse. *Id., XV, 13, 22*

Et sumus et nos esse novimus et id esse et nosse diligimus. . . . Sine ulla phantasiarum vel phantasmatum imaginatione ludificatoria, mihi esse me, idque nosse et amare certissimum est. *De civitate dei, XI, 26*

Constant inter Christianos veraciter catholicam tenentes fidem, etiam ipsam nostris corporis mortem non lege naturae, qua nullam mortem homini Deus fecit, sed merito inflictam esse peccati. *Id., XIII, 15*

Homo ita factus est rectus, ut non secundum se ipsum, sed secundum eum a quo factus est, viveret, id est illius potius quam suam faceret voluntatem: non ita vivere, quemadmodum est factus ut viveret, hoc est mendacium. Beatus quippe vult esse, etiam non sic vivendo ut possit esse. Quid est ista voluntate mendacius? Unde non frustra dici potest omne peccatum est mendacium. *Id., XIV, 4*

Fecerunt itaque civitates duas amores duo: terrenam scilicet amor sui usque ad contemptum Dei, caelestem vero amor Dei usque ad contemptum sui. *Ibid., 28*

The world's verdict is conclusive.

To wisdom belongs the intellectual apprehension of things eternal; to knowledge, the rational apprehension of things temporal.

God's knowledge is also His wisdom; and what is His wisdom is also His essence or substance; because in the marvelous simplicity of His nature, it is not one thing to be and another to know, but to know is the same as to be.

(*Tr. Walsh, Zema, Monahan, and Honan*)

We are, and we know that we are, and we love to be and to know what we are. . . . Without any illusion of image, fancy, or phantasm, I am certain that I am, that I know that I am, and that I love to be and to know.

All Christians who really hold to the Catholic faith believe that it is not by a law of nature that man is subject to bodily death—since God created for man an immortal nature—but as a just punishment for sin.

Man has been so constituted in truth that he was meant to live not according to himself but to Him who made him—that is, he was meant to do the will of God rather than his own. It is a lie not to live as a man was created to live. Man indeed desires happiness even when he does so live as to make happiness impossible. What could be more of a lie than such a desire? This is the reason why every sin can be called a lie.

What we see, then, is that two societies have issued from two kinds of love. Worldly society has flowered from a selfish love which dared to despise even God, whereas the communion of saints is rooted in a love of God that is ready to trample on self.

Condita est civitas Roma . . . per quam Deo placuit orbem
debellare terrarum et in unam societatem rei publicae le-
gumque perductum longe lateque placare.   *Id., XVIII, 22*

Incredibile est Christum resurrexisse in carne et in caelum
ascendisse cum carne; incredibile est mundum rem tam
incredibilem credidisse; incredibile est homines ignobiles,
infimos, paucissimos, imperitos rem tam incredibilem tam
efficaciter mundo et in illo etiam doctis persuadere po-
tuisse.   *Id., XXII, 5*

Quisquis adhuc prodigia ut credat inquirit, magnum est
ipse prodigium, qui mundo credente non credit.
                                              Ibid., 8

Intellectus merces est fidei.
                In Ioannis evangelium tractatus, XXIX, 6

Credimus enim ut cognoscamus, non cognoscimus ut credamus. . . . Quid est enim fides, nisi credere quod non
vides? Fides ergo est quod non vides credere, veritas quod
credidisti videre.   *Id., XL, 9*

Extra catholicam ecclesiam totum potest praeter salutem.
Potest habere honorem, potest habere sacramenta, potest
cantare alleluia, potest respondere Amen, potest evangelium tenere, potest in nomine Patris et Filii et Spiritus
Sancti fidem habere et praedicare, sed nusquam nisi in
ecclesia catholica salutem poterit invenire.
                Sermo ad Caesariensis ecclesiae plebem, VI

Noli credere, nec dicere, nec docere, infantes antequam
baptizentur morte praeventos pervenire posse ad original-
ium indulgentiam peccatorum, si vis esse catholicus.
                De anima et eius origine, III, 9, 12

Rome was founded . . . It was God's good pleasure, by means of this city, to subdue the whole world, to bring it into the single society of a republic under law, and to bestow upon it a widespread and enduring peace.

It is incredible that Christ should have risen in His flesh and, with His flesh, have ascended into heaven; it is incredible that the world should have believed a thing so incredible; it is incredible that men so rude and so lowly, so few and unaccomplished, should have convinced the world, including men of learning, of something so incredible and have convinced them so conclusively.

Anyone still looking for a miracle to help him to believe, in the midst of a world in which practically everyone already believes, is surely himself a marvel of no mean magnitude.

(*Tr. N.G.*)

Understanding is the reward of faith.

For we believe in order to know, we do not know in order to believe. . . . For what is faith, if not to believe what you do not see? Therefore faith is to believe what you do not see, truth is to see what you believed.

Outside of the Catholic Church everything may be had except salvation. One may have orders and sacraments, one may sing Alleluia and answer Amen, one may hold the Gospel, one may have and preach in the name of the Father, the Son, and the Holy Ghost, but nowhere except in the Catholic Church can one find salvation.

Do not believe, do not say, do not teach that infants who died before being baptized can attain to forgiveness of original sins—not if you wish to be a Catholic.

Qui recte amat, procul dubio recte credit et sperat; qui vero non amat, inaniter credit, etiamsi sint vera quae credit. . . . Regnat enim carnalis cupiditas, ubi non est Dei caritas.   *Enchiridion, sive De fide, spe et caritate, 117*

CLAUDIUS CLAUDIANUS

c. A.D. 370 – c. 408

Saepe mihi dubiam traxit sententia mentem,
curarent superi terras an nullus inesset
rector et incerto fluerent mortalia casu.

In Rufinum, I, 1

Sed cum res hominum tanta caligine volvi
adspicerem laetosque diu florere nocentes
vexarique pios, rursus labefacta cadebat
religio.

Ibid., 12

Abstulit hunc tandem Rufini poena tumultum
absolvitque deos. Iam non ad culmina rerum
iniustos crevisse queror; tolluntur in altum,
ut lapsu graviore ruant.

Ibid., 20

Asperius nihil est humili cum surgit in altum.

In Eutropium, 181

Armat spina rosas, mella tegunt apes.
crescunt difficili gaudia iurgio
accenditque magis, quae refugit, Venus.
quod flenti tuleris, plus sapit osculum.

Fescennina de nuptiis Honorii Augusti, IV, 10

The man who loves aright, without a doubt believes and hopes aright; whereas the man who does not love, believes in vain, even if what he believes is true. . . . For carnal lust rules where the love of God is absent.

CLAUDIAN

A Greek from Alexandria, Claudian wrote poems in praise of Emperor Honorius and General Stilicho, vigorous invectives against their enemies, and a large number of short pieces. He is admired for his technical skill and the purity of his Latin.

(Tr. M. Platnauer)

My mind has often wavered between two opinions: have the gods a care for the world or is there no ruler therein and do mortal things drift as dubious chance dictates?

But when I saw the impenetrable mist which surrounds human affairs, the wicked happy and long prosperous and the good discomforted, then in turn my belief in God was weakened and failed.

At last Rufinus' fate has dispelled this uncertainty and freed the gods from this imputation. No longer can I complain that the unrighteous man reaches the highest pinnacle of success. He is raised aloft that he may be hurled down in more headlong ruin.

Nothing is so cruel as a man raised from lowly station to prosperity.

Thorns arm the rose and bees find a defense for their honey. The refusals of coyness do but increase the joy; the desire for that which flies us is the more inflamed; sweeter is the kiss snatched through tears.

379

Si tibi Parthorum solium Fortuna dedisset,
care puer, terrisque procul venerandus Eois
barbarus Arsacio consurgeret ore tiaras:
sufficeret sublime genus luxuque fluentem
deside nobilitas posset te sola tueri.
altera Romanae longe rectoribus aulae
condicio. virtute decet, non sanguine niti.

De quarto consulatu Honorii Augusti, 214

Componitur orbis
regis ad exemplum, nec sic inflectere sensus
humanos edicta valent quam vita regentis:
mobile mutatur semper cum principe vulgus.

Ibid., 299

Ipsa quidem Virtus pretium sibi, solaque late
Fortunae secura nitet nec fascibus ullis
erigitur plausuve petit clarescere vulgi.

Panegyricus dictus Manlio Theodoro Consuli, 1

Me quoque Musarum studium sub nocte silenti
artibus adsuetis sollicitare solet.

De sexto Consulatu Honorii Augusti, Praefatio, 11

Paupertas me saeva domat dirusque Cupido:
sed toleranda fames, non tolerandus amor.

Carmina minora, XV

Felix, qui propriis aevum transegit in arvis,
ipsa domus puerum quem videt, ipsa senem;
qui baculo nitens in qua reptavit harena
unius numerat saecula longa casae.   *Id., XX*

Had fortune, my dear son, given thee the throne of Parthia, hadst thou been a descendant of the Arsacid house and did the tiara, adored by Eastern lands afar, tower upon thy forehead, thy birth alone would protect thee, though wantoning in idle luxury. Very different is the state of Rome's emperor. 'Tis merit, not blood, must be his support.

The world shapes itself after its ruler's pattern, nor can edicts sway men's minds so much as their monarch's life; the unstable crowd ever changes along with the prince.

Virtue is its own reward; alone with its far-flung splendor it mocks at Fortune; no honors raise it higher nor does it seek glory from the mob's applause.

I am a lover of the Muses and in the silent night I too am haunted by my accustomed task.

Biting poverty and cruel Cupid are my foes. Hunger I can endure; love I cannot.

(Tr. Abraham Cowley)

Happy the man who his whole time doth bound
Within the enclosure of his little ground.
Happy the man whom the same humble place,
The hereditary cottage of his race,
From his first rising infancy has known . . .

AMBROSIUS THEODOSIUS
MACROBIUS

fl. A.D. 400

Se iudice nemo nocens absolvitur, nec de se suam potest
vitare sententiam.

Commentarii in Somnium Scipionis, I, 10, 12

Hunc aiunt filios suos solitum devorare eosdemque rursus
evomere, per quod similiter significatur eum tempus esse,
a quo vicibus cuncta gignantur absumanturque et ex eo
denuo renascantur. *Saturnalia, I, 8, 10*

Vis tu cogitare eos quos ius tuum vocas isdem seminibus
ortos, eodem frui caelo, aeque vivere, aeque mori? Servi
sunt: immo homines. Servi sunt: immo conservi, si cogi-
taveris tantumdem in utrosque licere fortunae.

Ibid., 11, 7

Alius libidini servit, alius avaritiae, alius ambitioni, omnes
spei, omnes timori. *Ibid., 8*

Non ergo fortuna homines aestimabo, sed moribus. Sibi
quisque dat mores, condicionem casus assignat. *Ibid., 10*

MACROBIUS

Macrobius was probably born in Africa and may have been a high official at the court of Emperor Theodosius. His two surviving works were very popular in the Middle Ages. One is a philosophical commentary on Cicero's *Somnium Scipionis,* which reflects the author's almost Christian conception of the soul, and the influence of neo-Platonism. The other, *Saturnalia,* is a symposium. The subjects discussed cover a wide range—morality, health, dancing, famous *bons mots,* and mythology, among others. He often borrows from older authors. Apparently impressed by Christian criticisms, he maintains that the pagan gods are symbols of natural phenomena, and that all of them are incarnations of a single divinity, the Sun. The main portion of the book, however, is more original—it is a detailed examination of Vergil, who is exalted as the greatest rhetorician, profoundest thinker, and most erudite scholar. The medieval cult of Vergil probably began with this book.

No guilty man is acquitted when he is judged by himself, nor can he escape his own sentence.

It is said that he [Saturn] used to devour his children and then spew them out again. This, too, indicates that he stands for time, by which all things are in turn produced, destroyed, and in which they are born again.

At least consider that these men whom you call your chattels have the same origin as you, enjoy the same sky, live and die as you do. Slaves? no, they are men. Slaves? no, fellow slaves, when you consider that fortune has equal sway over them and you.

One is slave to his lust, another to his avarice, yet another to his ambition, and all to hope, all to fear.

I shall not evaluate people by their fortunes, but by their moral character. Everyone gives himself his own moral character; status is assigned by chance.

Non potest amor cum timore misceri. *Ibid.,* 12

Unde putas arrogantissimum illud manasse proverbium, quo iactatur totidem hostes nobis esse quot servos? Non habemus illos hostes, sed facimus, cum in illos superbissimi, contumeliosissimi, crudelissimi sumus. *Ibid.,* 13

Leges bonae ex malis moribus procreantur. *Id., II,* 13

Cumque conscii flagitiorum mirarentur quo modo similes Agrippae filios pareret . . . ait: "Numquam enim nisi navi plena tollo vectorem." *Ibid.,* 5, 9

Vis audire illum tanta brevitate dicentem, ut artari magis et contrahi brevitas ipsa non possit? "Et campos, ubi Troia fuit": ecce paucissimis verbis maximam civitatem hausit et absorpsit, non reliquit illi nec ruinam. *Id., V, 1,* 8

Quippe si mundum ipsum diligenter inspicias, magnam similitudinem divini illius et huius poetici operis invenies. Nam qualiter eloquentia Maronis ad omnium mores integra est, nunc brevis, nunc copiosa, nunc sicca, nunc florida, nunc simul omnia, interdum lenis aut torrens: sic terra ipsa hic laeta segetibus et pratis, ibi silvis et rupibus hispida, hic sicca harenis, hic irrigua fontibus, pars vasto aperitur mari. *Ibid.,* 19

Plebeia ingenia magis exemplis quam ratione capiuntur.
Id., VII, 4, 4

Omne quod dulce est cito satiat. *Ibid.,* 15

Love and fear exclude each other.

What do you suppose to be the origin of the very arrogant maxim, "We have as many enemies as we have slaves?" They are not our enemies by nature, we make them enemies when we treat them overbearingly, insultingly, cruelly.

Good laws are the products of bad morals.

When persons aware of Julia's adulteries registered surprise that her children were the image of Agrippa [her husband], she replied: "That's because I never take passengers unless the boat is full."

Notice how he [Vergil] speaks with such brevity that brevity itself could not be more concise, more compact. "The plain where Troy once stood." This is how in a very few words he levels and annihilates a very great city, leaving not even a ruin.

Yes, when you examine the world carefully, you discover a great similarity between this divine creation and our poet's work. For just as Vergil suits every taste—his eloquence is now terse, now abundant, now dry, now flowery, now all these things at once, flowing gently or rushing swiftly—so does the earth, here riant with harvests and meadows, there bristling with rocks and forests, here dry and sandy, there watered by springs or opened to the vast sea.

Vulgar minds are more impressed by examples than by reasons.

All sweet things quickly bring satiety.

CLAUDIUS RUTILIUS NAMATIANUS
Late 4th century (fl. A.D. 416)

Exaudi, regina tui pulcherrima mundi,
  inter sidereos Roma recepta polos,
exaudi, genetrix hominum genetrixque deorum,
  non procul a caelo per tua templa sumus.
De Reditu Suo, 47

Fecisti patriam diversis gentibus unam;
  profuit iniustis te dominante capi.
dumque offers victis proprii consortia iuris,
  urbem fecisti quod prius orbis erat.   *Ibid., 63*

Quod regnas minus est quam quod regnare mereris:
  excedis factis grandia fata tuis.   *Ibid., 91*

Atque utinam nunquam Iudaea subacta fuisset
  Pompeii bellis imperioque Titi!
Latius excisae pestis contagia serpunt,
  Victoresque suos natio victa premit.   *Ibid., 395*

C. R. NAMATIANUS

Claudius Rutilius Namatianus was the last pagan poet. Son of an imperial dignitary, he rose to the office of prefect of Rome in 414—his outspoken anti-Christianity was apparently no obstacle. In 416 he set out on a journey to his native Gaul, described in his unfinished poem *De Reditu Suo* ("On His Return"). The excerpts below, illustrating his love for Rome and his faith in her mission, are interesting as they were written only a few years after Alaric's sack of the city. The last two excerpts are characteristic of the attitude of cultivated pagans toward Christianity. The second of them was inspired by the island of Gorgona (today Urgo), where a noble Roman, scion of a prominent family, retired to live as a hermit—"buried himself alive," as the poet says.

Hear me, O Rome, most beautiful queen of the world you rule, received among the star-studded heavens! Hear me, Mother of Men, Mother of Gods, we are close to heaven for your temples.

You made one homeland for widely separated nations; under your rule, nations without justice were fortunate to be subjugated; and by making the vanquished partners in your law, you turned what had formerly been the world into one great city.

You are less great for ruling than for deserving to rule; by your exploits you surpass your own sublime destiny.

Ah, I wish Judaea had never been subjugated by the campaigns of Pompey and Titus' authority! Though the pestilence was excised, its contagion is still spreading, and the conquered nation presses hard upon its conquerors!

Impulsus furiis homines terrasque reliquit
et turpem latebram credulus exsul agit.
infelix putat illuvie caelestia pasci
seque premit laesis saevior ipse deis.
num, rogo, deterior Circaeis secta venenis?
tunc mutabantur corpora, nunc animi.

Ibid., 521

ANICIUS MANLIUS
SEVERINUS BOETHIUS

C. A.D. 480 – 524

Mors hominum felix quae se nec dulcibus annis
inserit et maestis saepe vocata venit.

De Consolatione Philosophiae, I, 1, 13

Quid me felicem totiens iactastis amici?
qui cecidit, stabili non erat ille gradu. *Ibid., 1, 21*

In omni adversitate fortunae infelicissimum est genus in-
fortunii fuisse felicem. *Id., II, 4*

Mortalium rerum misera beatitudo. *Ibid.*

Nihil est miserum nisi quum putes. *Ibid.*

Driven by the Furies, he turned his back on the world of men, and, credulous exile, lives in a shameful hole in the ground. The wretched fellow believes that filth nurtures heavenly thoughts, and, more cruel than the gods when they are offended, punishes himself. Pray tell me now, is not this sect worse than Circe's poisons? In her day bodies were transformed, now it is minds. [*Of an early Christian ascetic*]

BOETHIUS

Boethius was a dignitary under Emperor Theodoric. Falsely accused of high treason, he was thrown into prison and eventually executed. He composed a number of philosophical and theological works, but is best known for his *De Consolatione Philosophiae,* which he wrote in prison.

Death is kind to men when it comes not during the sweet but the bitter years: then, indeed, it is often prayed for.

My friends, why did you proclaim me happy? One who fell could not have been on steady ground.

(*Tr. W. Causson, 1732*)

In every kind of adversity, the bitterest part of a man's affliction is to remember that he once was happy.

(*Tr. N.G.*)

The wretched happiness of mortal things . . .

Nothing is wretched unless you think it is.

"Iam tandem," inquit, "intellegis me esse philosophum?"
Tum ille nimium mordaciter: "Intellexeram," inquit, "si
tacuisses." *Ibid.*, 6

Si quid est in nobilitate bonum, id esse arbitror solum, ut
inposita nobilibus necessitudo videatur ne a maiorum
virtute degeneret. *Id., III, 5*

> Felix qui potuit boni
> fontem visere lucidum,
> felix qui potuit gravis
> terrae solvere vincula. *Ibid.*, 12

> Quis legem dat amantibus?
> maior lex amor est sibi. *Ibid.*, 47

Aeternitas igitur est interminabilis vitae tota simul et perfecta possessio. *Id., V, 6*

CORPUS IURIS CIVILIS

A.D. 533

Iustitia est constans et perpetua voluntas ius suum cuique
tribuendi. *Institutiones, I, 1*

"I hope," says he, "you'll now acknowledge that I have proved myself to be a Philosopher." "You had indeed," replied the other sharply, "if you could have held your tongue."

I see no other good in nobility of birth, than that it seems to lay an obligation on persons so descended, to imitate the virtue of their ancestors.

(Tr. N.G.)

Happy the man who can view the clear fountains of joy, happy who can untie the bonds of heavy earth.

Who will give the law to lovers? Love is to itself a greater law.

(Tr. W. Causson)

Eternity, then, is a full and perfect possession of the whole of everlasting life at once and altogether.

CORPUS IURIS

The *Corpus iuris civilis*, compiled under Emperor Justinian, comprises the *Institutiones*, a summary of the whole law for the use of students; the *Digesta seu Pandecta*, a vast collection of extracts from the writings of eminent jurists; the *Codex*, and the *Novellae*, a supplement containing recently enacted legislation. The first work is largely based on the *Institutiones* by Gaius (c. A.D. 110–180). The other lawyers quoted below are Publius Iuventius Celsus (b. before A.D. 77), Sextus Pomponius (a contemporary of Celsus), Iulius Paulus (fl. A.D. 200), and Domitius Ulpianus (died in A.D. 228).

(Tr. Moyle, 1883)

Justice is the set and constant purpose which gives every man his due.

Iuris praecepta sunt haec: honeste vivere, alterum non laedere, suum cuique tribuere. *Ibid., 3*

Ius naturale est, quod natura omnia animalia docuit . . . Ius autem gentium omni humano genere commune est; nam, usu exigente, et humanis necessitatibus, gentes humanae iura quaedam sibi constituerunt. Bella etenim orta sunt, et captivitates sequutae, et servitutes, quae sunt naturali iuri contrariae. *Id., II, 1, 2*

Libertas . . . est naturalis facultas eius quod cuique facere libet, nisi si quid vi aut iure prohibetur. *Id., III, 1*

Scire leges non est verba eorum tenere, sed vim ac potestatem. *Celsus, Digesta, I, 3, 17*

Benignius leges interpretandae sunt quo voluntas earum servetur. *Celsus, Ibid., 18*

Vani timoris iusta excusatio non est. *Celsus, Id., L, 17*

Impossibilium nulla obligatio est. *Celsus, Ibid.*

Quae rerum natura prohibentur, nulla lege confirmata sunt. *Celsus, Ibid.*

Iure naturae aequum est neminem cum alterius detrimento et iniuria fieri locupletiorem. *Pomponius, Ibid.*

Semper in dubiis benigniora praeferenda sunt. *Gaius, Ibid.*

Optima est legum interpres consuetudo. *Paulus, Id., I, 3, 37*

Qui tacet, non utique fatetur, sed tamen verum est eum non negare. *Paulus, Id., L, 17*

The precepts of the law are these: to live honestly, to injure no one, and to give everyone his due.

The law of nature is that which she has taught all animals . . . The law of nations is the law common to all mankind: for nations have settled certain things for themselves as occasion and necessities of human life required. For instance, wars arose, and then followed captivity and slavery, which are contrary to the law of nature.

Freedom is a man's natural power of doing what he pleases, so far as he is not prevented by force or law.

To know the laws is not to memorize their letter but to grasp their full force and meaning.

Laws should be interpreted in a liberal sense so that their intention may be preserved.

Empty fear is not a legitimate excuse.

No obligation to do the impossible is binding.

What is impossible by the nature of things is not confirmed by any law.

According to the law of nature it is only fair that no one should become richer through damages and injuries suffered by another.

In doubtful cases the more liberal interpretation must always be preferred.

The best interpreter of the laws is custom.

Though silence is not necessarily an admission, it is not a denial, either.

Non omne quod licet honestum est.   *Paulus, Ibid.*

Libertas inaestimabile res est.   *Paulus, Ibid.*

Latius est impunitum relinqui facinus nocentis, quam innocentem damnari.   *Ulpianus, Digesta, V, 6*

Durum hoc est sed ita lex scripta est.
     Ulpianus, Id., XL, 9

Nuptias non concubitus, sed consensus facit.
     Ulpianus, Id., L, 17

Servitutem mortalitati fere comparamus.   *Ulpianus, Ibid.*

Multae hominibus at malitiam viae sunt.   *Novellae*

Leges neminem in paupertate vivere neque in anxietate mori permittunt.   *Ibid.*

Nihil est aliud falsitas nisi veritatis imitatio.   *Ibid.*

What is permissible is not always honorable.

Freedom is a possession of inestimable value.

Rather leave the crime of the guilty unpunished than condemn the innocent.

This is harsh, but thus the law was written.

Not cohabitation but consensus constitutes marriage.

To some extent I liken slavery to death.

Many are the ways of malice in men.

It is never the intention of the law that anyone shall live
in poverty or die in anguish.

The false is nothing but an imitation of the true.

AUTHOR INDEX

397

SUBJECT INDEX

Academus, 185
Accuse, 285
Achievement, 97
Action, men of, 17
Admire, not to, 177
Adversary, prowess shrivels without an, 241
Adversity, 29, 179, 317, 389
Advice, 35
Aeneas, 89
Aeneid, 215
Aetna, 319
Africa, 263
Agamemnon, 171
Age: ask not a woman's, 223; every age has its troubles, 355; golden, 123, 205, 223, 225; iron, 207; this dull coarse, 111
Agricola, 309
Agriculture. *See* Farming
Alcibiades, 85
Alexis, 121
All, we cannot do, 120
Alliance, 237
Ambition, 281
Ancient: ways, 31; writings, 183
Anger: of Juno, 129; short madness, 175; wishes to seem just, 213
Anguish, 395
Anna, 133
Ant, 125
Apella, 149
Apelles, 263
Apollo, 137

Applaud, I applaud myself, 145
Apple, 121, 127
Arabs, 177
Arcadians, 123
Architects, 251, 291
Arguments, 285
Arms, 51
Army, 271, 275
Arrogance, 97, 243
Art: laws of, 187; or Nature?, 193, 283; unveiled, 285
Artist, 319, 335
Arts, 75, 215, 309
Ascanius, 131
Ascetic, 389
Ashes, 115, 117
Asia, 41
Astrologers, 27, 157
Atheism, 69
Atticus, 85
Atys, 113
Auctioneer, 291
Augustus, 119, 333
Authority, 39
Autumn, 267
Avarice, 69, 105, 383
Avenger, 135
Avernus, 135

Bacchus, 37
Ball, 5
Bankers, 13
Banqueter, 95
Barbarian, 231
Barrenness, 283
Baseness, 75
Beard, 341

399

Desire: determines belief, 81, 253; each man his own, 267; inseparable from fear, 181; man does not want to have desires, 369; my desire reason enough, 352
Despair, 131, 255
Deucalion, 125
Devil, 363
Dialectics, 361
Dice, 38
Dido, 131–35
Die, the die is cast, 83
Dignity, 57, 77
Discipline, 275
Discord, 179
Diseases of the soul, 267
Disgrace, 7, 171, 325
Disgust, 61
Dissension, 311
Distich, 289
Distrust, 131
Doctor, 265
"Doing, a filthy pleasure," 269
Dolts, 91
Dominion, 317
Domitian, 335
Donkey, 237
"Do not stop," 371
Doom, 163
Dowry, 9, 13, 47, 347
Dreams, 123, 139, 207, 269
Dress, 225
Drink, 159, 201
Drones, 127
Drunk, 57, 103
Dullness, 61

Earth: exhausted, 93; no easy way to stars from, 253; O souls bowed to, 277; rewarding, 125; some say the earth revolves, 259
Earthquakes, 259
Ease, 59, 177
Eat, 15, 285
Education, 283

Egeria, 195
Electoral system, 55
Elegance, 87
Eloquence, 29, 67, 287
Emotion, 61
Emperor, 311, 361, 381
Empire, 311
Endure: be firm, 11; we endure neither our vices nor remedies, 195
Enemies, 31, 309, 385
Enemy, 67, 87, 105, 107, 275
Enmity, 141, 199
Ennius, 25, 285
Enterprise, 317
Envy, 99, 175, 267
Epicurean, 369
Epitaph: Ennius', 25; Naevius', 7; Pacuvius', 31; Plautus', 17
Equality, 13
Err, 59, 217
Error, 9
Escape, 317
Eternity, 391
Eurydice, 127
Events: greatest events obscure, 313; unexpected turn of, 81
Evil, within us, 249
Evils, 135, 197
Excellence, 331
Excess, 251
Excuse, 243, 393
Executions, 243
Exile, 161
Expectation, 39, 43
Expenses, 27
Experience, 211, 279
Exuberance, 283
Eyes, 215

Fabius Cunctator, 21, 243
Face, 225
Failings, 147
Faith, 159, 369, 377

False: definition, 395; shame,
179
Falsehood, 69
Fame: comes too late to the
dead, 289; desire for, 55;
fame's untruths, 229; hard
to hold on to, 79; nurse of
the arts, 65; posthumous,
75; starry, 141; wretched,
45
Family, 41, 311
Farming, 27, 71
Fashion, 187
Fasting, 361
Fate: blind, 257; leads the
willing, 251; rules all, 235
Father: be like your, 43; Father, perform a mother's duties, 217; father's longer
stride, 131; not master, 39
Fatherland: serve one's, 97; to
die for the, 163; wherever
we are content, 29
Fault, 189, 283, 285, 331
Favor, 11, 55, 103
Fear: and grief, 331; and hate,
23, 43; excludes love, 385;
first created gods, 267; of
death, 93; of gods, 195;
slave to, 383; whom many
fear must fear many, 79;
who prefer being feared, 87
Fearless, 163
Feeling, 287
Felicity, 259
Feminine sex, 141
Fictions, 211, 319
Fight, for country, children,
altars, 99
Filial affection, 317
Flame, scars of old, 133
Flattery, 35
Flogging, 283
Folly, 57, 159, 173, 175
Fools, 145, 179, 287
Forbidden, we strive for the,
219

Forget, 11, 307
Fortune: and wisdom, 69;
blind, 31; cruel, 31, 155;
easier to meet than to
hold, 105; fears the brave,
255; fickle, 31, 271, 273;
fights for the brave, 141;
foolish, 31; greatest good
fortune, 197; great fortune
is slavery, 197; like glass,
105; mastered by accepting,
135; nonexistent, 31; raises
high to bring low, 257;
saves the guilty, 297; stupid,
31; we make you a goddess,
325
Forum, 43, 301
Fox, 173, 237
Freedmen, 331
Freedom: all over with our,
79; and sovereignty, 307; a
pure heart is, 23; attribute
of Roman people, 59; legal
definition, 393; possession of
inestimable value, 395; to
obey God is, 245; valued
above money, 5
Friend: another self, 71; backbiting an absent, 149; delight of a, 149; indulgence
for shortcomings of, 147; in
need, 21; name of friend is
common, 239; portrait of a,
21; powerful, 181; to share
good things, 247
Friends: and your financial
status, 15; flattery wins, 35
Friendship, 71, 199, 221, 249,
267, 311
Frivolity, 55
Funerals, 243
Furies, 389
Future of science, 261

Gaiety, hard to pretend, 207
Gait, 129
Galatea, 121

Ivy crown, 155

Jackdaw, 339
Jests, 285
Jewels, 15
Jews, 149, 343
Judaea, 387
Judge, 151, 255
Julia, 385
Julian, 359
Juno, 129, 225
Jupiter, 119, 139, 141, 213, 235
Just, 163
Justice: as Christian virtue, 371; divine justice slow but severe, 273; holds provinces, 337; gives every man his due, 65, 391; more law, less justice, 71; queen of all virtues, 67; sister to Modesty, 159; source of justice fear of injustice, 147; undermines tyranny, 297

Kernel, 13
Kindness, 55, 73, 137, 275, 347
King, 257
Kisses, 13, 109, 379
Knowledge, 71, 259, 277, 281, 375, 393

Labor, 125
Lais, 355
Lalage, 159
Laugh, 145, 147, 185, 237, 245
Laughingstock, 243, 323
Laughter, 105, 157, 179
Law: at most rigorous, 35; break the law to seize power, 83; Caesar's vs. Christ's, 363; civil law, 56; common law of human race, 201; harsh but the law, 395; liberal interpretation prefer-able, 393; no law convenient to all, 197; of nations, 393; of nature, 393; precepts of the law, 393; reason in nature, 63; silent magistrate, 63; what law forbids not, shame forbids, 253
Laws, 43, 167, 187, 313, 385
Laziness, 27
Learn, 185, 245, 253
Learning, 347
Leisure, 3, 23, 67, 249
Lesbia, 113, 115
Letters, 73, 77
Leuconoe, 157
Liar, 283
Licinius, 161
Lie, 41, 323, 375
Life: a full life, 269; a long sickness, 369; a punishment, 263; common to all, 365; contempt for, 293; deceptive, 245; greed for, 259; life's comedy, 333; like shaking dice, 38; not just living, 291; prizes of, 149; shortness of, 141, 263; suit life to myself, 173; torch of, 93; untrodden paths of, 183
Light, of the faith, 367
Lily, 117, 213
Limit, 145, 175
Lion, 173, 237, 343
Literature, 55, 67, 251
Live: as brave men, 151; as you can, 33; do you have to?, 315; hastily, 253; nobly, 249, 251; today, 287
Losers, 131
Love: a kind of warfare, 223; alike for all, 127; all-conquering, 123; and fear, 385; and lust, 47; and modesty, 219; at last love has come, 209; easier to end than to moderate, 201; end to, 103,

410

411

412

Virtue (*cont'd*)
  perfect, 65; praised, 3, 181;
  true virtue the mean between vices, 181
Virtuous, 239
Vulture, 19, 267

Wallet, 277
Wantonness, 267
War: abhorred by mothers,
  155; and hero, 129; and
  laws, 57; contrary to law
  of nature, 393; easy to start,
  hard to end, 101; fear of
  war worse than war, 259; in
  war nothing is light, 197;
  madness, 205; prepare for,
  363; so much war, 125;
  war-god runs amok, 125
Warts, 147
Water-drinkers, 183
Weep, 231
Well-said, whatever is well-
  said is mine, 247
Whisperers, 7
Who gained?, 53
Wicked, 239
Wife: burden, 267; Caesar's,
  83; faults of, 47; loved, 139,
  351; necessary nuisance,
  339; prudent, 323; shrewish, 37, 207; with and without dowry, 11, 13; worried,
  37
Will, 213
Wine, 11, 165, 263
Winecup, 177
Winejar, 163, 165, 187
Wisdom: and beauty, 267;
  and fortune, 69; and knowledge, 375; driven out, 21;
  God's wisdom, 375; most
  men learn wisdom from
  others, 315; wisdom that is
  folly, 159
Wise: teachings of the wise,
  91; the wise alone are free,
153; wise in vain, 23; wise
man avoids excess, 177;
wise man is like a physician,
243; wise man loves, others
are lecherous, 47; wise
man second only to Jove,
173; wise men take old
wine and love old plays, 11;
would go mad if angered by
every crime, 243
Wish, I wish to love and to die
  with thee, 165
Witness, 17
Woe to the conquered, 197
Wolf, 121
Woman: chatterbox, 9; conceals desire, 219; cruel, 207;
  delay personified, 5; destructive, 337; either loves
  or hates, 103; enjoys revenge, 327; faithless, 207,
  351; in love, 133; ruthless,
  325; weathercock creature,
  135; what a woman is capable of, 135; who lost virtue,
  313; wily, 213; woman's
  nature, 29, 43
Women: better seen than
  heard, 15; distant journey
  changes women, 213; good
  when openly bad, 103; may
  my enemies love women,
  213; surpass men in evil,
  105; two worse than one,
  13; ways of, 37
Wooing, 223
Word: avoid a strange word,
  83; "had" is a dismal word,
  15; word once let out, 181,
  193
Words: a foot and a half long,
  189; plain words not
  enough, 147; renew well-
  known words, 189; unnecessary words, 193; will not
  be slow to follow, 191

LATIN INDEX

Every quotation is represented in this alphabetical index either by the opening words or by one or more key words.

415

Cerebrum non habet, 236
Cernis, ut ingentes, 304
Certum quia impossibile, 342
Certus amor morum, 222
Christianam religionem, 356
Christianos ad leonem, 342
Christus Tiberio imperitante, 316
Ciclops impius, 4
Cineri gloria sera, 288
Circumspecto iudicio, 284
Cito rumpes arcum, 238
Cito scribendo, 286
Cito virgo senescit, 336
"Civis Romanus sum," 52
Civitatem dare . . . verbo, 332
Civitates duas amores duo, 374
Civium domini, libertorum . . . servi, 330
Cogi qui potest, 252
Cognitio naturae manca, 70
Colamus humanitatem, 242
Commune vitium in . . . civitatibus, 86
Componitur orbis, 380
Condicionem . . . imperandi, 310
Condicionem principum miserrimam, 334
Condita est civitas Roma, 376
Coniugium vocat, 132
Coniunctio inter homines, 64
Conqueri . . . non lamentari, 28
Conscia mens recti, 228
Conscientia pluris . . . quam sermo, 76
Constant inter Christianos, 374
Consuesse . . . deos immortales, 80
Consuetudinem sermonis, 282
Consuetudo vicit, 340
Contemnunt novitatem meam, 100

Contempta res homo, nisi, 258
Contra verbosos, 346
Conveniet a litibus, 72
Convivarum numerum, 48
Corcillum . . . homines facit, 264
Corpus Priamo reddidi, 44
Corruptissima re publica, 312
Cras amet qui numquam, 350
Cras te victurum, 290
Credat Iudaeus Apella, 148
Crede ratem ventis, 350
Credere non possemus nisi rationales, 368
Credibilium tria genera, 370
Credimus? an qui amant, 122
Credimus . . . ut cognoscamus, 376
Credula vitam spes, 206
Credunt signis cor inesse, 40
Crescentem sequitur, 164
Crescit arbor gliscit ardor, 336
Crescitur amor nummi, 326
Crimine quo merui, 302
Crudele genus . . . femina, 206
"Cui bono," 52
Cui lecta potenter res, 188
Cui me moribundam, 132
Cui multum debeas, 72
Cui non conveniet sua, 178
Cui peccare licet, 216
Cui placet obliviscitur, 54
Cui Pudor, 158
Cui tradas . . . filium magistro, 290
Cui verba sonosque, 302
Cum ames non sapias, 104
Cum dignitate otium, 56
Cum glaucus opaco, 352
Cum iam fulva cinis, 116
Cum odio sui coepit veritas, 340
Cum rapiunt mala fata, 218
Cum sis incautus, 346
Cupiditas, 42
Cupiditas veri videndi, 64

O mihi praeteritos, 138
O miseras hominum mentes, 90
Omitte mirari, 166
Omne aevum curae, 354
Omne bellum sumi facile, 100
Omne ignotum pro magnifico, 308
Omne quod dulce, 384
Omnes humanos sanat, 212
Omnes . . . pari sorte nascimur, 344
Omne tulit punctum, 192
Omnia conando, 234
Omnia enim stolidi, 90
Omnia fert aetas, 122
Omnia Graece, 322
Omnia mortali mutantur, 234
Omnia tempus alit, 350
Omnia vincit amor, 122
Omnibus hoc vitium, 144
Omnis aut vetulas, 292
Omnis enim per se divom, 92
O nata mecum, 164
O noctes cenaeque deum, 152
Optatos dedit amplexus, 138
Optima legum interpres, 392
Optima quaeque dies, 126
Orator, 28
Oratores novi, stulti, 6
O rus, quando, 152
O saeclum insapiens, 110
Oscitat in campis, 20
Os homini sublime, 224
O si angulus ille, 152
O socii, 128
Ostendandae pietati, 316
Os tenerum pueri, 184
O tempora, 52
O terque quaterque, 128
O testimonium animae, 342
Otio qui nescit uti, 22
Otium, Catulle, 110
Otium sine litteris mors, 248

Pallida Mors aequo pulsat, 154
Panem et circenses, 324

Paratae lacrimae, 104
Parcus deorum cultor, 158
Par deo dignum, vir, 240
Parentum vita vilis, 46
Pars hominum vitiis gaudet, 152
Parsimonia, 66
Pars sanitatis velle, 256
Parturiunt montes, 188
Parvulus Amor, 48
Parvum parva decent, 178
Pastillos Rufillus olet, 144
Pater, avos, proavos, 14
Pati necesse . . . mala, 6
Patria, 28, 72
Patriumst, 38
Paucissimis verbis, 384
Paucos servitus, 248
Paulum . . . ultra primas, 280
Paupertas me saeva domat, 380
Pax optima rerum, 272
Pax secura locis, 300
Peccante nil est taetrius, 364
Peccare fuisset ante satis, 140
Peccare pauci nolunt, 104
Pectus . . . disertos facit, 286
Pecunia regimen rerum, 104
Peior est bello timor, 258
Pelle moras, 270
Pellitur . . . sapientia, 20
Per alta vade spatia, 254
Peras imposuit, 238
Per chaos occurrunt, 300
Percontatorem fugito, 180
Pereant qui ante nos, 362
Perierat totus orbis, 200
Per imbrem in villa, 26
Perpetuus nulli datur, 186
Persicos odi, 158
Pervixi, 268
Pessima sit, 220
Pessimum inimicorum, 308
Philosophia animum format, 246
Pictoribus atque poetis, 186
Pindarum quisquis, 168